*In honor of the houndsmen of the past
and in hope for the future*

Ed Barnes

IN PURSUIT OF HOG DOGS
By Ed Barnes

Tuskers PUBLISHING

281 Phoenix Ave
Tahlequah, Oklahoma 74464

Ed Barnes

First printing 2020

Tuskers Publishing
281 Phoenix Ave
Tahlequah, Oklahoma 74464

www.tuskersmagazine.com

Though yonder breaks, I spotted Lil Red
Up was his tail, down was his head
As I got close, I heard a muffled sound
It was Lil Red barking, his head underground
Dirt then filled the sky, to the left then right
Lil Red been digging, half of the night.
I smiled and laughed, no moment too dull
In the bottom of that hole, I could hear a hull
The sound got loud, and out he flew
Knocked Red down, he knew not what to do
Red came back and began to sull
Depressed like hell, out run by a hull.

~Pat Lewing

CONTENTS

Dog Health

INTRODUCTION

Hog hunting with dogs has been a large part of my life for the last 20 years. It has consumed much of my thought, a good portion of my money, and mountains of my time. It is not just something I do, it is who I am. It defines me. With that said, I do not consider myself an expert on the subject, but rather a student. No one comes into this way of life knowing everything, we all learn it in bits and pieces, sometimes large chunks come our way from veterans if we are lucky. Almost everything I know someone taught me. I do not want to seem that I am taking credit. Some things I did learn on my own, the hard way, usually after I refused to listen to the lessons a wiser man tried to teach me.

At one point I was the knot-headed kid, too proud to take well placed advice. I have grown a lot since then and now I find myself being the man that says, "OK, do it your way," when a whipper-snapper won't listen. When I was younger I took those words as a victory of wills, now I understand the thinking behind them and the background meaning that goes unheard saying, "OK, learn it the hard way." But I don't mean to belittle that youthful ignorance and stubbornness, lessons learned the hard way are more often etched into our thinking with such force that we will never make the same mistake again.

The human race has made it this far into history because of our brains and more specifically, our ability through language to pass on knowledge to the younger generation. Without language each generation would start at the same level of understanding as their parents started with and be forced to learn the same lessons for themselves. There would be no advancement because each generation would be a simple reset back to the beginning. As dogmen, we need to take this line of thinking and take that advice given, when correct, so that we can focus our learning on new areas - to continue the advancement of ourselves and the animals we breed, train, hunt and love.

In the following pages I will pass on my ideas and lessons, most of which were passed on to me. Much of this information is subjective and there is plenty of room for interpretation and expansion. Many of the ideas I will talk about are not fact, but merely personal theory. Everyone that reads this book will disagree with me at some point and maybe even from cover to cover. I am perfectly content with that. Some might say after reading, "That guy is an idiot! I got nothing good from the whole thing." But you don't have to agree with me to get something good from this book. Whether talking about hog hunting, or anything else, when we introduce ourselves to opposing views we grow by challenging our own ideas and putting them to question. I will introduce many opposing views.

You might be thinking, "Hog hunting isn't philosophy!" I say hog hunting with dogs is a very thoughtful game. The feral hog is the smartest animal in the woods, and you might catch a few with simple brute force and by overpowering a hog, but by in large we are playing a chess game. More than any other dog sport, ours is a balance of force and elegance. How many nights have you lay in bed after getting smoked by a hog, sleepless, planning a strategy to get that old boar hog under rope? How many days at work have you been running a conversation in your head of wind direction, terrain, and plotting a strategy with this dog and that dog? I know I have stared at the doors of a dog box, running factors over in my head trying to figure out which doors to open. If you are just swinging all the doors open you are arguably missing the best part of hog hunting with dogs.

I will do my best to keep these pages filled with a balanced account, showing multiple sides of a debate, but I am only one man and my opinions will be clear for all to see. I will lay the disclaimer here that these are just my opinions, I will not footnote my every sentence as merely my thoughts. My ideas about dogs are not set in stone, I am constantly learning and thus forming new opinions. Admittedly, some of my ideas on hunting dogs are a little out there. I am not one to accept many of the "facts" about hunting dogs, and if you want a reaffirmation that everything is hunky-dorry in the hunting dog world look elsewhere because I am not your man. I have a natural inclination to buck the system, and buck I will!

I am quite positive that one day I will look back through this book and think I was wrong. I hope I do. I hope I never get jaded and end my journey of understanding hunting dogs. I hope I never stop experimenting. I hope I never get comfortable and satisfied. I hope I never know it all!

CHAPTER 1
NAMESAKE

In the summer of 1973 a man named Edd Barnes died of a heart attack while calling a square dance in Braggs, Oklahoma. A couple weeks later a grandson was born and I took his name. Edd was a true outdoorsman, and a dogman - he ran Beagles, coondogs and occasionally running hounds.

A third grade education, coupled with a depressed Oklahoma economy left little options, though Edd managed to raise a family of 6 kids largely off of hunting and fishing and my grandmas hard work. My grandma, Mary Skinner Barnes held down a house full of kids with an often absent husband. Edd was a man of a different age, even for his time. My great grandpa, Alec Barnes would leave out of Caddo, County in southern Oklahoma in the fall to run traplines that stretched into far northern Oklahoma, not to return until the spring. By age seven Edd was running his own traplines in the absense of his dad, as was his mother Lizzie. Trapping supplimented their income.

Some of Edds' children resented his lack of adaptation to a more modern world, probably because of grumbling bellies, but one of his grandkids reveled and took pride in that refusal to bend to societies progress. Edds' love of hunting and fishing was seen as laziness, and without a doubt that trait was present.

Despite his lack of a formal education, Edd Barnes was

1

intelligent and many a senator, and senatorial candidate pulled up to the little log cabin in the hills of Muskogee, County Oklahoma to go fishing and hunting with the man. In the words of my dad, the cracks between the logs of that cabin were so big you could, "Throw a cat through them." Times were hard, and those hard times made hard men. Gold and silver are spent, but character built through hard times last a lifetime and those lessons can even last further into future generations when the lessons are taught and the kid listens.

Edd had the gift of talking, not a Barnes' trait generally speaking, and one I definitely didn't get. The politicians of the day knew that if they could get Edd on their side he would convince many in Cherokee, Sequoyah, and Muskogee County to follow suit.   Later in life his political influence afforded him 'leisurely' jobs with the wildlife department and the local sheriffs office. His skills of telephoning fish and gill netting were even used by the wildlife department in fish surveys, though the methods were illegal.

(Edd Barnes joking around on a mule)

In Pursuit of Hog Dogs

As a young boy the kennels behind grandmas house, though mostly vacant, fascinated me, like a ghost town for dogs. I can remember walking them, imagining the barking and howling that my grandmother used to shake her head at when recalling the racket. Grandma would describe the noise and then almost every time tell of the hardship of cooking dog food for her fathers foxhounds. My grandmas and my grandpas family ran old fashioned foxhounds together, one of the few social aspects of rural Oklahoma other than church. My dad would grudgingly tell the tale - "A bunch of old men sitting around arguing about who's dog was in the lead." He'd disgustingly say, "Ain't no way they could tell," and despite my arguments he wouldn't concede that those old men could tell the difference in the barking that echoed in those hollers and hills of northeast Oklahoma.

Occasionally a couple Beagles, a coondog or a bird dog would show up in my grandpas kennels, usually courtesy of one of my uncles, but for the most part those kennels stood empty. The bawling of a coonhound when one was penned touched me, that mournful sorrow in their voice spoke to me. Many years later I would understand, but at the time I only knew the draw I couldn't put my finger on. Sometimes today as I am walking to the kennels at my house I imagine them empty, with tall weeds growing in the dog fed soil, not unlike my grandpas kennels I knew as a kid. Hopefully that never happens, but we can only live our one life, the lives of our kids are theirs to do with as they wish.

When I was in my late teens my grandpa's kennels were bulldozed over, pushed into a pile and burned along with the brush that had reclaimed the area. A large, rusted 4" yard ring that the man used at a chain spot was his legacy left to to me, rusted iron. Though years later I realized he left me much more than material possessions. My family reveled at how much better everything looked with the eyesore gone and went back in the house. For me it was the end of an era.

For the most part Edd's sons didn't share his love of hunting with dogs, my dad surely didn't, but I can't begrudge him of that any more than someone can me for loving the sound of a dog race. My uncle George ran coondogs but he had moved off, like most, trading the hills for someplace where a man could make enough money to keep his kids' bellies from grumbling. So I waited, without knowing, without understanding.

I grew up all over the globe, traveling behind my parents. There wasn't much opportunity to hunt. My summers were usually spent back in the sticks of Muskogee County though and were always the highlight of my year. When I turned 18 we were living in Nairobi, Kenya in Africa. The United States government offered me a free plane ticket to anywhere in the world. My dad asked where I was going to go to live my life? "Oklahoma!" I didn't think about it for over a second. The old man knew the answer before he even asked, I think he understood, without approving. My die had been cast long ago. The old man shook his head and recalled the words of my grandmas dad, "Oklahoma is the armpit of the world!" I resented that, but kept silent. I felt a deep connection to that land.

Some things came natural and easy to me when it came to hunting and dogs, things that shouldn't have. At times it felt like I knew things that there was no logical reason for me to know. As a young man teaching myself about hunting with dogs I often thought of Edd, that man I had never met, but felt I knew. Sometimes I would just feel a push to turn dogs out at a random spot, many times it was the right spot. I am not an overly spiritual person, but I truly believe Edd was with me, teaching. Like the dogs we raise, we have a genetic connection and predisposition to our past, when the breeding is correct, but we will get to that later.

Grandpa, along with most of my old family is buried in the White Oak Cemetery in Qualls, Oklahoma. The cemetery sits back in the hills, near the unincorporated town whose post office was shut down in 1942. Qualls' claim to fame is an old fashioned general store that has been converted into a little restaurant. The restaurant appeared in the movie, "Where the Red Fern Grows," it is where Billy goes to pick up Little Ann and Old Dan, presumably in Tahlequah, but in reality fifteen miles south. One afternoon after hog hunting in the area just to the north of Qualls I decided to go by the grave of my grandpa. I had never been to it, the Barnes family is not overly sentimental. I parked my Toyota with my dog box loaded down with curs and began to walk the cemetery looking for the grave. After a bit of looking I noticed a Beagle sitting under a tree. I momentarily abandoned my search and walked over to the dog. The dog leaned into the ear rub I was passing out and I continued to rub as I stared off into space. I was thinking of old family lore and yearning for the past I am sure. When I brought my gaze back to planet earth I looked down and the Beagle was sitting next to Edd Barnes' simple flat grave marker. It merely read "Edd Barnes 1911 - 1973." In death, as in life, the Barnes' didn't give much up.

Years later when I told my grandma of the story she cried. "I am so glad you told me that Eddie," she said, she always called me Eddie, "Now I know he is in heaven." As a strict Christian she did not believe in dancing and had often told me she worried that Edd had gone to hell because he died at a dance. Grandma said the Beagle was a sign from him. In the old backwoods, Christianity is not a straight line, it is tinged with a dash of mysticism but in no way am I discounting my grandma's faith. Grandma was the most godly woman I have ever known, and she stood beside an old school dogman for nearly 50 years.

CHAPTER 2
MY FIRST DOGS

My first hunting dog was a Patch bred Beagle, a lemon and white and I hauled that dog all over. Many mornings I took her out at daybreak before I went to work. The time did pay off and she made a pretty decent rabbit dog for a young man who basically knew nothing at all. About the time I got her raised up and running hard she got ran over by a car. All the work I had put in was gone and it was a very hard blow. I was in the process of trying to gather up another Patch bred Beagle when I pulled into a gas station one day after gun hunting. There were three men in a truck with an old make-shift dog box. The rig caught my eye because something about it looked different from most. Even as an amateur dog hunter   I could pretty much at a glance tell what a man hunted by a look at his truck and box, but this setup looked different than anything I had ever seen. As I pumped my gas I stared. The dogs in the box perplexed me even more - big block headed cur dogs... and a bulldog? Being a naturally shy person I had to make myself go talk to them. "Hog hunting" was the answer and I was generally confused but my interest was perked in a very big way. We exchanged phone numbers and made plans to get together for a hunt.

At this time, modern hog hunting in Oklahoma wasn't just a baby, it was a new born baby, still covered in goop and looking nothing like a human. I met the guys at a gas station a week or so later and we went hog hunting. They turned a couple of those block headed curs loose soon after we turned onto the wagon trail that snaked around a lake and the dogs weaved across the road and into the edge of the brush as we slowly pushed them with the truck. I was still as confused as the day I had seen them at the gas station, but I knew we were after big game and something about it made my gut feel like it was turning inside out, in a good way. After a mile or so the dogs each let out a bark and took off down a small game trail that crossed the road. The man I was with had no more than stopped the truck and I came out of the door and shot down the trail hot on the heels of the dogs. I tried my best to keep up but I was left behind. I kept looking back expecting to see the guys coming... they didn't. You would think that after running Beagles I would have been waiting for that wide loop? I guess I will just chalk it up to youthful enthusiasm. I found my way back to the road and the truck and the boys had a good laugh at my expense.

We stood around and listened to the race veer far to the east around the lake. A man took out his beep beep tracker when they got out of ear shot and I thought, "Damn, this guy's a professional!" We drove... and drove, the tracking system hung out the window filling my ears with faint beeps that were as meaningless as Chinese to me. Finally one of the boys hollered out that they were "Bayed!" We made our way towards the barking, my heart about to give out, imagination running wild! Before we got to turn the bulldog loose the barking stopped. I was again confused and a bit heartbroken when it was explained to me. Shortly, the boy with the tracking system called out that ole so-n-so wasn't moving. There was muttered cursing and we all headed towards the signal on foot. As we neared I started seeing blood and I am sure my eyes were as big as saucers. We found the dog and it's guts were out! No rabbit had ever gutted my Beagles. They wrapped the dog in a shirt and we hauled it back to the truck. I was very concerned yet they seemed somewhat lax about the whole situation? At the truck we all held the dog down as one of them sewed his dog up after washing off the guts with some water and stuffing them carefully back inside the dog. I remember thinking that the dog had zero chance of survival, but I kept my thoughts to myself. We chased the remaining dogs all over two counties for the next 3 or 4 hours until we managed to get the dogs cut-off on a road and back in the box. We didn't catch a hog that day but I saw the damage one could do and my little Beagles just didn't measure up in the category of heart in my mind anymore. I called over the next few days expecting each time to get news the dog had died. The dog made a full recovery.

From that day forward I didn't have the enthusiasm I had before. Chasing a rabbit seemed empty. It wasn't but a couple weeks after that I started looking for some dogs that I thought could hog hunt. My sister had a cow bred Catahoula and on the next breeding of the sire and dam I got a pup. Somewhere along the line I got another cowdog and it wasn't long before they were old enough to start. My sister gave me her older dog and I had the start of a pack, although they knew absolutely nothing, not too far behind me. I had enough up-bringing to know I could not go back to the spot in Northeast Oklahoma the hog hunters had taken me, so I drove south. In those days southern Oklahoma, as close as you could get to Texas, was where you went if you wanted to hog hunt. I had been doing my research. I had been invited back to hunt with the guys that took me but my general stubbornness and my penchant for anti-social behavior pushed me to do it on my own, in my own way. I imagine that decision handicapped me and I would surely do otherwise today.

The first year that I walked those dogs all over God's green earth I caught nothing. I hunted almost every weekend, at least once and sometimes twice. I would come in the house and my wife would ask and I would hang my head and say, "NO." The second year I caught two, TWO! I was tickled pink, my wife didn't get it, and I didn't either but there was a desire there that I couldn't explain. I can't recall exactly, but the third year it was in the neighborhood of 20. By this time I had a fair amount of dogs and I started to get a pretty good feel for the type of dogs needed. I wore out countless boots. About the fourth or fifth year I was starting to get the hang of it and was at a point where I could start to gather dogs that hunted in a style I wanted.

In those days there was no GPS tracking, there was telemetry tracking but I was a poor boy so I slept in my truck waiting on dogs, left tee shirts with my scent in the woods, drove roads looking and rushed home to see if someone had called, there were no cell phones either. The first dog I got, a cow bred Catahoula, had by this time made himself into a dog and that big liver-spotted blue dog became my stud. "Rebel" was his name and he became my foundation stock. It is funny, because looking back I still regard him as one of my best, it might be purely sentimental, but you could put that dog on a track and he was going to bay it! In those days hogs were very hard to come by, finding them was the hard part but once located they didn't run. A typical race was 100 to 200 yards. There were lone boars on public land that would sure enough give a race but for the most part hogs bayed up very easily.

(Rebel)

With so few hogs in our area I was not about to kill hogs. In those days the Oklahoma Game Regulation book had no mention of the word "Hog." It was the wild west and we could lawfully do whatever we wanted. I had game wardens pull me over on public land and ask what I was hunting and they would laugh and look at me like I was totally crazy when I said, "Hog hunting." Today some of those same game wardens call me, encouraging me to hunt spots of public land where they are having a problem, and our regulation book is filled with hog hunting rules, tying our hands and making sure our "problem" grows. I consider myself truly blessed to have been a part of the 2nd guard of hog hunters that took over after the closing of the range and helped to push this new sport in new direction.

I hunted mostly by myself for probably the first 10 years, because of my anti-social nature. Hunting alone was a hardship I put on myself, but it did afford me an education. While I advise others to 'buddy up,' I wouldn't take a million dollars for my single handed beginnings. I learned very hard lessons, most the hardest way possible. It also gave me and my dogs no crutches to lean on - the shame and glory was all mine! There was no "social media" back then, thank God. Catching a good hog was not a means to bragging and puffing ones chest out to the world, it was an inner pride. The love of hunting was pure and self contained.

My old school Catahoulas would bay loose for hours but when I showed up they would catch. I didn't use a bulldog for many years. I would get the hog tied, then walk my dogs 20 or 30 yards back and tie them out. I would then walk back in and turn the hog loose, all the while breaking no laws. By this time in my hog hunting career I had talked it over with my great uncle Tom and received an education on free-range hogs. I had a feel for the old days. Tom was a dogman, and had free-ranged hogs going back to the mid-twentith century. Tom and my other great uncle, John Barnes were a sounding board for my dog questions, they were the link to my past and a resource I wouldn't exchange for anything. John Barnes gave me great insight into the old ways - a walking breathing Foxfire book of old knowledge - knowledge once common and in todays world rare.

As an old man Tom was surprised that there were still hogs in the woods and his eyes would light up a bit when I would tell of hog hunting stories. That glint in Tom's eyes were a driving force in my determination to hunt hogs. I can still picture the chewing tobacco dripping from the corner of his mouth as he smiled. If I had dogs with me when I visited Tom he would have me pull my truck over where he could see from the window and I would take the dogs out for him to give them a look from his recliner perched by a window. Tom was in his late 80's at this point but his eyes would light up like a teenager when we talked about dogs.

What I wouldn't give to run with him in his prime! Tom is dead now and I would give almost anything to sit next to his recliner and listen to his stories and knowledge again. If you know an old dogman I emplore you to go see them now! Ask the questions and listen to the stories because they pass on before we imagine.

I was hunting in Cherokee County one day around this time. The dogs had struck a hog on Spaniard Creek and took him up to a clearing to bay. I had three dogs on the ground but when I got to the bay there were four dogs giving the hog a talking to. My big blue dog, Rebel caught and I got the hog tied and all the dogs back. The fourth dog was a little dark brindle Mountain Cur, she wore a collar with the name Lee George and a phone number. At this time there were only a handful of hog hunters in northeast Oklahoma and while I didn't hunt with any of them, we all pretty much knew each other but I had never heard the name Lee George. I drove around for an hour or so after I got the hog taken care of, looking for a truck with this man Lee in it so I could give him back his hog dog. I had no such luck, so I hauled the dog home and gave him a call. I couldn't get a hold of him. Message boards had taken hold on the internet by this time and I posted on a big game board inquiring about "Lee." My handle was "Busch" and a few days later a man called me asking to speak to "Busch." Lee hadn't been on the message board, but he had been alerted. "This Lee?" "Yes." "Hey, I got your hog dog." By the sound of his voice I could tell he was an older man, and the roughness of his conversation confirmed his age. "I ain't got no 'hog dog.'" He placed an emphasis on the words 'hog dog', as if it was a slur. "The hell you don't!" I popped off and I then began to tell him of the previous days happenings. The little dog had been a squirrel dog that had gotten out of pocket. Lee told me to keep the dog and get her started on hogs for him. Lee called me "Busch" for the remainder of our friendship and we had a couple decades of running hog dogs together.

Lee and I hog hunted together for many years after that. Lee was in his seventies and had run dogs his whole life, mostly coondogs, squirrel dogs, and beagles. He was originally from Arkansas and he and his father had woods hogs they caught with dogs in the old days. Lee became my best friend and in many ways my mentor, though we fought about dogs at nearly every turn. We shared a million meals of beans and vienna sausage on the tailgate of a truck, or under a tree beside our mules, as dogs made their tracks over the hills in search of a hog. The old man would take a bite, chew a bit and start, "Did I ever tell you about the time..." Of course I had heard the story but I would always shake my head "No." I didn't mind to hear the story again and it gave him great pleasure to tell his hunting stories. I was accustom to old men.

Lee taught me a lot about dogs but the biggest thing that hunting with him taught me was that the personal relationships we make while hunting are as much a part of the sport as the dogs are. This came as a great surprise to me. The bond that men make while hog hunting together is a very tight one. When you go into dangerous situations together, time and again, having each others backs, you cannot help but feel a strong kinship. That bond rivals that of a man and his dogs, and it is every bit as important. Often when I think back on my past as a hog hunter very few hogs pop into my head, a few great dogs do, but the majority of my thoughts center around the great men that I have shared time with and the strong bonds we have forged in hard and trying times. Those trying times are the reason I hog hunt.

In 2013 I became the editor of Tuskers Magazine. That experience shaped my understanding of hog hunting with dogs more than 50 years in the woods would have. The connection with a hog hunting magazine brought me out of my small corner of the world. I traveled over a good bit of the southern states talking with hog hunters and hunting very different hogs and terrain. That broadening of my understanding of hog dogs without a doubt made me a better hog hunter. It opened my mind to different methods, but in many ways it left me longing for the old days - hunting by myself back in the hills when it was more pure and simple.

Tom Barnes and "Lonesome" with bear

CHAPTER 3
FREE★RANGE

We cannot have a discussion about hog hunting in America without paying honor to the men and women of the South that free-ranged hogs in our not too distant past. Without these often poor, southern men, our sport of hog hunting would still be relagated to the elitist, white collar guided "Boar hunts" inside high fence game ranches, conjuring up our European past, and the Kings Forest, where hunting was a right only afforded to royalty, or in America's case the wealthy elite. Imagine hog hunting being a banker on a horse, in an English saddle, spear in hand - slipping it past past 20 sight hounds mounted on a boar. It is sickening. In America we took a past time of European nobility and transformed it into the most blue collar of all dog hunting. The fact that hog hunting with dogs in America has shed that picture and landed in the hands of common men is largely because of the men and women that free ranged hogs for survival and not sport. It is our duty to carry that lineage! That lineage deserves to be in the forefront of our minds at every turnout.

Hernando De Soto came to America in 1539. He was here for the long haul and planned ahead bringing cattle and hogs. De Soto, in his funny metal hat, was the first man to free-range hogs in the Americas. It was a matter of survival. De Soto knew the value of a woods hog, before us rednecks even knew about these hills and hollers, when my Barnes clan still worked the stables and barns of England. These hogs were the first in America according to mainstream science, and are our original seed stock. A couple hundred years later when Europeans started settling the south they were still reaping the benefits of the hogs and cattle that De Soto planted. While technically hogs are not native to North America, they were here before us.

Whether the early settlers learned from the hogs they killed in the woods, or whether they learned it organically, it became the custom to let hogs run loose in the bottoms. The hogs were quite adapt at making their own living in the woods, and it made no sense to pen them and feed them when they could be turned loose and find a way to thrive on their own. Free-ranging hogs was simply a matter of economics, and conservation of energy- common sense.

This tradition of ranging hogs carried on in the south largely until the 1950's and in some areas until the 1980's, yet again it still continues to this very day in limited pockets around the south, though illegal. Many scoff when I mention personally witnessing these places where free-ranging hogs still exist. The tradition does carry on and I have had the great honor to witness it. I will leave it at that. There is "illegal" and there is "immoral," sometimes the two intersect, sometimes they do not, but those two words are not interchangeable. Mans law and Gods law are often at odds.

Ranging hogs remained in style across the south until the closing of the range. It was a state, or even county issue so there is no set time that the tradition stopped in America. Oklahoma is always behind the curve of history, one of the many reason I am proud to call myself an Okie, and in Oklahoma our range was closed January 1, 1966, our "hog problem" began January 2, 1966.

My great uncle, Tom Barnes (1913 - 2007) was an old school man of the world. When speaking of northeast Oklahoma you are safe to take at least 50 years off of a date to get a feel for the time and conditions of the day. So when I say Tom Barnes was old school I mean in 1940, northeast Oklahoma was still the wild west. I remember asking him once where he ever got the money to own as much land as he did. Tom spat, and gave a short answer as was his way, "Hogs and moonshine," yet logging the pacific northwest played a role too. Tom never gave up much, and if you wanted to hear a lot you were going to have to coax him out of every single word. My uncle George talked often of the conversations he heard while the 'old men' thought him to be asleep. Information in those days was not as loose lipped as today, men were silent and thought before speaking.

Tom, like a lot of old southern men, kept hogs in the woods. In those days the range was open for stock, now 'Free-Range' means that dozen eggs will cost three times as much as the 'regular' ones, but in the old days it meant that a man need not own a single acre of land to have 3 or 3,000 head of cattle, horses, or hogs. Fences were meant for keeping things out, now we have turned that idea on its head and fences are meant for keeping things in, but that is a very recent idea. In past days you put up a fence to keep stock out of the garden or to keep them off a hay field, if they got in it was not the liability of the man that owned the stock, it was your own fence building shortcomings . The beast of the world are meant to roam at will, when we confine animals disease rears it's head. I will mention it many times throughout these pages, there is a natural order. Fighting nature will get you nowhere fast, and very tired.

So you have to ask yourself why America, and the South in particular, turned away from such a democratic idea of land ownership? Of course those fast moving automobiles had a say so, but fundamentally there was another driving factor in the closing of the range. Like with most things, it was greed. If you have ever watched a western movie then you have undoubtedly seen the theme occur over and over of land rights. Land rights were a large factor in the very creation of this country. When our ancestors left the feudal system of Europe and loaded themselves on ships to come to America they were in no big hurry to duplicate the European class system in the new world. "This land is OUR land," as the communist, (and Okie) Woody Guthrie sang - taking an American sentiment further to the left. The bodies that came to America were human though, so greed followed, and as always the rich and powerful wrote the laws and reaped it's benefits. In the northwest, where a majority of land was owned by the state, and the people, these ideas of 'common' land existed well into the late 20th century, in the form of grazing rights. In modern times we have witnessed a federal land grab of these state lands, pushing us even closer to our European past, but I will steer clear of my political hate speech.

Most everyone knows the practice of ranging hogs, but I will give it a brief description for those that don't. In the days of the open range most families had hogs in the woods. In the spring they would round up their hogs to ear mark the new arrivals to show ownership, cut lesser quality boars, de-louse and vaccinate. Every family had their own ear mark and they also knew the marks of other family's. Honesty was not at a premium as it is today, and for the most part marks were honored, meaning you did not take a hog holding another mans mark. Just as with cattle though, some threw a 'wide loop,' as John Wayne said in some old movie. Many a feud was started over those 'wide-loops!' The famous Hatfield and McCoy feud was in fact started over a free range hog.

The hog is the fastest evolving animal on the planet. In three generations a domestic hog in a feral state starts reverting to wild traits, so often all boars were barred and a blooded boar was turned in to the sounder to settle them back down. Today this is illegal, and in part, that recent legislation is responsible for our current 'hog problem,' though the blame is more regularly laid at the feet of hog hunters.

Some used stock dogs to gather hogs and some penned, some did both. Of course these hogs were not as wild as what we generally deal with today. These hogs would wad up pretty easy and could even be driven. Bulldogs were not used as these hogs were stock to be sold and a chewed up hog brought less at sale, and bite marks on a hog turned back were an invitation to disease. Loose dogs were the norm of the day, and many a dog was culled for one offense of mouthing a hog. By in large, the dogs of this period where more herding influenced than the dogs we use today. Often dogs were trained to 'cut' a hog from the wad on command, and working was done in the woods. My great uncle Tom Barnes had Catahoulas, though he didn't know them by any other term than stockdogs, and if you dared call them curs you better be ready to fight. Back then there were not specialized dogs as we have today, a dog might tree coon or possums on Monday night, (with no preference to either) gather cattle Tuesday morning, round up hogs Wednesday and bite a stranger Sunday through Saturday. Tom had catch pens and the dogs would locate a sounder, then he had a decoy dog that would lead them into a pen and jump out the back after a hidden man slammed the gate. I have had the pleasure of seeing the remains of log catch pens in the woods of south Arkansas. These traditions are not placed as far in the past as you might think. The law often uses the illusion of distance as a defense of their new laws. The men and women that know the past are a burden to their 'progress.'

Being a liquor man, Tom Barnes also had another trick, he would take his left-over mash and the tailings and put it in large feed bins he had at the edge of the woods. After calling the hogs, he would go to the house and return in a couple hours. Tom would laugh a little as he recounted, "They'd be so drunk you could just walk up 'n grab em." Conservation of energy is a southern tradition, not to be equated to laziness but rather intelligence.

When I was younger an old man in his nineties drove me to the back of his pasture, we got out and he hollered for his hogs. We stood leaned up against the truck and ever so often he'd go to calling mid-sentence, interrupting our conversation. Shortly he perked up, pointed and nodded his head in a direction. At the wood line a boar poked out and looked towards us. The old man made his call a time or two more and the edge of the woods erupted with black mulefooted hogs, if there was one there was 200. That image is burned into my brain and I hold it dear. The man was a famous hogman, but I will withhold his name, though he is now dead. "Best pork you ever throwed a lip over," he laughed at himself and I laughed with him.

In the fall the hogs were again rounded up and barrs were selected out of the sounder for butchering and others to sell to buy the barefooted kids shoes for school. In rural, poverty stricken Oklahoma a kid got one pair of shoes a year, in late summer before school started. Those kids tried to stretch them the whole year but most years they were barefooted by summer and not by choice. The hogs in the woods were like a savings account for poor country folks and when times got hard they could make a withdraw. Without the free-range hog many more Okies and Arkies would have starved during the great depression and the dustbowl, and during the fallout that lasted for decades after the rain returned. The rest of the nation got back to normal, while we reaped the seeds of the dustbowl for generations more. We forget the lessons of history all too often.

The Russian boar was introduced into the woods at different times depending on location. Generally speaking, the Russian was not widely an influence in range hogs until the 1960's, although in some areas it was much sooner, oddly enough further north. When they did show up, by their nature, they rode most of the sows and pushed our feral hogs in the Russian genetic direction. The introduction of the Russian hog - escapees from hunting clubs most often - was in effect the death nail of wide scale free-ranging of hogs.

When the range was closed for good, folks had a deadline for getting their stock out of the woods, after that date the hogs were fair game. Around Oklahoma people didn't stop ranging hogs, they just went out of sight. The stock that was left in the woods, unclaimed or un-catchable is our foundation stock. Everyone knows you can never gather every single head from the woods. Nearly every family that ranged hogs has a story about a particularly mean boar, or a sow that when with pigs was a handful, these in part, are the type stock that was left, and what we deal with today - the most wild.

When the government and 'progress' tied our hands from working these hogs, constantly taming the blood, they set the mold for our current hog problem. It was the law that created our new found 'hog problem', not us.

Most everyone has caught a barr. Where I live it is rare, but we still see marked hogs ever so often too. I for one will not harm a hair on a marked hog. There are folks that disagree, but in my eyes that is no different than walking up to a mans house and stealing. Ear marks show ownership, don't be a thief.

There are very valuable lessons in the origins of our sport. To be ignorant of our past is a slight in the face of our ancestors. If we as hog hunters wish to pass this life on to the next generation we must educate ourselves on our past and pass on the lesson to the next generation. There are moral decisions we must all make, as our lifestyle has been largely marginalized, and outlawed. No one can make those decisions for you. Despite the law, I will still advocate for hog management in place of hog eradication and strive to become a Hogman and not a hog hunter. "Eradication" is a dirty word in my world, and is likely to be met with four knuckles and a thumb at their side, leave that word to the urban deer "hunters" and folks at the wildlife department.

Common Earmarks

Steeple Fork	Crop	Swallow Fork	Shoestring

RIGHT LEFT	RIGHT LEFT	RIGHT LEFT	RIGHT LEFT
Over Bit	**Split**	**Under Half Crop**	**Jingle Bob**

RIGHT LEFT	RIGHT LEFT	RIGHT LEFT	RIGHT LEFT
Under Bit	**Crop Split**	**Over Half Crop**	

RIGHT LEFT	RIGHT LEFT	RIGHT LEFT	

Illegal Marks
Used to cover anothers mark

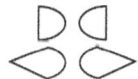

These marks were usually combined to create a readily noticeable mark of ownership. For example; right Under Bit left Swallow Fork (more commonly pronounced Swaller Fork) or right Split left Crop. In areas where many owners ranged hogs they got more elaborate ; right Under Bit Crop left Over Bit Split.

CHAPTER 4
OUR FATHER OF THE HUNT ⋆ ESAU

Genesis 25:22-23 - The children struggled together within her, and she said, "If it is thus, why is this happening to me?" So she went to inquire of the Lord, and the Lord said to her, "Two nations are in your womb, and two peoples from within you shall be divided; the one shall be stronger than the other, the older shall serve the younger."

Two "nations" were in fact born of Rebekah, two societies, two opposing mindsets and two outlooks on the future of society, and the older did in fact serve the younger.

Rebekah gave birth to twins, Esau and Jacob. Esau grew to be a hunter. He was strong, and hairy; a man's man, and he was favored by his father Isaac. The father usually favors the one that beckons back to his past. Esau was impulsive and prone to wondering. Jacob on the other hand was a momma's boy, and instead of hunting and wondering he stayed close to the tents and tallied the sheep and grains. Jacob played it safe, he was a sissy. Jacob was favored by his mother, as mothers often favor the "future" over the past.

Esau, being the oldest was in line for the birthright, but returning from a long unsuccessful hunt, tired and hungry; he traded his birthright to Jacob for a bowl of stew.

This story is often taught to show the folly in

21

impulsiveness, or thinking in the short term. Most preachers recall the story with a strong slant in favor of Jacob, despite Jacob's trickery in cheating his older brother out of a birthright. When Isaac, their father, was old and blind and about to die, Jacob wore Esau's clothes to smell like him, and he put animal furs on this hands and neck to trick his father when he touched him into thinking he was Esau. Jacob's tricks worked and his father unknowingly gave his blessing to Jacob instead of Esau. Honesty was not one of Jacob's Godly traits as he had manipulated Esau out of his birthright and then tricked his father into giving his blessing to him instead of Esau. The future was stolen.

This story has always struck me in a different way though, more as a fable that told of the conflict of man's place in the world. Esau represents the hunter/gatherer, and Jacob represents the farmer. The farmer and the hunter have been at odds since the first nomadic hunter spoke up and said, "Let's stay here, it's nice." I see this story in that light. The hunter undermines the farmers market, he has little need for buying the farmers harvest. The hunter embodies the masculine qualities that the city - a product of the agricultural society, fights to repress. It is commonplace to hear folks talking about the "war on masculinity" now a days, but this war is not a new one, it has been going on since the first permanent structure was built. The city suits the female, it is stable - like Jacob, while the hunting culture is impulsive and uncertain, feast or famine - like Esau. Freedom verses security, it is an old debate.

In Romans 9:13 God says, "Jacob I loved, but Esau I hated." Surely God could not "hate" a man for being manly? Some would say God hated Esau's traits, but those traits are at the base masculine traits. It is common to explain this by saying Esau did not respected his birthright and his fathers blessing, yet those blessings where stolen by trickery and deceit, so who held them as less than sacred? It could also be said that Jacob did not respect Gods order, and used trickery to steal a birthright and a blessing that did not rightfully belong to him. Another explanation could be in the translations of the bible. Kings translated the bible time and again, they used this as a chance to mold their subjects into more easily managed servants. Nomadic hunters have no use for a government, governments are a product of cities. Cities need order.

Cities demand land ownership. Hunters defy that ownership. How can a mortal man own a piece of immortal land? A man that subscribes to an older order bows to no mortal man as master, but sees the natural world as more whole. The modern world is built on the ideals of man and not nature.

I bring up this bible story because it parallels the battle that many hog hunters face today. Many of our main hardships in hunting hogs have to do with finding property to run these dogs. Often it seems the farmers don't want us and the governments don't want us on "their" land either - though both camps complain about hogs until they have to come up for air. The reason lies deep in their collective "farmer" brain. The dog hunter is a threat to modern society. We hearken back to days gone, we threaten weak models of modern masculinity, and unconsciously, we are a threat to progress, as we go against the grain of a progressive society, a feminized society that trudges onward into the future searching for "easier and safer."

We need open land, like we had before civilization! We need the old human mind, before the ideas of land ownership took hold and mortal man staked claims on the globe like gods. We need a whole, not pieces, cut and divided into mans claim with barbed wire. We need room to roam as part-time nomads, chasing the herd and not obstructed by societies boundaries. The hunter doesn't need a fence, or land ownership, those are creations of the agricultural society, kings and governments - people like Jacob that horde and count, "own" and rule over.

Our culture of hunting with dogs is a culture that is rooted in the past. Our fight to secure that culture is a long one, and the fight steams full force into the future. Dogs were the first animal that man domesticated, and we didn't bring them to camp to pet, we brought them back to camp to help us hunt. We saw traits in the wolf that reminded us of ourselves, traits we wanted, traits we needed. The wolf is not welcome in the city. The wolf steals the farmers flock in the night. The wolf is everything the farmer hates - as we are as dog hunters - the dog hunter has invited the wolf into our being and that has seperated us from our 'human pack.' The wolf and the hunter are after a natural order, while the farmer seeks to dominate nature and create unnatural orders. The wolf and the dog hunter are brothers - the wolf brought us in as much as we brought them in.

The wolf was domesticated 33,000 years ago, give or take a few thousand years. We did that before agriculture, before literature, even before we wrote a language, and before the advent of iron or bronze. Domesticating the wolf helped to secure mankind's future, yet "progress" has reduced the vast majority of dogs today to little more than useless oddities to be petted and trained not to pee on the rug. The dog hunter maintains that age old partnership with our first animal companion and that puts at us odds with the majority of our society. Modern society has brought the dog closer into camp; all the way into the house, and even the bed. We evolved the dog to help us hunt, today the farmer society has evolved the dog to mere companion and emotional crutch, some calling them "family." That family is artificial. The dog hunter holds that relationship in perspective.

The dog, more than any other domesticated animal is born with the ability to read our facial expressions, and understand the tones of our voice. The dog understands us, this comes from living beside us for tens of thousands of years, and is a very special thing. Dogs can read humans. This ability didn't arise from sleeping in our beds and getting petted, it came from working beside us, a tradition the dog hunter carries on today. The pet breeds are more likely to bite you, partly due to terrible breeding and partly because they have been too far removed from nature- the pet uses the human as an emotional crutch as much as the modern human does the pet - two species that are defying nature and reaping the mental disorders that follow such disconnect. As much as modern society urges, don't get wrapped up in the humanizing of dogs. We are the master, and they are here to bend to our will and do as we ask! Man has dominion, we are not in a Disney movie!

The dog hunter even yet finds himself at odds with most of the still hunters of today, in part because they have bought into the fences. The still hunter is little more than a vacationing agriculturalist. The still hunter "owns" game because it is on his part of the earth, behind his fence. Like Jacob, they want to horde, and count because of their feminine outlook. The still hunter also, probably without knowing, is jealous of our masculinity, as we hunt in a more primitive manner, with dog and knife. Many still hunters recall tales of getting in touch with their primitive side when hunting, so it stands to reason they would see our more primitive encounters as superior in that respect- they are jealous of our birthright and are willing to sink to trickery and deceit to get at it, if they cannot get it rightfully then they will stoop low enough to try to rid us of it, not unlike Jacob. The birthright is ours!

Thom Hartmann, in his book "Attention Deficit Disorder: a Different Perception" proposes the theory that ADHD is a lack of adaptation of members of the hunter/gatherer societies into agricultural societies. Hartmann says, in simple terms that people with ADHD are left with a hunters brain. Like Esau, these people are accused of being impulsive, short sighted, with no focus, poor planning and organizational skills. A key component to ADHD though is also hyper-focus, as hunters we all know this feeling and can see it's value in hunting - when everything slows down and you can hear the slightest sound and catch the smallest movement - that conversation that abruptly ends with a faint dog bark half a mile off. It also comes as little surprise that ADHD is far more common in boys. While Thom's theory is not proven it seems plausible, and causes thought.

Farmers complain about hogs, and that might be the understatement of the year. I can empathize with them, to a point. Farming is an un-natural state though. You cannot plant fields with crops that have very high nutritional value and then become aghast when hogs, or any other wild animal takes advantage of that readily available food source. The farmer needs to understand that what he is doing is creating a false reality in the natural world, it will not be without hardship. Those of us that subscribe to an older order are not to blame, we are just beacons to the folly. Often the farmer wants to blame the hog hunter for the hogs, but going further back the farmer is responsible for the domestication of the pig. The hunter did not domesticate swine for his pens, we were content to hunt the wild pig. Dominion comes at a cost, and begs responsibility.

You might be thinking I have a problem with farmers, I don't, but I am not fond of our farming society though. That farming society is responsible for cities, jobs, governments, money, taxes, and an over populated globe - I am not in favor of those burdens and those burdens do not fall at my feet. It is not my burden! But that is purely academic, and water under a 50,000 year old bridge. Our type lost that war, so now we have to kick, claw and scratch to keep a tiny hold on to our distant past. We re-create that past every chance we get, then are forced to return to the agricultural society that beat us out, heads dropped.

I have had Christians curl their faces when I tell them I claim Esau over Jacob. Many see that as a slap in the face of God, and the "good" men. Esau's father favored him over Jacob, and Isaac was a Godly man, so I will side with the man of the house in determining which son was fit for carrying on the family name, because that is really what we are talking about - a choice between a masculine society and a feminine society, and the feminine society has won. Fences rarely come down once up.

It might be said that I disdain "feminine" society, but I wholly understand the duality. Our future as a species depends on that duality. The woman seeks security for her offspring, while the male seeks freedom for his offspring. It takes both. The key is in not letting one over-ride the other.

(Jarrett Martin and Ella Barnes)

CHAPTER 5
HOG PROBLEM?

The notion that we have a 'hog problem' in America is up for debate. Many of the men that wear suits to work in large cities, men who rarely, if ever get to the woods would emphatically disagree with my idea that we do not have a problem, but a great resource in our feral hogs. For the sake of argument I will assume in the following passages that we do have a hog problem, though I see that much as saying we have a 'free money' problem, though "Free Money" is a very large problem when viewed from their perspective! The goal of governments is to subjectify us - they do this by bonding us to their money and not by making us truely free.

It is commonly accepted that Hernando De Soto brought hogs to the Americas in 1539, by some accounts in numbers increasing to around 700 as they reproduced in his captivity. The Spanish released some hogs as they marched, either deliberately as seed stock for their return journey or in some cases by escape as they herded them along their trek. There is documentation of hogs in Desha County Arkansas as early as 1543. In 1543 local Indians captured or killed the animals and delivered them to De Soto's returning party for rations. (The narrative of the expedition of Hernando De Soto by the gentleman of Elvas. 1907 Lewis TH)

The free ranging of hogs began in America by the settlers as early as 1770. For nearly 200 hundred years American society was accepting of the practice of free ranging hogs. Ranging hogs benefited the common man, and current law favors not the common man, but the elite. The numbers of hogs in the woods of past was kept in check by simple economics, there was a value to these animals that were fit for the table. Modern legislatures have suceeded in stripping these hogs of monetary value in an attempt to reduce thier numbers, while history tells us that increasing their value keeps them in check. Imagine hundred dollar bills laying in the bottom lands, folks are going to go pick them up. Even in the early years of our country there were cases of hogs destroying crop land, though it was more rare than today because of the lack of numbers. In addition, it was not looked at in the same way as we do today, because the hogs were of equal value to the crops, even possibly the hogs were seen as having more value than the crops they destroyed. Today crops are seen as money, where they used to be food, here in lies the difference. In todays world we only place value on neatly packaged meat for sale by large agri-companies. Our ancestors knew blood, today the buyer of meat is disconnected from the blood.

Pork used to be the meat of the common man. Pigs were a small enough animal that a family could process them easily and store the meat, more so than the cow. Much of the hog was cured which made it easier to store. The pig is, and always was, a cracker staple in America. That simple fact places the hog hunter at a disadvantage in todays world, where the class system is not only alive and well but on the upswing. The poor cracker is a mere footnote in modern American culture, though once a staple.

The range was widely closed across the nation from the 1940's to 1960's. Almost immediately there was a drop in the number of feral hogs, mostly because their rightful owners removed them. By the 1980's in most areas hogs were back on the rise though, and these hogs were not looking like grandpas hogs! After generations of being feral these hogs were taking on characteristics of their wild ancestors. Man was not managing them as before, cutting boars and introducing new boars to keep the blood tamed down. Also, the influence of the Russian hogs, escaped from hunting ranches, was starting to show in clear hybrid hogs - feral x Russian. The hybrid hogs gained hybrid vigor making them grow faster, and making them less apt for disease.

In cases I have documented wildlife departments across the south were instrumental in introducing Russian hogs into the ecosystem! These facts stir strong emotions from current state wildlife departments as you can imagine and I have personally seen cover-ups and even had threats uttered towards me when I exposed them.

The mold was set for a perfect storm. If an organized plan was ever hatched to create a hog problem in America it could not have been planned any better. The range was closed right as the influence of Russian hogs was being seen in large numbers. If the range would have stayed open it is likely that hogmen would have had success in weeding these wild hogs out as their numbers were relativley low, after all, the livelihoods of poor folks depended on it. The wild hog grows much slower than the more domesticated breeds, and their bodies are built for survival rather than built for the table. With few feral hogs in the woods, and the men that worked them, the wild strains of hogs recently introduced had free rein and they used that to their advantage.

As dog hunters we get the blame today for the release of hogs, but it wasn't men in our class that imported and released the Russian and Eurasian boars in America, it was the super rich, the wealthy elite. It wasn't our lack of desire to work hogs in the woods and keep the wild hogs in check, a tradition 400 years in the making, it was the lawmakers that closed the range and tied our hands. Yet, history has a way of laying blame on the littlest man in the fight, and when it comes to feral hogs the dog hunter and poor hillbilly are low men on the totem pole so the blame was thrusted upon our backs.

The first documented case of Russian hogs in America was in New Hampshire. In 1889 the founder of the Long Island Railroad and Coney Island, Austin Corbin, imported 14 European wild hogs from Germany. The hogs were released into a 23,000 acre "Boar-proof" enclosure. They did not stay inside the fence by all accounts. By 1941 the number of these wild hogs, inside and outside the enclosure was estimated to be around 200.

In 1902, millionaire Edward H. Litchfield imported 15-20

wild hogs from Germany and turned them out into his 8,000 acre enclosure in Hamilton County, New York. Again, it is reported his fence building skills were not up to Russian boar standards.

1912 brought yet another introduction of wild hogs into Graham County, North Carolina, by the socialite business man George Gordon Moore. Moore created a European style shooting preserve. He imported many big game and exotic animals including 13 wild hogs that he acquired from Europe. The split rail fencing on the 1600 acres had little success in holding the hogs. Around 1924 Moore rounded up a dozen of the hogs and had them transported to his property in California, where they were released, and by all accounts refused to stay penned.

I will not bore you with the details, but the trend continues of our American upper-crust being responsible for the lions share, if not all introductions of wild boar into the United States. I have scoured every resource at my disposal and I find not one instance of a poor cracker shipping over wild boar from Europe.

Most of the hogs in the woods today are a hybrid of domestic (feral) and Russian/ European hogs. We can see the influence of range hogs in the spotted hogs, listed hogs, red hogs, and white hogs. The head tells the story best though. Looking at a true wild hog from the side of the head there is a straight line between the top of the skull and the tip of the nose. The head will be long. In a domestic hog the head is very short and stout, with a deep curve from the top of the head to the snout. In hybrid hogs, as you would guess, the profile is somewhere in the middle with a little bit of a curve and an in-between size in length.

In 1971 president Richard Nixon declared America's war on drugs. I don't have any statistics to share, but common sense tells me that half a century later I can clearly say that war was a loss. While I will agree with the idea of a 'war on drugs' I have to say that the methods we have used were the wrong ones. Many companies, governments and individuals in suits have made millions off of America's war on drugs though. I will leave it up to you to decide if the government thinks the war was a loss, taking into account the money they made off of it.

Nixon proclaimed, "America's public enemy number one in the United States is drug abuse..." While no 'war' has been officially declared, America's wildlife officials aren't too far from an all out declaration of war on pigs - rural America's new public enemy number one. Like the war on drugs, this too will be a failure, because the methods they are using are the wrong ones, and again money taints the picture. As with their war on drugs, they seek to punish the low man, all the while proping up, and turning a blind eye to the men that make millions.

If total eradication is the goal, flying helicopters to shoot pigs isn't working, trapping isn't working, and the poisons they are proposing won't work, yet those 'solutions' make many men rich. Just as with the war on drugs, or the war on poverty, or the war on pigs - America must love the idea of entering social / ecological wars that it has zero chance of winning. Is winning the war the goal or is it just a means of enriching a few?

In my little mind, before declaring this war on pigs the powers that be should take a hard look at the situation and see if there really is a problem. I say there is not. I'll pull a switch on an old saying and say, "Don't look a gift hog in the snout." We have an amazing resource in feral hogs. Hernando De Sota understood the value in having woods hogs in 1540. From 1540 up until the 1960's or so, rural American's understood the value in a woods hog. What changed after all those years? Crop damage most would say, others would say all the damage wild hogs do to native wildlife, a few would tow the tired line of the undocumented lie of the disease spreading feral hog. But we started growing crops before 1960, and our wildlife is the healthiest it has been since the white man showed up at Plymouth Rock! Maybe America just needs an enemy? Maybe just a war? Maybe just a revenue stream? Maybe big agri-business sees feral hogs as a dam to their profits?

In all my years at this I have only heard of two cases of a man contracting a disease from a feral hog, and both cases were the same man. But the anti-hog clans want it both ways - they want to say that feral hogs are reservoirs of disease and they want to say that feral hog populations are exploding. It does not take a PhD in biology to understand that those two ideas oppose each other. Diseased populations don't explode - ecspecially when the two big diseases they are supposedly infected with are reproductive diseases - Brucellosis and Pseudorabies being the two main hog diseases touted. Brucellosis causes abortions of litters early on and later perminant infertility. Pseudorabies or Herpesvirus Suis also causes abortions of litters, fetal death and death in shoats. If feral hogs commonly had these diseases, as government agencies claim, this hog problem would be taking care of itself, yet it seems not to?

Anyone that has experience with animals understands that if not from breeding, from simple standards of survival - a wild animal is more hardy and healthy as a whole than it's domestic counterpart. Man cannot improve nature! Sorry Jacob. Industrial farm pigs are fed a constant diet of antibiotics to ward off the disease that their environment creates. If given the choice between eating raw pork from a wild hog or a Tyson hog I am hands down picking the wild pig. Sure, the 'wildlife' experts tell us wild pigs are disease ridden, but I have been chasing, catching, and eating these feral pigs for more than 20 years and I have only seen a handful of feral hogs that looked like something was seriously wrong, out of thousands of feral pigs. How many feral pigs have these proclaimed 'experts' laid their hands on? On an average year I probably talk to 400-500 hog hunters, hardly any ever bring up a conversation about diseased hogs they are catching. I just don't buy it, not because I can point to facts on paper, but because my personal experience tells me otherwise, and my personal experience is extensive.

It is no secret that I have no hate for pigs in the woods. Often when I talk like this I am bombarded with stories of farmers getting crops decimated by hogs. I understand their plight. I understand their hate of feral hogs. I hear stories of farmers planting and that night having hogs come in the fields and root every single seed, row by row. I can only imagine what that must feel like, and I understand the financial hardship that must be.

I want to be clear that I mean no disrespect to farmers, I

do not mean to minimize the damage that hogs do to agricultural crops. Fences before the closing of the range were built to keep animals out, historically the concept of a fence to keep animals in is a relatively new concept, and in my mind a flawed one. Hogs are by no means the only animal involved in crop damage and I would even go as far as to say that nationwide deer damage more crops than hogs do. I have never heard of a farmer trying to fence hogs out? I don't mean to place the blame on them, but from a strictly monetary stand point, it might make sense. For the millions on millions the federal government doles out to the southern states to combat feral hogs they could probably build six foot hog (and deer) proof fences around every agricultural field, and I bet they would if there were large, politically active fence companies lobbying, and tossing money at politicians hob-knobbing around.

There are farmers and ranchers that have noticed the gift horse that feral hogs can be, and changed their thinking and used them as a resource. When life hands you lemons, make lemonade they say, well; when life deals you feral hogs (tearing up you land) sell hog hunts at hundreds of dollars a pop! This is an adaptation. Fortune rewards those that adapt, the future rarely rewards those that whine. Currently the hog is winning the adaptation race against man. They say hogs are smart, but what does that say about man? Fortune rarely rewards the men with their hand stretched out.

"We have to learn to get along... or at least co-exist," as the liberals say. I do find it ironic that wildlife departments adhere to this slogan as they re-introduce mountain lions, bear, and wolves into ranching country, yet when it comes to a hog, total eradication is the goal. They tell the rancher to grin and 'bear' it as his livlihood is reduced by bear, mountiain lion and wolf, yet they cradle his head about feral hogs? Will history absolve us? I understand, mountain lion, bear and wolves are 'native,' while a feral hog is not, but hog hooves have been making tracks in America's woods for going on 500 years. At what point do they become 'native?' If the line of logic goes something like "since they aren't native here then they should be exterminated" then are we to apply that same logic to ourselves? White man is not 'native' to America. If you go back far enough Indians aren't even 'native' to America, they came over on an ice bridge. It is not my field of expertise, but I am fairly confident that many of the animals we consider 'native' were at some point introduced to America, if not by man then by their own migration. I'm just curious, at what year marker we deem an animal 'native?' In the list of non-native animals of North America we also have to add horses, pheasant, bovine, and many more. I hear no cry to exterminate horses or cows? The history of the world is in large part a story of transplanting, man and beast alike, but we tend to look at things as a picture when they are really a moving picture. Nature trudges on, despite our limited view of history.

There is a widely circulated picture of a full-blood looking Russian hog running with a dead fawn in it's mouth. I am not sure about the origin of the picture, but it hints at coming from Europe. The picture is 'proof' that hogs kill fawns. Every deer hunter sees the picture and imagines the minutes before, when the evil hog bum rushes Bambi and steals it's fresh born, healthy fawn. That must be the reason Johnny Bass-Pro didn't bag a trophy buck last year! Despite the fact that our deer population in America is at an all-time high, feral hogs are decimating the deer population? Deer hunters pour bag after bag of corn out and then complain about hogs. If you don't want hogs don't feed them! It is quite possible to hunt deer without corn, a revolutionary idea I know, but foreign to the farmer brain of Jacob I guess. Hunt deer like a hunter, and not like a farmer, and you won't have a hog problem!

So, at least in my mind, I have excused away the reasons why hogs are a problem (with little to no facts and just my person views). Why then do the outdoorsmen of America want to exterminate this resource? Aside from the farmers, I say it is because of a well orchestrated smear campaign that they have swallowed; hook, line and sinker. But why? Two reasons - money, and money!

The USDA has a fund in Washington DC that the states can apply to, in order to receive funding from the Federal government to combat their 'hog problem.' The USDA only has a set amount of money to pass out, so they look at data to determine which states have the biggest problem, line them up in order of importance and dish the money out proportionately. So each state has a financial incentive to blow their 'hog problem' up as big as they can. The states get their allotment then tap their pencils on the desk trying to think of a way to use it. Some rent helicopters at hundreds and hundreds of dollars an hour to shot (and let lay) literally tens of hogs. Literally tens! A few years ago the helicopter was going to be the silver bullet, then these fast adapting hogs got wise and stopped running, now helicopter shooting has got to be one of the least effective methods when looking at the cost verses kill ratio. Some states hire professional trappers. Most of the trappers do an amazing job of catching the shoats and young sows and boars, hardly capable of even maintaining the current population at a stalemate. Some states use the majority of their budget hiring companies to do further 'studies' on hogs that they can in turn use the next year to get an even larger portion of the USDA funds... to conduct even more 'studies.' I had one of these studies leaked to me, it was very comprehensive with all kinds of numbers, and projections but there was a whole side of the 'problem' that was not even mentioned. The study focused on the red-ink side of the equation, but neglected wholly the money that feral hogs brought into the state! Accounting is a relation of revenue and expense, to deny one side of the equation is to perpetuate a falsehood and a fraud on the American public.

Hogs do contribute to a states gross revenue. Out-of-state hunters flood to the south from the cities and the north to kill a 'Russian Boar,' usually which ends up to be a pen raised domestic hog. These wildlife tourist of course spend their money with an outfitter, they get hotel rooms, in some cases they buy game tags / licenses, they visit the local outdoor super-store because they forgot to pack their favorite scent-lock camo undergarment, the wives are at home so they hit the liquor store for some top shelf single-malt scotch and a cigar to smoke as they recall their brush with a deadly beast, and they almost always get a speeding ticket. They do their best to shake their Jacob brain as the play act a scene from Esau's life which they deep down admire.

Dog hunters spend on average a few thousand dollars a year on the basics of dog food, gasoline and veterinary care, not to mention the modern electronics necessary, ATV's, dog boxes, cut-gear, collars, leads and we all know the list never ends. Wild hog buyers spend money buying the feral hogs that trappers and dogmen catch, to send the disease ridden meat to Europe and New York City where it is prized and served in the finest restaurants. I guess the propaganda hasn't reached them yet, or the diseases only effect guys in bib-overalls? The dog hunter gets litterally tens of cents a pound while restaurants in big cities charge $40 a plate for ounces of wild boar created dishes. The high end diners mind wanders to men horseback in red blazers and knee-high riding boots, yet a more accurate image is a man with a big chew of Redman yelling, "Come on Bubba! They bayed!!!"

The Pork Council isn't too hot on feral hogs either, and why would they be - with a more healthy version of their product walking around in the woods free for the taking? The USDA colludes with the Pork lobby to ramp up the disease claims, and grossly over inflate the 'risk' that feral hogs pose to commercial hog 'herds', when the real risk to commercial hog herds is in their living conditions; animals living in mans' conditioning. In reality the commercial hogs are the reserviors of disease, as is evident in their constant diet of medications. If we were to take 10 commercial hogs, and 10 feral hogs and pen each in a barn, with no medication, which group do you think would have the highest mortality rate? Anyone who has ever raised domestic hogs can tell you unequivically that the domestic breeds are suseptible to disease.

Don't take my word for it! Just as you shouldn't take their propaganda at face value, don't take mine either, do your own thinking about it. Don't listen to words, watch a man's actions if you want the real story, and follow the money. They catch murderers by looking for who has the motive, who has something to gain, usually money, control, or power! We have no money, power or hopes for control.

CHAPTER 6
DOG STYLES

We have gotten much of the history, background and political ramblings out of the way. Now we can get down to the meat and potatoes of hog hunting with dogs!

If you put 10 hog hunters in a room together and ask them how they hunt, after the fist fights get broken up, you are likely to see 10 different ways to hunt hogs with dogs. At the risk of sounding like a left-wing panty-waste; "Our diversity is our strength." How boring would it be if we all hunted the same dogs in the same way? There are a million ways to skin this cat. Do yourself a favor and go watch some other people skin cats.

You can hunt close dogs, long range dogs, rough dogs or pure bay dogs; tight bay dogs, loose bay dogs, or you can use running catchdogs. You can free cast dogs, track cast dogs, walk them, road them, rig them off a truck, a boat, or an ATV. You can use night vision to spot hogs and turn dogs in, or just drive crop land looking for hogs. You might have feeders out and turn dogs into feeders at times you know pigs are coming to them. You can bay and tie, bay and shoot, or bay and stab. Some kill everything, others yet manage hogs. The options are almost limitless!

While it is easy to think that your way of hunting is hands down the best way, and it obviously is... for you, it is a huge mistake to think that what works for you will work for everyone. The way we all choose to hunt is based on our terrain, our properties, our hog populations, our physical limitations and simply put, what we find enjoyable. When we pass judgment on others for the way they hunt we are only showing our ignorance.

Lets say for example you hunt in the mountains and take three dogs and start walking. Your dogs hunt close and you cover from a few miles up to ten miles in a night. Your dogs jump very hot tracks and shut hogs down fast. You're a young fella, ex-military and you can walk the miles up and down without so much as a pant. You enjoy it and it produces hogs. That is great, but would that method work for an older man, lets say 60 or 70? Would that method work for a man who hunts with his young children? My guess is those kids would be turned off from hog hunting with dogs after just a couple marches. They might even prefer to sit on their phones in a deer blind and deer hunt. So, what is right for you, doesn't make it right for everyone.

When I hear people start in on a man because of the way he hunts, more times than not the man casting the judgment lives in a very small world and has never hunted but one place and usually one way. There was a time when I would not hunt with someone that hunted different than me. Now, I still have my favored style and that is how I hunt from day to day, but I have to say I enjoy hunting with other people in different ways, though my dogs will more than likely stay in the box. I have no problem admitting that I have learned stuff, and even taken some new direction over the years after exposing myself to the methods of others.

Sometimes watching another mans' dogs hunt reaffirms the pride you have in your dogs, and sometimes it raises the bar that you measure your dogs against. I remember a time when my chest was puffed out pretty far, and then I saw a mans' dogs work that popped my bubble! If I had just stayed in my little world I would probably still be walking around thinking my pot-lickers were as good as it got, resting on my laurels. My dogs, and myself, are better today because I saw a man that raised the bar. My quest is not to be the best, but to continue to find that man that raises the bar and spurs me on.

It is easy to get a big head! We are all very proud of our dogs, and we should be. We must remember that others are also proud of their dogs, and there is room enough for everyone to have good dogs. If you have to knock someone else's dogs to feel better about your own dogs then you probably need better dogs.

If you get yourself well-rounded you will be a better hog hunter, even if you do not adopt any changes to your dogs or methods. In the very least, when you have hunted different terrain, and different dog styles you will likely find yourself a more open minded person and less judgmental of others - yourself and your dogs will be better for it.

I am constantly preaching the notion that you have to match your hunting style and dog to the terrain and conditions that you hunt. I evolved from hunting all by myself, to hunting with just a couple very close friends, later yet to hunting all over with all kinds of people after becoming the editor of Tuskers Magazine, it is just part of the job. So I hauled a set of dogs all over and they almost always made me feel proud. While I talked about how no one type of dog could produce hogs everywhere, I somehow kind of thought these dogs of mine were the exception and could do it everywhere, so far they had, until one weekend in west Texas!

Myself and a couple friends hitched the trailers and headed to West Texas to hunt with a friend that lived there. My buddy had cut his teeth hog hunting with us in Oklahoma, using these very long range, loose bay dogs. In Northeast Oklahoma we are blessed with a good number of large tracts of land to hunt, but they are not loaded with hogs like many places in the south, so we need dogs that will get gone and cover a lot of land to find pigs. After moving to west Texas my friend had changed his dogs up to suit the way most hunted there. He was rigging dogs, mostly on crop land.

The first night in West Texas we hunted my buddies dogs off the hood. We did catch a couple good hogs and it was fun to hunt in a way that was so foreign to me. Walking to a bay didn't involve crawling and chopping our way through saw briers, watching for snakes, or sliding down 60% grades on our pant seats. It was easy, though it felt slightly uneasy going to a bay in the middle of cropland with no trees to climb if we had to. The change of terrain and dog style was nice, but we had not driven all the way down there to hunt his dogs, we wanted to turn some dogs out. The next day we loaded up our dogs and headed out to hit a couple ranches.

The terrain was like an old western movie and I kept expecting to look up to the cap rock and see ole Blue Duck straddling a paint stud bareback, Winchester buttstock rested on his thigh with the barrel pointed to the huge sky. It was dry and dusty. Everything that grew out of the ground had some kind of point on it that it just couldn't wait to bury in our skin.

We followed behind our two guides in the pickup as we made our way to where we were going to hunt. Shortly they stopped and got out, walked back to our truck window and said, "Let's drop 'em here, looks piggy." I gave the scene another look, looking hard. I couldn't see anything that would have given me the idea to use the words, "Looks piggy." It was cactus, canyons, washouts, dust, and what they called "thickets." The "thickets" weren't very thick. It looked like Arizona to me. We trusted their knowledge of the area though and turned a brace of dogs loose.

After a long day of hunting we had nothing to show for it! I don't even recall a single strike. Our dogs were limping, sore and their noses were caked with dust. We didn't look much different. (Throughout the day we would have to catch dogs and flush their noses with water, just to give us the hope they might strike.) The dogs had hunted hard, covering miles and miles at a loop, not unlike home, but the terrain had sure taken a toll on them. I felt defeated. One of my friends that had come felt more defeated than I did, and he headed back to camp to sleep, and no doubt lick his wounds. My brother-in-law and myself loaded up and set out to do as the Romans. We hooded dogs and had a good night of striking hogs off the road.

The next morning we loaded up and headed north to God's Country. The long drive gave me plenty of time to ponder. I understood now that rigging the dogs gave them an advantage in a couple ways. For one, it got them a little higher off the dust covered ground and kept their noses in better shape so that they could strike a hog. Secondly, rigging the dogs conserved their bodies so that they were not out there beating their feet up looking for something to strike. It just made sense.

While I never had anything against rigging, I had never done it and to be honest, I kind of saw it as cheating. Later I adapted and started to use rigging in certain cases here on the home ground when it made sense and I thought it could benefit us. This sport is tough enough without limiting ourselves and with some basic understanding you can enlarge your toolbox. When we head out to hunt we usually have a game plan of where on a piece of property we intend to send dogs. Sometimes as soon as we go through the main gate I will put a dog on the hood as we inch our way back to the place we are going to turn out. Usually we make it all the way there without a strike, but every so often the hood dog will strike in a place we never intended to even hunt. You could also road a dog or two on the way to the place you intend to hunt, though in my mind rigging gets it done faster and without using any of the dogs energy.

In life, and in hunting, we scoff at what we don't understand much of the time. It seems the easiest solution, but if we educate ourselves we open doors to new methods that can make us better hunters, and people. Almost everyone hunts the way they do for a reason, if we don't understand the reasons then we shouldn't criticize the methods.

CHAPTER 7
RANGE

Before we get started here let me explain range. Range is simply how far a dog hunts, not how far a dog will chase a pig - that is bottom. It seems like a simple enough idea but I hear folks misuse the term all the time. It usually goes like this - a few guys are standing around talking about range, fists balled up and someone chimes in that their dogs are long range, "Yeah, last night we struck a hog and when we finally got it to bay up we were 3.2 miles from the truck!" That is bottom, not range.

If you want to know your dogs range you need to take the dog to a place that you know there are no hogs and there has not been any for at least a few days, now hunt him. Range is how far that dog will consistently hunt looking for a hog to strike.

A key word in that last sentence is hunt. No matter what a dogs range, he has to HUNT! I have seen, and even owned a couple dogs that were very long range, 2 miles deep at almost any given drop, but they were not hunting, they were just running. I have also seen a pile of close range dogs that would take a hog if one jumped out of a bush, but they weren't hunting, they were just along for the walk. A dog that is not putting his nose to the ground or to the air and actively looking for a trail is not hunting, he is just there. Life is too short for such nonsense! Hunting dogs need to hunt - plain and simple with no room for excuses.

If you are pleased with a dog that is just there and will

give chase to a hog then the pound is full of free dogs and 9 out of 10 will suit you fine. Of course that is not what we are looking for in a hog dog but I would encourage you to look at your dogs and think about this. I have personally witnessed hundreds of 'hog dogs' that did not hunt! Most of the time the owner of the 'there' dog was happy with the dog, more than likely it was a pile of money and rose colored glasses that kept the owner from seeing the dog for what it truly was. But a dog is a mans property, and if it suits him, no matter how worthless I think the dog is, it is none of my business! I will not criticize any mans dog, but if asked I will give my honest opinion.

In psychology there is a term called "Buyer's Stockholm Syndrome." In a nutshell, if we buy a Chevy (or a Catahoula) we immediately associate positive things about the product (or dog) and discount any information that would make us think otherwise. This wiring inside the human brain is there so that we do not second guess our choices. You have no doubt been driving and seen a squirrel in the road up ahead. He has plenty of time to get out of the way, however about the time he makes it to the edge of the road he darts back into the middle, then runs right and then changes back to left and then you hit him. This is why humans are wired with the Buyer's Stockholm Syndrome, or more accurately a broad term called "Principal of Commitment." It is a safety mechanism. While our commitment might help us in picking a path out of the way of stampeding water buffalo, it can limit us too. The successful dogmen are constantly evaluating their dogs and are not afraid of loosing their investment on a dog. As with most things, it takes a middle of the road approach. It is a very easy trap to fall into but when that truck passes find yourself on the side of the road and not the middle! In dog hunting this principal is often referred to as "Kennel Blindness."

There are benefits in long, medium, and short range dogs, just as there are hindrances. Property size alone is a very large deciding factor in the range you want out of your dogs. If the properties you hunt are 200 or even 500 acres then a long range dog is going to cause a lot of trouble and headaches! Before long you will for sure be on a first name basis with the local game wardens. On the flip side, if the hog population in your area is pretty low, then a short range dog is going to become very tiring, and you will probably be on a first name basis with your local boot repairman.

Range is decided by necessity... if you are in charge of it. I say that because many hog hunters use close range dogs because that is what they have and they do not have the information to know how to change a dogs range. Again it goes back to the psychology I mentioned earlier, they convince themselves of the benefits of close range dogs because it is what they have. While many will disagree with me, range is a trained habit. And yet again, we will get to that training at a later time.

Range is also decided by other traits in your dogs. Typically long or medium range dogs should be loose baying. A long range running catchdog or even a long range rough baydog is not going to live very long, or at the very least spend a lot of time on the injured reserved list and pile up large veterinarian bills. It is asking a lot of a dog to hold a hog at one mile while it takes us an hour and a half to find a road that gets us close so we can lend a hand. I have seen it first hand many times. If you have a dog whose natural inclination is to be rough when working a hog then the options are to try to take the rough out of him, limit his range, or just cut him loose and hope the veterinarian can put Humpty back together again.

In an ideal world every hunting dogs range is unlimited. A dog naturally wants to hunt as deep as is necessary to find game. Any limiting of range in a dog is a man made inhibition, either directly or indirectly. Of course, this does not include physical limitations that a dog might have. If your dog is fat, naturally that is going to affect his range. If your dog only has two legs that too is going to limit range. (I have seen more than a few three legged dogs that were more than a hand)

When we train for long range dogs the biggest hurdle is keeping ourselves from unknowingly putting limits on the dog. There are plenty who say range is in the breeding, I disagree. It is just plain common sense that we can reduce a dogs range, very easily, so why would it not stand to reason that we can add to a dogs range, or not limit the dogs range? I have trained a good handful of dogs from the pound, the side of the road, and "Uh-oh" breedings, and while all those dogs did not make the final cut, all but just a couple hunted very deep, not as my testament, but as note to my theory that dogs naturaly hunt as deep as necessary when not inhibited.

Range of course increases the ground a dog can cover in an attempt to locate a track, but it of course does not increase a dogs ability. Despite range, a dog must have a good set of tools to use. Without ability range means nothing - range is not ability!

The use of tracking collars has also affected range in dogs. Before I ran tracking collars on my dogs I wanted them to stay about 300 to 500 yards, it just made life easier and allowed for more time in my bed. After I started tracking my dogs I began to push them further, out to a mile plus. Knowing where the dogs were made the rangier dogs more manageable. A silent cur dog ranging a mile plus with no collar left you sitting at the truck straining your ears hoping for a bark to give you an idea of where to drive. Logically, back in the day, most all of the men who ran long range hog dogs were hunting hounds, or open dogs.

Whatever range you look for, or train in dogs, pick it and don't let it pick you.

SHORT RANGE

A short range dog is hunting anywhere from 1 foot to 300 yards from the handler. A short, or close range dog can be rough, loose, tight, or running catch. You can hunt a short range dog by walking the woods as the dog ventures out but stays close until striking a hog, you can road hunt a close dog, or even cast a close dog. A short range dog really is the most versatile dog as far as the sheer number of styles he can be hunted, and it opens up almost any size property as hunting grounds.

I would venture to say that 75% of hog dogs are short range. I do not mean this as a negative. Short range dogs can be a huge benefit when hog hunting. It seems that day by day the large chunks of land in America get fewer and fewer. It is sad but I guess all we can do is chalk it up to progress. Short range dogs are needed for hunting smaller properties. Short range dogs can also be an asset because in theory it keeps you closer to the action, though with many of the hogs today, where a hog is struck and where a hog is bayed is often miles apart, no matter what the dogs range that struck him.

When a short range dog gets out towards the outer limits of his range he will likely show back up, or check in, and then go back out. If you are walk hunting, the progress you make through the woods will keep him in 'new dirt.' If you are casting the dog, after a check-in you will have to send him another direction or change spots.

The check-in can be handy when hunting, and in the days before tracking systems it was a must. Some short range dogs will check in every 15 minutes, 30 minutes, and even as long out as hour or more, while a long range dog may not check-in for 4 or 5 hours, if at all. While the 'check-in' is widely viewed as a cur dog trait, I somewhat disagree, it is a trained behavior and I have seen plenty of hounds that check in. Where my disagreement comes from is mostly in the misuse of the word. Sometimes the dog always being around is called a "check-in." For a dog to "check-in" he has to "check out" for a while. If a dog walks by your feet, then darts off for 30 seconds and then comes right back - he isn't "checking-in," he's dependent on you.

Sometimes dogs that "check-in" aren't really checking in, but are really just confused. A dog that checks in runs up ahead looking back at the handler, maybe gets out of sight for a few seconds and then comes back to start it over again is not sure of things. From the beginning of his hunting career he went hunting with his pack, handler included, and they took off. From the hunters stand point he was just walking, from the dogs standpoint the hunter was hunting. When the dog checks in he is wondering why the leader of the pack is not leading? The dogs' check-in is almost like him saying "Come on! Get up here. Lead us, you're the leader of the pack!" This is a dependent dog

The check-ins, despite the dogs range, should be spaced long enough apart to give him enough time to thoroughly cover the ground within his range. By that I mean if a dogs range is 100 yards we don't want a check-in every minute, it should be spaced long enough for him to guarantee that there is not a hog within that 100 yards.

I want to be clear that I am not against a dog checking in, what I don't like is a dog that hangs around! A dog that checks in is very handy. Many times a handler may not even notice the check-in, the dog doesn't have to come sit at your feet or nudge your hand, instead most dogs that have a true check-in just fly by, or they even just get close but not where you can even see them and they are off again, they are checking your position not necessarily letting you check their position!

Many of you probably cocked your head, like a smart dog thinking, when I mentioned casting close range dogs. It is rare, but folks do cast close range dogs. All that means is that you are taking the dog out of the box, and you are picking the general direction he goes to hunt, either free cast or track cast. The hunter that cast a short range dog is not walking with the dog. "Cast" is more often associated with longer ranged dogs though.

MEDIUM RANGE

A medium range dog is hunting around 300 - 1000 yards deep, too far to be considered close and not far enough to be considered long range. These yard measurements are just approximations of course and five hunters will likely have five different definitions of the ranges. It really isn't important anyway.

For quite a few years medium range has been my goal in dogs, but it is a tough one. Usually a dog that will go 500 will go 2 miles. I have had some success in getting dogs to cast in this range, but every time the dog has begun to get deeper and deeper with age and experience. Some guys use the tone button to keep a dog inside of the range they want the dog to hunt, and from what I hear it is working in some cases. I don't have strong enough feelings either way to use my energy to limit a dog so I haven't tried it. A medium range dog though, in my mind is the ideal, they are covering plenty of ground but remain within calling distance and are still within easy walking distance.

Like the close range dog a medium range dog can be hunted about any way. Terrain will determine whether you want rough or loose dogs. If you can usually cover the dogs range fairly fast a rough medium range dog may work. On the flip side, if your terrain is thick and it takes you 40 minutes to get 1000 yards then a rough dog might have a tough go of things.

LONG RANGE

A long range dog is hunting around 1200 yards deep or up to two to three miles from the handler. In the curdog, non-hound hogdog world long range dogs are the most misunderstood dogs! Long range dogs are not for everyone. First you need large properties, 1000 acres is close to the bottom limit. Secondly you need free time! If you have to be at work in two hours, turning long range dogs loose is not going to be conductive to keeping your boss happy!

My buddy Pat Lewing said a fella that runs long range dogs needs to be Christ-like, with patience, and carry a sack lunch. I would have to agree.

Long range dogs are my preferred style, not because it is best for everyone but because it is best for me, in my conditions. This type of dog allows me to cover as much ground as possible with the littlest amount of work. Typically we will turn out two or three dogs, we point them in the general direction that we want them to cover and they go. We sit on the tailgate, inspect GPS screens, laugh at each other and wait. Many folks cringe when they hear long range and say, "I ain't walking THAT far!" But that is a misconception, we walk very little, rarely over 300 yards to a bay. When the dogs bay we drive and get close. In fact, hunting long range dogs is the laziest way to hunt!

A good long range dog does not immediately head for the next county, he hunts out, covering the areas close fully before inching deeper and deeper. Not all deep hunting dogs do this and many times I have seen closer ranged dogs come in behind long range dogs and strike hogs that were missed. It goes back to the notion I mentioned earlier that dogs must hunt. When these type of dogs burn the countryside down and miss hogs it is usually a case of two dogs racing each other. You can take two great dogs that hunt very good, put them together and they forget the hunt and just race. This problem is easily noticed, and easily remedied by simply not hunting the dogs together. Often times, this just occurs with the excitement of the first turn-out.

It takes a change in mindset to hunt deep dogs. When I first started my nerves were a mess! Hunting deep dogs has a different feel to it, we are more removed from our dogs just due to distance, we are less involved and not readily available to help the dogs - they are on their own. For me, I love the beauty of it. When everything goes right it is amazing, like a fine tuned machine. We free cast a couple dogs, they hunt out ever deeper, we hear a strike faintly and watch the game on our tracking system, they bay, we drive close, listen for a bit, turn a bulldog to them, flip and tie. When it goes off clean like that it is simply beautiful! When it doesn't go smooth it is game wardens, 10 hours without seeing dogs, trespassing, folks shooting at dogs, and dogs ran over in the road. Like Easu it is feast or famine!

Tanner Herr

CHAPTER 8
TRAINING FOR RANGE

I view range, in part at least, as a side effect of the bond or connection a handler has with the young dog. In most cases a strong connection with the pup, because we are setting range in as the dog is young, will yield a closer dog. Some will adamantly disagree. Almost everyones grandpa told them when they were kids to not pet their hunting dogs because it was going to ruin them. Where did that notion come from? It wasn't divined from thin air. We want Esau dogs that are not afraid of the wild, not Jacob dogs that are content to mill around the tents. A strong bond with a pup sets a partnership, which is fine for the closer range dogs but in long range dogs we are after a more independent dog - a dog a little closer to a wild animal, but not without handle!

I liken the long range dog to the racehorse. The 'breaking' is just at a bare minimum, we want a dog that we can handle, but we have to leave all the spirit in them. We are just hanging on, not controlling. But this is often misunderstood. Long range dogs can have great handle, and should, but that training comes after the habit of hunting deep has been set in. Habit is an important word. We train with behaviors and if we are successful we instill a habit. When a behavior becomes a habit it is more solidly set in a dog, this is why we can 'break' or put a good handle on a dog after they have the habit of hunting deep without limiting range. This backward method bucks every dog training book you will pick up, it bucks common sense, and it bucks our inclination to start training handle into a pup from day one.

A good example of habit is familiar to most; When a male dog likes to fight other dogs it is most often recommended to castrate the dog. Castration limits the testosterone levels, and when done while a dog is young it will usually stop the dog from fighting. In most cases when you band an older dog for fighting it does almost nothing to limit the fighting. This is because the dog is largely fighting as a habit and not as an instinct - or result of testosterone. Breaking a habit in a dog is like quiting smoking, it can be done, but it is very hard and takes a re-wiring of sorts in the brain of the dog.

Some claim that long range is bred into lines of dogs. I agree, in the sense that I believe all dogs are naturally long range, and I also disagree. The guys that claim it is a bred trait are hunting long range dogs. It might seem to be automatic because their training methods are so ingrained that all the pups are going long. I also promise that one of these 'long range pups' placed in the hands of a hunter not familiar with training long range dogs will end up hunting close. It is commonly accepted that we can limit a dogs range, probably because it is easy, yet it is not widely accepted that we can lengthen a dogs range, probably because it is hard. Old dogs can be taught to hunt deeper, but it goes back to that word 'habit,' and it is not easy.

I am going to explain about training for range here. It might seem out of place as we have not even gotten into any training yet, however, we have to know what we want in range before we do any training with the dog. There are many very small details about range that if we overlook and do not think about in every aspect of future training will lead to confusion in the dog, and effect range. Before we start any training we have to thoroughly understand how our actions effect range, otherwise we are just rolling the dice on what the range of our dog will be. When training a dog it is seldom the large things that run us off course, it is almost always the tiny, seemingly inconsequential things. We have to train ourselves to be aware before we start to train the dog.

We should only train in calm situations, this goes for us and the pups. If you are in a bad mood then save training for another day. If you just brought home three new dogs and everyone is barking and growling and sniffing butts then train after things calm. Limit distractions. Don't invite five buddies over with all their pups and think you are going to train. The best training is done one on one. Dogs can read human emotions and even movement, keep your emotions in check and stay still as much as possible. As my buddy says, "Don't be waving your arms around!" It sounds weird, but there is merit. Arms at your side. Our role is mostly in setting up proper training scenarios, once the pup is in motion our main goal is to stay out of things. At a kids basketball game parents and coaches are screaming as the kids run the court, "Like chickens chasing a grasshopper" as an old man in a cowboy hat laughed at one one of my kids games many years ago. Those kids don't hear the parents, at best they are reverting to their training, at worst they are just running. When we train dogs it is no different. Once the dog is in motion you are on the sideline. If you have done the background work the sideline is a comfortable position, if you have not you will likley find yourself screaming.

TRAINING FOR SHORT RANGE

Unless you luck into one of these 'automatic long range pups,' training for a short range hunting dog is the easiest range to train. As you lay drags, bay in a pen and mock hunt you are free to do as you please. You can talk to the dog, walk with them, push them on track etc. While training in the woods when the dog gets to the outer limits of where you want his range to be you can call the dog, or even tone him with an E-collar. When the dog returns ignore him, don't pet him, or talk to him. If the dog wants to just hang around start walking, still silent and pay him no mind. Don't even look at the dog! When the dog starts to go out stop and wait, silent as a church mouse.

Walking the dog in the woods, where he is not likely to get on a hog, is also a good exercise in setting range. Allow the dog to range out and just call him back at the outer limits. When doing this you can praise and pet on the dog upon returning, however when we are really working the dog on tracks don't pet and keep talking to a minimum.

If you are training a casting type dog then use your lead to build up 'want to.' Lead the dog to the head of a laid track and when you are pretty sure he has got a good whiff of the scent just hold him back, not so long he loses interest, but long enough to build anticipation. If he is pulling and wanting to go then un-snap him and give him a verbal command like "Hunt 'em up" or whatever. You stay put! You stay silent. We do not want to distract the dog in any way. Even the sound of walking around can pull a young dog off a track if he thinks his ears have located the game, or if he thinks he is being left behind. The casting type dogs need to be assured that we will be where we sent them from when they return. We are setting a habit here, so you will keep the drag under the desired range. This is using bottom to set range, so just a few goes at this exercise is all we will do. If you over-do this method you can limit bottom or make a lazy dog, you are not always going to be able to lead him to the mouth of a hot track, we don't want the pup thinking that is the game. We want these drags and mock hunts to be very easy. If we make them too hard then what do you do if the pup goes further than you really want but hasn't found the end of the drag or lost it? We sure don't want to make a quitter, but we also don't want a 300 yard dog wandering out 1200 yards. So make them very easy, later on, after range is somewhat loosely defined in the dogs head then we have all the time in the world to really test the dog on hard hunts. Using the verbal command mentioned above, when we know the young dog has a nose full of hog scent will be helpful later down the road, it will become a signal for the dog get busy later in life when we feel they are being lazy.

After just a couple goes on the drag then set a new drag. Now we will cast the dog 'x' amount of yards off of the mouth of the drag depending on how far you are pretty sure he will range and find it. If you already have an old dog that hunts in a range you are after then by all means pair the pup, remember, this training is only about range, but again, just a couple times, we are not after 'me-too' dogs.

If the dog is not wanting to go then walk him slow, on the lead, down the track and see if the 'want to' is starting to show. Walk slow and even pull him off the track side to side. If he isn't showing signs of wanting to go then you need to back up and get him in the pen, or wait for some maturing. If the desire is not there then we don't have many tools to work with on setting range. Training with dogs that do not have desire yet can be frustrating and can even set up failure and make future training, when the desire is there, even harder. If the want-to isn't there don't push things!

Never shock a dog in an effort to effect his range! If you are using the tone on your e-collar then you need to have already set the groundwork with the dog to teach the meaning of the tone - and not just as a precursor to a shocking. The tone should be used as an attention getter, used in pair with vocal commands and with praise and positive re-enforcement. As training gets further along, as in trash-breaking, the tone will be used as a warning, but at this point in training range we want to be very careful with any negative training because we can effect 'hunt' without knowing or meaning to. When we shock a dog we are rolling the dice - it is a gamble as far as what behavior the dog will link the shock to. If a dog is at 301 yards and we shock him there is practically no chance he will link that pain to getting 1 yard too far from you. The dog might have just got a big ole nose full of hog scent at the second he was shocked, in that case you are ten steps back. He might link the pain to the act of hunting. Anytime we shock a dog we have to wait for the moment that a dog is so involved in a behavior that 'chasing that skunk,' or whatever, is so consuming every ounce of his brain that the correct link will more likely be made. Again, never shock a dog to effect his range unless you are looking for a dog scared to hunt that won't get out from under the truck or under your feet.

Most well bred dogs will have enough desire to hunt in them that training handle will not effect close range dogs. With that said, don't over-do it. Hunting dogs can be pets, IF they become pets after they have been made into HOGDOGS! For pups I am happy with a good 'COME,' and them knowing their name, for closer range dogs the handle can be more expansive.

TRAINING FOR LONG RANGE

I jumped from short range right into long range, skipping over the medium dogs, that was on purpose. Training medium range dogs takes some aspects from short and long range, so I figure it is best to understand both first.

As I said earlier, I believe all hunting dogs are born with the desire to hunt as deep as they need to in order to find game. Man limits a dogs range either through training designed to, or on accident by creating dependency. The dogs physical condition and body type can also limit range. A long range dog must be built for endurance, have the nutrition for a long haul, be sound, and be parasite free. (All hunting dogs should fit this criteria, though some closer range dogs can catch hogs in lesser condition.)

When training for long range dogs first we have to not put limits on the dog. Staying out of the way is hard one for most humans when it comes to animals - we always want to get our hands in there! This reduces the dogs you can buy cruising the interwebs for long range prospects. You cannot buy a 3 month old pup from Jimmy The Hog Hunter. Who knows what harm has already been done? Unless I know the guy I won't even waste my time on an 8 week old pup, I just don't know how many times they have been kissed and peed on the floor, although at this tender age the dependency that may have been created is easily corrected. This is where the fight starts when talking about long range dogs! It is a balancing act between socializing the pup, getting a tiny bit of handle and having an uncontrollable mess of a dog that runs off and you never see again. Of course there has to be some kind of bond if you ever plan to catch the dog in the woods. That said, unless your pups are in the back 40, on automatic feeders and you never give them medications there is going to be a bond there. When we feed a dog we are creating a bond. I like a dog to know their name, so I usually talk to them as I feed and with pups I call their name a couple times as I do. I even pet them a touch as I feed. Long range prospects are not laying on my couch, the kids don't get to drool over them, they aren't licking plates, they aren't wrestling around with me in the yard or hauled to town in the passenger seat of the truck. I can already hear the soft pitiful inflection of the sad "Ahhhs." In an attempt to quiet those "Ahhhs" I will say that my older dogs are afforded many luxuries after they get in the habit of hunting deep, with no ill effect on their range. I wait to put the handle and give the love to a pup until I am certain it will not hinder their range. A huntingg dog must be made a hunting dog first before other ventures are attempted - i will love on a hunting dog but not just a regular old dog - I leave that to the Jacobs.

We start the long range dog on mock hunts, in the bay pen and with drags just as with the short range dog, but with less of it. Usually one drag and one mock hunt is all they get, if the performance is there. Laying a one mile drag just isn't practical, so the majority of their range training is 'on-the-job.' The mock hunts and drags are not so much about range as they are about confidence. When training with limiting range in mind our drag and mock hunts are dual purpose, with long range dogs the training is about opening them up to the joy of hunting. With the close range dog, most of the training is done one-on-one, with long range dogs that is a very tall order so most of the training is done with two dogs. With close dogs the training can start pretty early in life, but with long range training, just due to the distances, a dog needs to be very well matured. I usually don't start a dog until 11 to 12 months. Ideally the tandem training is an old dog that knows which way is up and a pup, but it can be done, though much harder, from scratch with two pups. Extreme patience is required! When we talk about training with two pups it should be evidently clear that we are talking about "pups" on the older end of that spectrum. Two immature pups is a recipe for a bunch of playing and not much work. You can get one 8 year old boy to work if you crack a hard whip, to get two 8 year old boys to work together you got to lay that whip leather on some back ends - not much different with dogs, except if you lay that leather on pups it will likely shut them down and nothing positive will come from the exercise. Maturity is a must.

I will come at this from the angle that you do not have long range dogs to train your pups. You have avoided humanizing your pups, you both still know they are dogs, they have matured physically and mentally and they have had the musky scent of a boar hog sucked in through their nostrils more than a couple times. The baypen has taught them the fun of baying and they have an elementary understanding of a hogs movements coupled with a healthy respect for the danger they impose - it is time to go to the woods!

You have got to do your homework! In successful training we set dogs up to succeed, if we set dogs up to fail, and they fail, the failure belongs to us, not them. In long range dogs it does not start out by getting pups to cast 3/4 of a mile to strike a hog. Maybe surprisingly, we do not want that! We are after dogs that cast and hunt close to us, venturing deeper and deeper when they aren't finding hogs close. Dogs that light out and end up at a mile deep in two minutes are not the goal. Our first time to the woods we want pups to cast and bay a hog,or at least give chase; the distance is not a factor. We do want to set it up where they cast though. The best way is with feeders. If the hogs are tending to your corn charity know the likely times and know the direction they are coming from. Now you cast the two pups from as long a distance as you highly suspect they will go before hitting a track. When you turn them loose you have taken them from the box without talking, you haven't scratched an ear or done anything to get the attention back on yourself. You must snap them to a lead. Lead them as far as you have to in order to get them pulling and you see want to, hold them back letting anticipation grow. Pups want to run, use that. Don't worry about the distance. If we cast from 50 yards or 500 it doesn't matter much at this point. The idea we are pressing home to a pup is that getting away from the dude that feeds him isn't a big deal, and it actually can be really fun. I have to hammer it home- that first hunt is so important! We really, really... really want the first hunt to involve at a bare minimum looking at pork. We want a race or a bay - ACTION! It is a huge leg up, but if it doesn't happen it's not the end of the world.... but do your darndest to make it happen.

If the pups cast from 150 yards and hit a track an give you some barking count your lucky stars! If they quit or are not able to finish out the track and return just load them with no talking, no emotion, total blankness. At this point you can go back to the mock hunt but make it a challenge. The "gimmies" are gone. We are after total success, so only give praise when a hog is bayed. Repeat the next day if at all possible, or two days later at the latest. On the rare instance that you catch a hog with the pups then give them one or two days and repeat from a greater distance, importantly - at a different location, this encourages hunting and not just checking. I have seen many dogs that just checked thickets for hogs - while it is merely slightly different than hunting, it is a lesser venture.

If you send pups and they just come back then you casted from too far, so lessen the distance next time, but for now ignore the pups. When they come back load them in the box as fast as possible. Don't go straight home. Make them stay in the box. If you have older dogs go try to catch a hog as fast as you can! Leave the pups in the box and let them see all the fun they are missing out on. Even if you don't catch a hog, letting the pups stay in the box while their friends run is a good lesson. Give these pups a few days in the kennel and then it is back to mock hunts. It is important to remember that we are ignoring the pups, not disciplining them. You are disappointed, I have been there, but just stay neutral. We punish when a dog knows what to do but chooses otherwise, we cannot punish a dog that doesn't know better.

Sometimes the pups will go out to 200 or 300 yards and one will get left behind while one pup circles around hunting. Eventually the hunting pup will return to the pup that quit. Don't pick favorites! Often the lax pup will take off with the hunting pup, or they might just hang out at 300 yards, messing about. This is a good thing, and though I understand I sound like a broken record, keep quiet. Getting dogs comfortable with being away from us is also a goal here. If they lay down and take a nap then you do the same and take a nap in the truck, the longer the better. Do not call the pups in! If you have to stay there all night then measure that up to success.   On the off chance your pups light out and go miles you stay put unless they are bayed. In long range dogs we need that added security that dogs will return to where you cast them from, so make them come back to you. It might turn into a long night, if so count your blessings. Of course if the pups are in danger get them, or if they do not offer to come back then go get them, but give them plenty of time to have the opportunity to come back to you.

Not too long ago me, Jarrett Martin and Seth Cobb rolled though a gate, we cast Jarretts' Bo and my dog Fuzz. Shortly after turning dogs out I realized that I did not have a track on Fuzz. I had forgotten to turn her collar on. It's a bad feeling in this new world. Bo hunted out, as did Fuzz I guessed. Bo deepened out to a mile plus and we made our way in trucks closer in case he bayed. We chased the dog for a couple hours, as I vocalized to Seth to reassure myself - "Fuzz is with him." After a couple hours Bo was making his way to us on the road. When he came in I kept shining the field, looking for the reflection of those eyes of Fuzz. The light didn't bounce back at me. I was sick. We returned to the spot we had cast them and we all reclined in our seats expecting a long night after Seth blew a dog horn a few times, just enough to get all the house dogs within a couple miles cranked up. Shortly Fuzz showed up. She reverted back to her training. Sometimes the ability of these dogs amazes me; we turn loose and they travel upwards of 5 miles and find us on a road 3 miles from where we cast them, sometimes they travel a great distance and come right back to us from a different direction. With that said, it is important to instill the notion that we will be where the dog was cast from, this comes from our small clues we give in early training.

I had an old dog that this notion of returning was so instilled into that you were not going to load him from any place other than where you turned him out. At times it was a pain, being 300 yards from him and watching him back-track himself and he wouldn't come in to a call, but you could bet the farm he would be where you cast him from 3 miles away.

On the flip side - a long time ago I had a catahoula I named Plott - he was a dead ringer for a Plott, black with brindle trim and above average ear. This dog was a 100% hogdog, but he had no sense of direction! These were the days before a Garmin, and I was too poor for a beep beep unit. I lost that dog half the time I turned him out. Many a night I spent sleeping in my truck on some old forgotten wagon trail waiting for him to return, most dawns broke with the rest of my dogs asleep under that Toyota, but not Plott. Like I said, he seemed to have no sense of direction, but bottom was not a foreign concept to him! One day my old friend Lee George and I were hunting around McAlester,

Oklahoma. We were driving roads looking for a track to cut. We found one and sent the dogs, headed by my old "Rebel" dog. The dogs cut out down a dry creek and in an hour we had a bay. As we approached we saw it was a sounder and upon our entrance into the picture Rebel grabbed a hold of a good boar, aided by Lee's Mountain Fiest, Tex. As we were running in pigs were pouring out of the bottom and I caught a glimpse of a sow with Plott close behind. I was cussing in my head. We caught the boar and once back on top I began calling for Plott, though I knew it was pointless. The sun was down and we were whipped when I pointed that truck towards Tahlequah and my bed warmed by a woman. "Someone will call," I told Lee, and he played along with a "Yeah" through his old lips. He knew the dog. The next day I made the two hour drive back to McAlester, cruising those oil well roads calling and cussing. There was no response. That was on a Sunday. Tuesday a man called me from the town of Kinta, a good 15 miles from where we had lost Plott. "I got yer dog," he relayed. I was relieved. "Where'd ya pick him up?" I came back. "He was in the back yard with my beagles," he responded. I called the wife and she loaded kids to go get the senseless dog. Such were the days before tracking collars, when a phone number on a collar meant something.

One night I sent dogs and they struck and got out of hearing. It ended up being a longer night than I had accounted for! I drove, stopping to listen in the silence that tens of thousands of acres free of a house could offer. I imagined baying far off more than a time or two. Mile after mile I grew tired and returned to the place I had sent those darn dogs. I always hated that return trip, because more times than not it was the sign of not catching a hog. There is no telling how many hogs we bayed back then and didn't know. I kicked my seat back and was asleep in no time. Around 11pm I was awoken by a bobbing light coming up behind me. Now take into mind, I was in the middle of NOWHERE! I clicked the safety off my 22 rifle hoping it was sufficient firepower and exited the truck with it at ready in the direction of the light. Shortly three kids come into view, surprised of the rifle aimed at them. "Hey..." was all they could get past shaky lips. I retorted with a "Yeah," and they came back, "What are you doing?" I could read the naiveness in them and dropped the barrel, slightly. "Waiting on my dogs, what are YOU doing?" "Man, we're stuck in the mud hole up ahead. Think you can pull us out?" I knew the hole they spoke of, " I doubt it." This mud hole was one I wouldn't take my old Toyota through without a dire situation pressing me into foolishness. We approached the hole and there sat a brand new, paper tagged, two wheel drive Chevy pick-up. The new truck was sucked in the mud, water over the door jams with about three inches of water in those new floorboards. After some coaxing they got me to ford the mud hole past them to try to pull them out. The small truck couldn't budge that heavy truck, despite my best attempts. I gave up and returned to go back past them to get to my resting spot in hopes my dogs had returned. I got stuck. After much mud wollering a plan was devised and me and their leader would walk overland back to the WMA road where I could get cell phone reception to call my wife. As me and Mr. Off road 2 wheel drive made our trek across hill and holler my coon light give out, and he didn't have a light! He was in the lead, as I directed him, and before too long he held a branch and let it go and by god if that thing didn't get me right in the eyeball. I have a tendency for things getting in my eyeball. It was bad! One eyed, I took the lead and got us to the road. It was probably 1am when I awoke that woman, "Go out to the barn and get two log chains, and the come-along and meet me at 'such-n-such' road." We were good I thought. After some waiting she showed up, with one small kid in a car seat and one in the womb. She wasn't happy and I wasn't any happier. I pulled the log chains from the bed of her Ford then boldly asked, "Where's the Come-along?" "It's back there!" She was short from lack of sleep. I dug around, knowing it wasn't there as she approached me. I grabbed a fence stretcher and held it up, "There," she said and my heart sank! "Ok," I said and through clamped lips asked her to drive us as close as I figured the two-wheel drive truck would get us. She did, reluctantly. At the end of the trail I told her to go home, knowing I still had a long night ahead. After a hike I got my truck unstuck with no aid of the fence stretcher that had been mistaken for a come-along, all the while one hand cupped over an eye that was swollen and dripping tears. My dogs had all returned by this time, they were curled up in the leaves, waiting for a ride back to their doghouses. I promptly told the boys I was headed back to Tahlequah and if they wanted a ride they better jump in. They didn't, afraid to leave that brand new 2 wheel drive. I rolled into the house after sun up, with a hand cupped over that messed up eye, driving like a drunk. I downed some pain pills, slept, then went to the eye doctor. Point being, dogs that return are good, and don't help fools - they will only drag you to their level of foolishness!

A very large piece of getting dogs to cast is not letting them hang around - seems pretty logical. When a dog comes back to us we load them in the box, no if's, and's or but's! When we let dogs hang around with us at the trucks pretty soon our anger subsides, and we start talking to the dog, and then we, or one of our hunting buddies rubs an ear and without thinking we are training a dog to hang around. A well driven dog will train himself to get gone if the alternative is to sit in the box and miss out, but at some point we will probably have to pass out some scolding and maybe even dust the fleas off his back end with a switch. When I see a young dog tracking himself back to me after not really hunting out like I would like, I start making my way to him so he doesn't make it all the way back to the truck. I will catch him without calling and then physically correct him and re-cast him immediately down the same track towards the dog or dogs that are hunting out. The dog will sometimes just make a large loop around you and come back to the truck from a different angle, if so load him. Sometimes the dog will get gone and just pout around away from you. This is a good thing so let him. If the dog or pup stays out, pouting around, 100 or 500 yards let him stay there. If he wants to stay an hour or three hours let him. We have to use our patience and wait him out, we don't want to call him back. When he does come back we stay neutral and just load him, no praise and no punishment.

I will say it here unless I forget later, when we punish a dog we have to be clear about the purpose. I have seen a dog trash on a skunk or a diller and the handler holler their name at them and when they come in punish them. That is only teaching a young dog not to come in when you holler. The best approach is to haul your butt to where the action is and punish them at the scene. This gives the dog a better chance of understanding exactly what you are unhappy with. Boot soles are cheaper than trained dogs.

Many years ago a lady tagged along on a hunt with me and a friend. She had a cur dog I will call "Slow." She brought "Slow" up to us and our dogs when we cast the dogs down a trail. The dog had never been cast hunted before, it was clear as the dog jotted out with the other dogs about 30 yards then returned to us at full speed, like the boogieman was hot on his heels. The woman screamed, "GO HUNT!" kicked, and mashed the button on a shocking collar sending the dog howling in a bee-line under the truck. I would have got under that truck too, where she couldn't kick at me. Possibly from guilt, shortly the lady was down on her hands and knees petting the dog under the truck and sweet talking him with sentences so long that they needed commas. With tail tucked and a low hung head the dog came out and milled around us. The woman petted on the dog as it hung around and made excuses for him not hunting. "He hasn't hunted with your dogs," she reasoned, my buddy replied, "These dogs haven't hunted with him either." I pushed my grin back, that was a good one! It wasn't but a couple minutes and "GO HUNT!" was again yelled as the lady attempted to toss "Slow" down the trail like a lack of forward momentum was the problem. Of course the dog just whirled around and headed for that truck again, and again he was given that electric. I don't like to tell people how to do things but I politely told the lady the dog was confused and it might be best to just wait and try again at the next turnout. She was insulted and continued on the same line of confusing directions for the rest of the night, in a manner that I took as a jab at me trying to instruct. That poor dog was shell-shocked and had no idea what was wanted of him. At times he was punished and at other times he was loved on. I was confused myself. If I ever find a dog that understands English I won't be hunting that dog, I will be rich. Dogs read our actions, and maybe a few simple verbal commands... sentences spoken to dogs are a waste of your breath unless coupled with a good sense of humor.

That last bit reminds me of a good dog joke. Bob and Jim went hog hunting one night and Bob took out his cur dog and told the dog, "Them hogs oughta be down in the bottom huddled up in the crook of the creek." The dog responded, "Ok, I'll check there first" and took off. Jim's jaw dropped and he stammered around, "That dog just talked!" Bob returned in a humdrum voice, "Yeah." In an instant the dog was bayed and the two men took off. At the bay Jim grabbed the dog and spoke, "You can talk?" The dog said, "Yeah, I've always been able to." "That's amazing," Jim retorted and the dog shrugged it off. "I used to lead an exciting life, I worked for the CIA, and traveled the globe working with spies. I could listen in on secret conversation and then tell my coworkers what was said. People would say anything around a dog. I traveled the globe and saw all kinds of interesting things, but now I just hog hunt with Bob." Jim turned to Bob who was rolling his eyes, "I'm gonna buy this dog Bob!" "Why in hell would you want him?" Bob said with a sigh. "He can TALK Bob!!" "Yeah, he can but he's a damn liar." Bob shrugged, "I've owned that dog his whole life, he's never done any of that stuff!"

A common mistake I see when hunting long range dogs that are early in their training is turning them out with other peoples dogs that you do not know well. If hunting anything other than rock-solid real hogdogs, turning loose with dogs you do not know is generally a very bad idea. Trashy dogs can set your young dog back so fast! Training dogs to hunt in a manner you want them to is hard enough without pairing them with dogs that will be a bad influence. To the opposite effect, pairing a young dog with good dogs is the best training there is, if done in moderation.

A few years back I had been hunting with a man a good bit. This fella had a hound that loved a deer race. I don't mean a bump, 3-400 yards and quit, I mean half a day! Other than that one small fault the dog was the real deal though; hunt to spare, unlimited bottom, a nose and legs that paired with the nose! I had an old red dog that when coaxed, would run deer a spell, but generally wouldn't start one. The man was convinced my red dog was dragging his dog into the races. One day we were hunting and the guy walked off to visit the little boys room as the dogs made close circles around us in a hay meadow. He had his deer dog out and I had two out, one being my red dog. When he was away I saw a doe disappear into the wood line at the corner of the field and I promptly whistled to my dogs quietly as they circled past me. I had a plan. I loaded my two dogs in the box. No sooner than my hunting buddy returned his dog hit the corner of the field where the doe had been and tossed about a few barks and left in a dead run. The man and I loaded in the truck and eased down the road. It was becoming apparently clear to both of us that the dog, or as he thought, the dogs, were on a deer. The man lit into me! "Now gawtdamnit Ed, I like hunting with you, but if you can't get that red bitch deer broke I'm gonna stop hunting with you!" I stayed silent and let him dig the hole. "Hell, I'll come help you break her one day. It just ain't no fun chasing these dogs all over AND we ain't catching hogs when we're running deer. That red dog is gonna ruin my dandy!" I broke my silence, "How many dogs I bring today?" The question took him off guard. "Well, two I think, that red bitch and that hairy dog," he answered quizzically. I stopped the truck, "Go look in the box." He sat motionless. "Go look," I said with a grin. When he returned to the passenger seat he looked like he had seen a ghost. "Imagine that, my red dog starting a deer race from the box?" I jabbed at him, but laughing as to not seem mean spirited. "I never in a million years woulda thought that dog of mine would start a deer race," he said, humbled. We left it at that. We did keep hunting together, and we did get his dog deer broke, eventually, but it zapped something from the dog. She ended up a good solid hogdog, but some spirit was gone. In hind sight it would have been better to kick her down the road to country where deer dogging was legal, but it is hard to give up those dogs with something special. "Jill" was something special. That one dog left a soft spot in my heart for redticks.

I understand that some of this information seems to contradict. It is very hard to play out every scenario with dogs of differing training levels and give the appropriate method of dealing with each behavior. Rather than looking for a step by step methodology, understanding the psychology of what we are doing and how our actions and re-actions effect that psychology of the dog is the better strategy. The key here is putting yourself in the dogs shoes, with the dogs understanding and figuring the correct re-action from their point of view. Some accuse me of putting human thoughts in dogs minds, and I know I am guilty of this to some extent, but it is just a side effect of trying to understand a dogs mind I guess.

TRAINING FOR MEDIUM RANGE

The medium range dog is kind of the holy grail, and it is a tough one. The drags and mock hunts will mirror the short range training, but obviously we will increase the distances to a point. As with long range training we want the dog comfortable with being away from us, and this comes about from getting them away from us and having fun with a hog trail or a hog, as well as not being dependent on us for their sense of security.   Unlike with the long range dogs, we will call or signal to the dog when the outer limits of the desired range are hit. Again, not punishing, just signaling. We do however want slightly more handle than the long range dog. A good "come," is needed! Training will be done one-on-one and note it will take a special dog! If we train two dogs that will go medium distances they will likely follow out to long distances. The key is an independent dog not afraid to wonder but with enough handle to come back. As we set range by getting the dog to go and then come back at the desired range we have to be very careful not to call the dog off when tracking or chasing. Hog hunting today is largely a game of bottom and limiting that bottom is a move in the wrong direction in any range of hunting dog.

I have to disclaim myself here, I have not had much success with medium range dogs. I have trained a couple dogs into medium range dogs, and both those dogs ended up long range later in life. It just seems a dog is either close or long and the middle ground is hard to hold. A dog comfortable to be away from you for an hour, at half a mile ends up comfortable to be away from you for 4 hours, at 3 miles. Part of my failure in holding medium dogs into medium distances could be that I never had two at the same time to hunt together. I hunted each by themselves and then paired them with young dogs in an attempt to train the younger in the medium range ways. Each time the influence of a running partner lengthened range. If I was to try medium dogs again I would train two dogs independent of each other and then pair two medium dogs to see if the range held true, though I have a feeling the range would again grow.

Range is most commonly seen as something in the dog from birth, it is not. Range is the outward expression of our training methods and actions when interacting with the dog. Pick range, don't let range pick you.

CHAPTER 9
ME⋆ LEE AND BEN LILLY

We saddled mules by what was left of the moonlight. A brutal Oklahoma summer had left us cracked feeling and the cool air of the hours before the wretched sun showed back up felt like a tall glass of water. I tossed my saddle up on the back of my mule, Kate and jostled it back and forth letting it fall in the sweet spot of her back, "Think he's beddin' there by the creek?" My hunting partner, Lee George, grunted and dropped the stirrup off the saddle horn as he tighten the girth, "Yeah. Hot. Seen his track two days in a row. Wallowin'." The summer months always pushed our hog hunting to the background, it was far too hot to run dogs anyhow, and aside from very early morning hunts, we didn't do much but ring our hands and wait for fall, curse the sun, and reap the grass seed we had sewn.

It's hard to say who was more excited, us or the dogs. The dogs couldn't help but let a couple small choppy barks loose when we un-snapped them, and I was tempted to hoot a little too. I defied my animal nature and repressed the desire staying silent. We set three on the ground; Ruby, a full blood Mountain Cur that was as equally good as a tree dog as she was a hog dog, Tex, a half Fiest, half Mountain Cur, that despite his small size cast a man sized shadow, and Blonde, a three quarter black mouth cur and one quarter Kemmer cur. Blonde was the veteran, but not the leader of the pack as old age had reared it's head over her and was slowly putting on the brakes.

Greenleaf Creek was 300 yards in front of us. The dogs were at the creek when we kissed our mules up and eased in. "Prolly go down," I said, "Towards the cane." Lee pushed his mule up beside me and after a slug of coffee poured into his cup from his thermos, "Yeah." It felt good out there and we were content to sit atop a good mount, far from cell phone towers, surrounded by nature, and forget about the work and commitments of modern life. I imagined we were two old mountain men, like Ben Lilly, with nowhere to go after the hunt but on to another hunt, chasing that chicken hawk. My soul ached for those times past. As far as we were concerned there was no city, no phone bill, no mortgage payment. "Like desperados waiting for a train," as David Allan Coe had sung so many years before - a song that aways conjured up the old men in my life and often begged a tear in my eye.

Ruby let out a few quick, short barks loose down the creek, maybe 700 yards and then Blonde sounded in once as a locate, despite her cur breeding. They were running the hog. "Better start movin'," Lee was turning down the creek already. When a man knows his dogs he can read those faint barks like a book. Without speaking Lee and I both knew it was a hog, not a hot track, they were looking at him. We knew it wasn't going to be one of the long races that lasted half a day and snaked the hills and hollers, how I can't explain, but the information was all in the voice of the dogs. We knew it was a good sized hog. In the days of satellite tracking collars and goggle earth, what still really told a man the information he needed was that dogs mouth. It's the slight tones and frequency of the bark that let us know if we should move that direction, wait for a circle, or (cough) whether we needed to cut a switch.

"Whooo." We stopped, and not moving, afraid of the sound our clothes might make, we listened. "They bayed!" I said in a soft tone and we sat motionless listening to the three dogs hammer on that hog. People in the city pay big money to go listen to an orchestra, and while I have never heard one, I can say with certainty that it can't be any more beautiful than the sound of a pack of dogs baying a big nasty boar hog on the banks of Greenleaf Creek. The fevered pitch of the dogs, the hog grunting and snapping his cutters, telling those dogs he means business, how do you orchastrate that? You can't. Beethoven couldn't have written anything prettier. The bulldog tethered to my saddle britchen following was about to have a coniption fit. He was whining, and starting to pull, eager to do his end of the hunt, yet one stern look from me and he got back in line reluctantly. "Let's GO!," Lee was done listening and I agreed with his sentiment.

At 100 or so yards we tied up the mules, readied the bulldog, and gave the bay one more listen to make sure everything still sounded 'right'. Chunk, a long legged, muscular pitbull, dawned in a Kevlar vest was released and he sped to the sound of the baydogs. In the dense underbrush of Northeast Oklahoma a hundred yards might take a man 10 minutes, Chunk made it in a couple. The baying stopped, and we could hear the deep grunts of what was now definitely known to be a boar hog with a bulldog earring. The hog wasn't squeeling, just giving off those grunts - not from fear, or pain, but merely as a vocalizing of the fight in him. Off we went, running like wildmen, parting saw briars, hoping logs, crawling for a spell.

Old Chunk sure enough had him but this wasn't going to be an easy catch! The hog had picked a fallen tree top to bay up in. It was a mess of limbs grown over with vines and briars and he was backed up in there about as far as he could get without having his hind end hang out in town. I made a quick tour around the flank, and with no way in, it was clear I was going to have to go in facing the hog. Now I had the utmost faith in ole Chunk, he was NOT going to let go, but it was still a bit un-nerving going in to catch a hog from the front. I made my way through the mess of limbs and vines and the bay dogs, seeing my predicament, lent a hand in keeping ole McNasty focused on them and not me. With both the hogs back legs gathered up I hollered to Lee to pry Chunk off that hairy black ear. Out into the open we went, and once flipped we gathered his legs up and tied him like a calf. With adrenaline pumping, Lee and myself recalled the details back and forth to each other despite the fact that we had both seen the fray, all be it from different perspectives. Our modesty was gone, faces about to crack from the smiles we dawned.

We had caught a nice feral hog, about 225lbs, with a good 2" of cutters. While everyone that hog hunts is on the prowl for that

300lb plus wall hanger, hogs in the 175lb to 225lb range are by far more dangerous. Hogs of this size have less fat, and are more quick, they can spin on a dime and thrust forward 20 feet before you even have time to string together a decent set of cuss words.

It wasn't even 8am, but that Oklahoma sun was already turning us to sweat by the time we got him removed of his manhood. The now barr hog would make some lucky hunter a nice meat hog some day with no honor thrown our way. While the barr hog ran to the deepest depths of the Greenleaf creek bottoms to lick his wounds, Lee and I mounted up, dogs in tow and headed to the house. We weren't Ben Lilly, we had work to do.

(Lee George and Ed Barnes)

CHAPTER 10
ROUGH DOGS VERSUS LOOSE DOGS

When I first started hog hunting my dogs were loose baying until I showed up at the bay and then they would get rough and catch. I didn't train them to do this, it just happened and it suited me fine as I was hunting by myself and not having to lead a bulldog around was a blessing. I had the best of both worlds. Occasionally I would have to put fishing line and needle to a dog though. In all honesty, my dogs weren't that great so I saw the risk and reward as a pretty even trade off.

Today I prefer a bulldog to do the dangerous work. My reasoning is that I can get and train a bulldog in a fraction of the time it takes me to replaced a trained baydog. I do value a good bulldog, but I value a baydog more. If my bulldog gets killed I can still go bay hogs, maybe call dogs off the bay, maybe shoot if I need meat or get in a pinch. If all I have is a bulldog my hunting is on hold.

Over the years as the pressure on the hogs intensified, and the hogs learned the game, things got tougher. In the early years most all the hogs would bay up very fast and busted bays were very uncommon. I could bust through the woods like a bull, coon light on bright and bouncing all over and the hog would stay put, my dogs would catch and we were done. Slowly things progressed and slipping into a bay quiet as a mouse became necessary. Often I would get in so unnoticed that even the dogs wouldn't know I was there and I would have to talk them into catching. It got to the point we all know now, and often if the hog heard you coming the race was on. Some nights were long, walking to busted bay after busted bay.

One night at Cherokee Wildlife Management Area the dogs struck at around 10pm in the bottom. The hog took the dogs to the top of Persimmon Hill. They bayed up. I took off afoot thinking I'd be home at a decent hour. As I navigated my way up my ears were filled with the baying. At 100 yards I stopped to catch my breath and get rested for the battle. It was a good boar, I could smell him - that musky, sweet smell; maple syrup and dirt. The baying stopped and I heard the dogs coming back down in my direction, barking with every breath. They were hot on his heels. I never caught sight of them but I could hear them headed down. I stayed put, listening. At the bottom they bayed up again so I headed back down, thinking all was fine as I was going to have to go back down anyway. As I neared the bay at the bottom I slowed way down, watching every foot step and being as quiet as I could, light off, there was a good moon anyway. The baying was so loud I figured I was about to step on dogs. I crouched down to get under a patch of saw briers and when I stood back up they were in sight, for a second. The hog busted and my big dog tried to stop him but he just got dragged through the mess of jungle. The race was back on and they were headed back to the top. I had never seen anything like this.

Over the course of the next 4 or 5 hours the pattern continued... bay at top, break to the bottom, bay at the bottom break to the top. The hog bayed up 7 or 8 times, sometimes for 5 minutes sometimes for an hour. I was done, simply trying to get my dogs caught. I eventually got my dogs wrangled up, wore smooth out, and we went to the house to lick our wounds. The sun was up when I got home and I didn't bother to go to bed. I was cat-napping on the couch keeping an eye on the smokehouse filled with meat. Later that afternoon my phone rang, it was a hog hunting friend of mine, James. He proceeded to tell me the story of his hog hunt from two days ago at Persimmon Hill. "We were out ALL night! This hog would bay at the top then go to the bottom. Bay at the bottom then go to the top!" I was smiling, not at his frustration, but at the humor of the situation, "Didn't catch him did you?" "Hell NO!" he said, disgusted. I recalled my hunt the night before to him and we got a good laugh. I hung up and dozed off, to only wake to a glare coming off the window - the smokehouse was on fire! It wasn't my day.

That hunt was a turning point. The hogs were changing. The hogs were gaining mental ground on us. The "Good ole days" were behind us in northeast Oklahoma. Over the next year the story continued to play out with running hogs and busted bays. Like any hog hunter worth his salt I started calculating and came up with a plan to get my dogs rough as a cob! Brute force! We were gonna MAKE these hogs sit down. It worked sometimes, mostly on the smaller hogs, or even the larger boars if they caught in a place where I could get to them fast and lend a hand. My cut kit got more elaborate. My homegrown veterinarian skills got better. My injured list was ranked in order of severity and dogs towards the bottom had to just tough it out and hunt anyway. I wasn't turning many hogs back out though, they were getting the knife because they weren't going to live anyway, or my dog's lives were in danger and I didn't have time to waste dealing with a hog. I ran rough dogs for probably around two years.

One day in Muskogee County I 'bayed' a young gilt on Greenleaf creek. She was about 150 pounds and piggy, she was sure enough healthy with good fat and a shiny coat, a blooded hog. The dogs had her chewed down pretty good when I grabbed a leg and hollered them off. I held her by one leg and she didn't give me any fight. I was leading dogs back to the truck in a pretty sour mood. That wasn't fun? As I thought back, the last few hunts hadn't any fun! Driving home I had about talked myself into quiting hog hunting. I didn't hunt for a few weeks. I'd lost that loving feeling, as the song goes. All the while I was having this inner dialogue with myself trying to understand how something that I had loved so much was now empty feeling. I went as far as making plans where each dog should go.

My friend Lee called on a Friday night with a plan for a hunt the next morning. I tried to talk him down as I just didn't want to go but he would hear nothing of it, I was going! I hadn't told Lee, or anyone of my plan to quit. To be honest I felt a little ashamed of myself, it felt like blasphemy to even think of it.

Lee and I turned three dogs loose and I went through the motions of acting like I was having fun. Before too long the dogs were bayed and we drove in closer. When I got out of the truck I could hear the dogs hammering at about 400 yards. They were lighting it up! It had been about a year since I had heard a bay sound like that. My heart got back to ticking. As we neared the bay I didn't hear the gnawing, growling and squealing that I had gotten used to, it was a full on bay. The boar had backed himself against a small bluff. The dogs were baying, no one was trying the boar on for size! Lee got out his pistol, "I'm gonna try to get a shot." "Lee, no! I'm gonna catch him," I didn't know how but I was going to get him legged. Lee tried to dissuade me but I held my ground. After a good few minutes I did manage to get a hand latched on to the boars leg. The excitement was back! That is what I had been missing, the adrenaline and danger - the selectiveness of a real 'bayed' hog!

It took me about another year to get me a pack put back together that was loose. I added a bulldog and have not looked back since. For me, the fun isn't in piled up hogs, or pictures with big nasty boar hogs, for me it is about watching dogs work and that rush of adrenaline when you hear the bulldog hit. You pull up your socks 'cause you know by the grunts this hog is gonna rattle the shirt off your back. Laying hands on a hog that is half dead feels empty to me. Watching dogs gang up and chew a hog turns me off, it seems cheap and easy. I am after beauty, dogs that know their role - a well orchastrated plan.

I hear it all the time, "You can catch more hogs with rough dogs." I will agree, you probably can. If hog hunting is strictly a game of numbers for you then rough dogs might be the way to go. Sometimes it's a matter of quality of life. For me the joy in hog hunting comes from little things like watching dogs sit back and bay on a hog for an hour, or two hours. I like to leg a hog that is full of life. I love that slight moment of eye contact a bay dog throws my way as the bulldog hits and the baydog rolls out in search of another hog for the day. I like choosing what to do with a hog, not having my hand forced because he is chewed up and is going to die either way. Management is a dirty word in hog hunting, but it is a word that needs to slide off every hog hunters lips at least once in a while. Rough dogs can manage hogs in one direction - death, but management requires more than a vector in one direction.

It seems a logical jump to say that rough dogs are needed

to stop running hogs, but before we pick a solution to the problem we first have to know what is causing the problem. Hogs run for a multitude of reasons.

Why are hogs running?

In a nutshell, running hogs is a matter of dog pressure, breed influence, and last but by no means least -evolution through our selective culling- breeding hogs to be runners! Yep, we are largely responsible for all these track stars. Hogs are evolving or adapting to our hunting pressure, the pressing question is, "Are our dogs adapting at an equal pace?" I have to say they are not!

Dog Pressure -

Hogs run when they feel like the dogs are putting their life in danger, it is a simple survival instinct. I will put it into terms we all know. I might not be the toughest guy that ever walked the earth, but I am not afraid of anyone. So lets say I'm sitting in a bar drinking a beer and a skinny little dude walks up behind me and starts popping off at the mouth. I'm probably going to give him a look over and tell him to pipe down then go back to my beer. I'm not worried about him. Now that same guy comes back with six of his friends and they go to talking trash. Now I know if they all jumped on me they could wear me down, but I also can tell they don't have any "jump" to them, so I go back to my beer, but I am also looking for signs it might be time to slip out the back door. On another day I am nursing a beer and three big ole 250lb meat heads come up to me. I have a blackjack in my pocket. I whirl around and start swinging that leather and lead and put one on the floor and keep the other two past arm distance after a time. They put knots on my head, and dot an eye or two, but I hold my own and make it out to my truck to drive off fast. I lick my wounds and a week later I am back at that barstool and a different group of three meat heads show up and start crap. I remember those knots on my head, I don't particularly want more if I don't have to get them, so I just bolt for the door as fast as I can. I have been trained.

Breed Influence-

When I talk about 'breed' here it is really not an accurate word. The domestic hog (Sus Scrofa Domesticus) is a descendant of the wild hog (Sus Scrofa) they share the exact same DNA. They are the same thing! A domestic hog will revert, somewhat, back to his wild traits after years of living in a feral state, so what we are really identifying is the hogs relationship to domestication. I want to be clear that a hog is a hog is a hog. "Feral" defines his relation to fencing and is not a breed. For ease in writing I may refer to "feral," "domestic," "wild" and "Russian" but these terms are ambiguous and often inaccurate. A hog is seldom that clear cut.

Anyone who has ever been on Russian type hogs can tell you they will stand and fight! Not only will they stand and fight, but others will come in to get in on the fight. We call this a rally, and it is not a pretty sight, though it can be fun. Run of the mill feral hogs used to do this too, but it is less common, and now almost unheard of. Russian hogs will run, of course, but running is generally something we attribute to their lesser cousin the feral hog. Hogs run more now than ever, and at the same time our hog population is leaning more towards the "Russian" side of evolution with each generation? It doesn't make sense until you start looking at their bodies.

Many years ago a neighbor called me and said a Russian hog was visiting his domestic hog pen every evening. This guy was forever "seeing" mountain lions, wolves in the black color phase, and bigfoot - so I took it with a grain of salt. That evening I came over with a dog box of three curs and when I pulled in I saw the hog standing at the back of his pen! It was a true russian. The boar didn't run, he stood and fought, and whipped the ever loving hell out of my dogs! There was at least one dog airborn at any given moment. He whipped those three dogs and I was scrambling to get them caught. I went home and doctored dogs - one died. The next evening I went back with a loaded dog box. I got him caught, but dang my kennel had empty spots after!

The Russian hog is high in the shoulder and thin in the back end. Maybe it is because man runs on his back legs that we attribute running with the rear of an animal, but for hogs, just as in dogs, it is the front that is the machine. If you don't believe take a piece of rope and push it, now take it and pull it. The front end is where speed lives. Of course it is not that simple, but I like the analogy. When man domesticated Sus Scrofa he did so for food and through selective breeding increased the hams. They taste good, but they are an adaptation that flies in the face of thousands of years of natural selection that made them thin in the wild. The wild hog has a thin backside for a reason, and it doesn't have anything to do with breakfast sausage. In fact most wild animals are larger in the shoulder than the back end - wildebeast, wort hog, wolf, and in part mules (though not fully wild.) Just to name a few.

What I am getting at is that breed influences running simply because when a hog does run it is the more Russian leaning hogs that can really turn on the speed and endurance, not to minimize the speed and endurance of a feral hog.

Evolution through selective culling-
Whether for the table, or just as part of that evil word "eradication," when we kill hogs that bay up we are tinting the future of hog hunting for running hogs. We kill what we catch and the hogs that beat us go on to breed. It is that simple! This is like free-range management in full-blown reversal. For kids that just want a year or two of hog hunting for the hog hunter patch to hang on their jacket this doesn't matter, but for those of us that are in it for the long haul, this short-sightedness is a real problem. It takes patience, and thought to drop the leg of that hog that bayed right up, but it needs to be done. Plunge the knife into the hog that you chased for 15 hours and through 3 counties.

NO HOGS LEFT TO KILL * BY PAT LEWING (from October 2014 issue of Tuskers Magazine)

Once upon a time in a not so distant land, there was an old cowboy and his dogs. His name was Glen, and he wasn't a rodeo star, but a working cowboy. He trained horses and used his dogs to carve out a meager existence in an ever shrinking wilderness that was giving way to progress and political correctness. After they passed the stock laws and the last of the bad tiger striped F1's were made extinct in the piney woods, Glen and his scatter bred brindle mongrels grew restless and yearned for the good old days of running through the woods and bringing a bad adversary to bay. So Glen started to travel, and switched his mongrel noses from bovine to swine. As he caught and tied hogs, he relocated them to areas as far from civilization as possible, and kept a close eye on the population, managing them like a good hog man should. When they would venture off too far, he would take a couple of bay dogs and drive them back. This went on for decades without incident.

Then came cable tv, hunting shows, and programs featuring some of the most moronic pig hunting drama that the world has ever endured. This is where David comes in. He is a decent kid and loves the woods, too young to remember a time when there were no swine. David indulged in watching these scripted debacles, believing this to be what it takes to be a true hog man. He went out and bought dogs from all over the land. He started to pursue the wild swine, as if they were placed in the woods by some unknown entity that had a fabled stock yard that burst forth swine on the full moon of every month.

He began to pursue the number of slain hogs in which their carcasses were only used to add to a number killed since the first. Then their pictures adorned the pages of FaceBook along with a caption that the hunter didn't even know the true meaning of. He posted pictures of piggy sows and piglets torn half in two on the ground before him. As time passed, David noticed the hogs had begun to run a lot farther before baying, and he switched from the traditional cur dog to something with a little hound blood running through its veins.

All the rookies sat around listening to David at the country store, he told them it was getting harder to hunt because of the Russian blood that made the hogs run. Glen, overhearing, looked up and told them they were idiots and it was survival of the fittest and simple evolution that had taken place. Glen told them since the only thing left alive to breed were the hogs that were able to out run David's cur dogs. David responded, "How do you know old man?" Glen snapped back, "Because I didn't go to Russia and catch any hogs to stock this land with." David said, "You don't own these hogs old man. They are wild and belong to whoever catches them." Glen responded, "Catching them ain't the problem. You punks are killing them." David's face turned red and he advanced toward Glen but stopped short because he loved living. Glen had put his right hand into his pocket where that yellow handled Case pocket knife rested after a long day of barring bad boar hogs. Glen chuckled as David backed away, "What's the matter boy? Are you afraid to catch and release something that eight dogs aren't holding?" David left with his tail between his legs. He had been curred out by a feeble old man that was only a couple of weeks from finding his reward at the end of life's struggle. It had been almost a year since Glen had passed that David was posting his last post on FaceBook. It read: "Finished Hog Dogs for Sale along with Garmin Tracking System." Reason for selling, "NO HOGS LEFT TO KILL."

Pat Lewing

CHAPTER 11
BULLDOGS

Bulldogs is a very large topic, and I will do my best. For a good many years, as I have already told you, I didn't use a bulldog. Here in ranch country the bulldog is either loved or hated. The majority of the old timers coming in on the hate side. Now "hate" is a strong word, but along the way I kind of soaked in the anti-bulldog sentiment, not from experience but just from rubbing elbows with the old men that were not in love with them.

When my dog pack went to the totally loose side I needed a bulldog. A neighbor had picked up an APBT pup for free at the tire shop down the road and after the "puppy" wore off they grew uninspired and offered him to me. He was a looker for sure. I put him in my most iron-clad kennel and kept a sharp eye on him. I was weary to say the least. I named him "Chunk," and he was a chunk! Luckily for me he was a natural, because I probably would have ruined a lesser dog. To this day I measure bulldogs off Chunk's back. This dog would blow into a bay, then slow way down or even stop as he got within seeing distance. Chunk would look the situation over and plan an attack. Most times he would circle around behind and come in from the right side, hit the ear and body up to the hog and ride him like a pony. He'd drop his back end and anchor, and never shake or thrash around. A hog would spin trying to get a jab at him but he stayed stuck to the side and out of harms way. I caught countless hogs for 6 years with Chunk. In those 6 years I put stitch or staple to him no more than three or four times, all the while wearing no vest! Chunk died in his prime in a four-wheeler wreck. I haven't owned one better, or even equal since and I seem to go through about 2 a year.

Over the years I have acquired a fondness for bulldogs. You just can't watch a breed with so much heart and gameness and not admire it. Their fierce loyalty. Their total and complete lack of fear. Their strength. Their willingness and eagerness to do battle with another animal that by numbers alone should be able to handle them, but cannot because of the bulldogs mindset!

I hear it all the time, folks bragging that their bulldog "Hits like a freight train," I usually smile and nod, all the while wondering what they are thinking. Now it's kind of entertaining to watch a hard hitting dog, but it's not the best way. The bulldog I have now does it, and I don't like it, and his life will not be a long one because of it! "Gumbo" flies in head first, hits an ear from head on and half the time he is caught on the right ear with his body across the snout on the left side of the hog. More times than not he looks like a rag doll getting tossed around. He gets cut on sows. He's no star obviously, but he's a solid dog that gets the job done most nights. He doesn't miss too awful much, never lets go and has no dog aggression. For these reasons he will eat my dog food and do the job he loves and the job I ask of him, however sloppily. (While writing this book Gumbo died.)

I have often wondered if the catchdog vest is in part responsible for sloppy dogs? Before store bought vest were readily available we did without, or made do, sloppy and unintelligent dogs were culled by smart hogs in the woods. Years ago I took an old canvas army tarp and cut a pattern and had the wife sew me a vest. I really thought I had something, and it was better than nothing, but of course it cannot compare to the vest we have today. I remember well when I first showed it to a man I was hunting with and he was confused. "A shirt for a dog?" he questioned me. I felt kind of silly when he put it that way, but it worked. A couple weeks later I met him at his house to go hunting and he came out of the barn with a scrap of army tent, "You think Michelle would sew me one?" I'm not sure who was more proud, the bulldogs or us! We really thought we were on to something new, yet later I discovered that hog dogs had been wearing vest of various sorts going back hundreds of years.

But are these hi-tech vest saving the lives of lesser dogs that go on to breed yet more lesser quality dogs? I would have to say they are, the only question is on the impact it is having on the catchdog breeds as a whole.

I lost Chunk and I began the search for a replacement and nothing seemed to stack up. After years of lesser dogs I had somewhat found myself accepting of the fact. A couple years ago, after catching a hog and watching sloppy bulldog work I found myself thinking back to Chunk the next few days. I wondered if Chunk would have even been the kind of dog he was if he had worn a vest. Since that day I do something different with my new bulldogs. When I start a bulldog he doesn't wear a vest until I see that light click on, where he gets tired of being cut-down all the time. Some wise up, they get a style, some never get that light bulb moment, but they all get the opportunity. A vest is an earned milemarker at my house.

We cannot talk about bulldogs and not talk about gamebred dogs or even dog fighting. Yes, I said it! No matter which side of the dog fighting fence you are on we have to all agree that fighting dogs made the APBT. Without the fighting the breed would not be where it is today, that is not even up for debate! The money and the fame fueled the flames to breed better and better bulldogs, and those men did. I am not going to go deep into gamedogs, but I have had the honor to sit and talk with some of the old guard and some world famous dogmen and I have yet to meet one that did not love the dogs to the center of their being. The gamedog men have taken the science of breeding, nutrition, and care further than any other dog sport and they hold a wealth of knowledge that cannot be rivaled in the dog world. To shun that knowledge because of it's source is a waste. I have never been to a dogfight, I have no desire to either, but I respect a man's freedom to do as he pleases as long as it doesn't infringe on my rights, and I will gladly take any well placed advise from any source.

A gamebred dog is the difference between a .22LR and a .22Mag. The two best catchdogs I have seen, after Chunk, were both gamebred; Mongo and RJ. Mongo was owned by my good friend and hunting partner Kolby Ingram, he was out of Bob Scoggins' line of dogs. He was Carver / Eli bred and hell on a hog. I only saw the dog miss one time in two years, though he lacked the smarts of Chunk he was a fine canine. RJ was owned by a man I used to hunt with a lot and he was an equal of Mongo though I can't remember his breeding. Both of these gamebred dogs had a level head, they both had a switch and as long as the switch didn't go off we were fine, but if the switch got flipped it was going to be ugly! I could toss my grade bulldog in the same box hole with either of them and not worry about a fight. RJ and Mongo both would be considered 'hot' but they had the intelligence to go with it. Not all 'hot' bulldogs share this trait though! The "trigger" is key.

Whether a 'hot' gamedog, or a 'cold' gamedog, or a side of the road bulldog, socialization is the key! I will not take a bulldog over 4 or 5 months old unless I know where it came from and I am 100% certain it has had the right handling, by an adequate dogman. Bulldogs take a heavy hand. A bulldog that has ruled the roost the first year of his life is a handful! One time I was in bad need of a catchdog. I had an acquaintance, who was by no stretch of the imagination a dogman, and he offered me a bulldog about a year and a half old - perfect age to start. I looked the dog over, made some fast movements around him, grabbed him in the flank hard, showed dominance and the dog was fine, just happy go lucky. I took the dog home and staked him out on a chain spot. I kept an eye on the dog for a week and saw no warning signs at all. One day I was out in the yard and my boy, about 6 at the time, walked past the dogs chain spot and this bulldog came alive! The dog was mid-air, mouth open wide right at face level with my boy and my heart sank. The dog hit the end of the chain and I bet his mouth wasn't 4 inches from the boys face. I was already at a run and pushed the boy back. The dog shrank with me around and went back to normal. That dog never ate another scoop of my food, and I never took an old dog from someone I didn't know and respect again. Most run of the mill Johnny home owners can't handle real bulldogs, or even real Catahoulas. Don't take their trash, it will only lessen your yard! DONT" TAKE THEIR TRASH!

The feed bowl, like most times, is the best training tool in your toolbox. I like to feed a bulldog pup with an older grouchy dog, while standing right there. You want a dog that will exert dominance but not take it too far! (This method will work with some bulldogs, but not most 'hot' bulldogs, even as pups their heart will overpower their body.) I let the old dog whoop the pup off the food, then after a bit let the pup finish it off. After a dozen times of this I feed the bulldog pup by himself, but this time I whoop him back. He eats when I LET him eat. As always, it can't always be punishment, you have to show these dogs a lot of praise. I am against hunting dogs, and dogs in general, in the house except when it comes to bulldogs, bring them in, pet them and let them sleep in your bed if your of that mindset. The very best catchdogs you will ever see spend a ton of time with their owners. Haul the pup to town, get him around people, dogs, horses, cows and bigfoot - show him the whole world and show him you are the center of it. This is a total 180 degrees from my views on baydogs.

A good handle on a catchdog is golden. No one likes a pulling dog as you walk to a bay. No one likes a dog that can't be tied back near other dogs after a catch. No one likes a dog that squeals at the truck when he can hear a bay. It's all pretty simple stuff yet many just deal with it and don't put in the work to make their hunt more enjoyable. A few years back I was eating lunch at a gas station and ran into an old friend. We got to talking about hunting and I let it slip I was in need of a catchdog, seems I'm always looking for a catchdog when everyone is looking for a strikedog. "Hey, I got one you can have," he sounded eager, "She's old but she will catch good!" I figured as he usually had a good slew of bulldogs. "Only thing is, keep her away from other dogs after a catch 'cause she will sure grab another dog." I was forcing interest. "And if you gotta whoop on her just give her two swats, third one she's gonna eat your lunch!" I weaseled my way out of that very politically. Why feed such a dog? Life's too short. I would bay and shoot before I messed around with junk bulldogs.

Squealing at the truck is usually a simple fix, even in a hard headed dog, though it can take a lot of determination on your part - when training hard headed dogs you're head has to be harder! A shock collar or a stick will do the trick. Often with age they will settle into things on their own. It's not rocket science you don't need me to tell you how to do it. Pulling is simple too, it just takes the time. Take about 20 feet of rope, roll the tag end up and leave about 4 feet to use as a lead on the dog, keeping the very end of the rope tightly in your hand. As you lead him if you notice he is pulling or even not taking note of where you are, drop the slack in the rope, grasp the tag end hard, put it to your chest and take off running as fast as you can in the opposite direction. When the slack is gone you will have the dogs attention. Repeat. After just a few times you will notice the dog keeping a visual reference on where you are, he doesn't want to be surprised to find you running the other way. Repeat every day for a few days and most dogs will lead much more comfortably. Use a wide collar when doing this, the object isn't to snap their neck, but just to get close. When you 'lead' a dog you should be in front, with the dog slightly behind you or at least even with you. If the dog is at the end of a rope 4 feet in front of you who is leading who?

Another trick for stopping the pulling dog is simple to do, but hard to explain, I will give it a shot though. Snap the lead to the dogs collar. Run the lead down his side and at the flank put it under the dog and loop it around over the back. Now loop the remainder of the lead around the part you ran down his side, the tag end going in front of the lead going down his back and then behind the dog for you to lead from. This makes a 'second' collar that goes around his flank. The slightest pull from you tightens it. The first few times you tighten it some dogs will lose it; flip over and flop like a fish. It is not terribly painful, but the flank is a dogs soft spot, it is vulnerable. If you want to see a dog's real temperament grab them in the flank - weak spots expose the real dog.

While we are on handle let's talk about a catchdog releasing on command, it is often spoken of as the holy grail of catchdogs. It takes a great deal of training to get a bulldog to release on command, I doubt I could do it. I respect the time and effort invested in such training but I don't want such a dog! I don't even like the dog that can be pulled with constant pressure off a hog. I want to physically break a bulldog off a hog. I do not want to run into a bay, guys screaming at each other and the bulldog 'think' he heard the signal to release. Things could get more dangerous than they need to be! While we are talking about breaking dogs off lets discuss the proper way, because I've seen far too many boys put a breakstick in my dogs mouth and get yelled at. A breakstick is not meant to be used like a crowbar, that's just a good way to break teeth.

The breakstick should go well behind the canines, towards the back 2/3rds of the mouth. To get the dog to release it is not a prying action, it is a twisting action, like revving a motorcycle throttle, just enough so that as someone else is holding good pressure on the dog lead the dog slips off the ear. My friend Ronnie Creek turned me on to an even more gentle way to break dogs off a hog, and while it hasn't worked for me on all dogs, when it does work it is very simple and easy. Ronnie fashions a deer antler, about 7" long or so, at a sharp angle you put it in the dogs mouth and reach to the back of his tongue with it, a little bit of pressure on the base of the tongue and the dog will release. It is almost a gagging reflex. I've seen old timers blow in a dogs ear to get them to release, I have also seen old timers about get their face bit off doing so! I've sat back and watched kids choke a dog off, all the while shaking my head in dis-belief. I have also seen guys kick dogs, punch dogs, and beat them with a lead - obviously that is sending mixed signals and should never, ever be done. If you are ill-prepared for catching hogs don't take it out on the dog that is performing his job and training. In a bind you can place your hand over the muzzle of the dog and use your thumb and middle finger to push his lip over the top teeth. You then apply upward pressure to mimic him biting his own lip. Some dogs will let go with this approach, but you will likely get a pinch also when he does release. Blood is paid for with blood.

I came across the single most elegant way to break a bulldog off a hog while a sow chewed on my fingers! We were hunting around Texarkana one night in a light snow. The dogs were on fire! We got a nice sow caught and the dogs were rolled out on the next one. As usual we had a bulldog latched on to an ear and no one had a breakstick. I was observing as another man handled the hog. The dog wouldn't release. I started gathering up a tree limb to use as a make-shift breakstick like I always do when I noticed the dogs were bayed in the distance. I found me an appropriate stick, and in a hurry reached across the hogs head to break it - a move I KNEW was wrong but I was in a hurry to get to the next hog. This sow flung her head in the blink of an eye and had my two middle fingers between her teeth before I could string a decent set of cuss words together. Everyone just laughed as I screamed. This sow must have been half snapping turtle as she wasn't letting go and there was little chance of a lightening strike. Through the screams I managed to get the words out, "Cut this bitches ear off!" The sow was grinding and the bulldog was yanking and my two fingers were caught in the middle. After the bulldog was off I managed to get the sow off me after repeated punches with my left hand to her head. My left hand hurt almost as much as my right when it was all over. Of course everyone laughed, except me!

A bulldogs adult teeth do not set in until they are about a year and a half old. While we can do a little bit of training to catch before then, with small pigs, we do not want to put the dog to a true test until the teeth are fully set. The canine teeth are important, but not as important to holding a hog as many think, still we want to protect them. I have seen old bulldogs with little to no canines left, and I trusted them to hold a hog as much as any dog I ever have. There is no rush, and the first year and a half of a bulldogs life is time to get his basic training and socialization done anyway. I like to haul a bulldog pup along on hunts, in the box just to get them around the baydogs and other catchdogs, with no expectation of doing anything else with them. Haul the pup to town. Expose the pup to as many other dogs as you can. Teach them basic commands. Teach them to lead properly. It's like training a horse, you expose them to as many things as possible so that when the situation comes up in the real world you don't have a rodeo on your hands.

When our bulldog is old enough to start with his teeth fully set we will start with a pig about the same size as the dog. I like to put one or two baydogs in the pen to bay, then hold the bulldog outside of the pen for a good while. You want to see the bulldog wanting to get in there! If the bulldog is not consumed with the desire to get in there then amp the excitement and anticipation up. If time does not do this then get the hog to squeal.   You can also talk the dog up.   Sometimes the squealing will kick in a dogs prey drive. If our dog is losing his mind we are almost there, but we aren't just throwing him in to see if he catches! Instead we catch the pig, remove the baydogs from the pen entirely and lead the bulldog to the pig that is being held down on his side. Lead the bulldog to the ear! Keep the dog lead tight in a way that enables you to stop him from catching anywhere but the ear. It may seem like a small thing, but habits start with small things! Two or three times in a single day is as much as I want to do this. If the dog is going in straight for the ear, I will stop here with the hog held down and move on. If the dog is wanting to catch anywhere, or anywhere other than the ear then we will repeat the training with the dog on lead. The goal here is to increase our odds of making an ear dog. We remove the baydogs to not start bad habits. A bulldog is a wired animal, and once wired some dogs just want to see action and they may grab a baydog simply from excitement. We need to avoid these situations to avoid bad habits.

The next step is letting the dog catch a hog in a pen without the help of us. We can use baydogs to bay the hog and send him, like in the woods, or we can just let the bulldog in the pen on his own. I prefer to bay the hog first, it cuts out the chasing the hog around and mimics our hunting better. The hog should be close to, or slightly larger than the dog at this point. When the dog catches we move in fast and break him off the hog. We are not testing his dexterity! If the dog catches ear then we can ease our way on to larger hogs. After a few goes he can be hauled to the woods. The first few times in the woods I like to send an older catchdog first, then stagger the younger bulldog in, so that the hog is caught when he gets there. This serves a couple purposes; 1. We don't lose a hog, and 2. It is a confidence booster for the young dog.

If the bulldog doesn't catch ear in the pen the first time he has to catch without us, then we can back up and go back to holding the hog and focusing him on ear. Do NOT reprimand him for not catching ear, nothing good will come of that!

If you have a 'hot' bulldog that you are worried about catching another dog in the pen then we have a big problem! If you 'think' this may happen then save yourself the trouble, heartache, and liability and find another catchdog prospect! Trust your gut, don't think but rather let intuition guide you.

Many hog hunters 'like' a jaw-dog, or leg-dog but I tend to think most 'like' that because that is what they have, instead of having a jaw-dog because that is what they like. Chicken or egg I suppose? An ear-dog has a few benefits, for starters it is the safest spot for a bulldog to catch. An ear-dog also causes much less damage on a hog then a jaw, leg, snout or 'wherever I land dog.' Snout-dogs can control a hog a little better, but it is dangerous and often a hog caught with a snout-dog has to be killed because of a broken snout. I have seen very large boars scream like little girls when a snout-dog has them. In a way, it is almost like twitching a horse. I still opt for the old fashioned ear-dog. Ears are dispensable but snouts are not, and I have seen many an old fat woods hogs with little to no ear still thriving.

I prefer to send two bulldogs to a bay. On what I believe to be a single hog I will stagger turning the bulldogs in according to their speed so that they get there at the same time - in theory. On a wad of hogs I will send the lesser quality bulldog first (the first catch is the easiest) and hold the better bulldog back so that he gets there a few moments after the first dog. This, again in theory, is so that each dog will catch his own hog, although it seldom works, but I still try.

In today's world there is a whole mini industry when it comes to vests. Catch vests come in a wide array of styles, sizes and materials. Despite the advertising campaigns there is no 100% hog proof vest. If there was a 100% hog proof vest it would likely be a death sentence for the dog that had to wear it. I will not advertise for any vest makers, but there are definitely 'better' vest around. They are not all the same! The hog hunter has to think for himself though, the 'best' vest in one climate, and terrain is not the 'best' in another situation. The ideal vest does not limit the dogs movement, it does not hold in heat and it does not take on water making a dog drown. The ideal vest will stop most cuts, and minimize the severity of others. One thing I will say is get a vest with a built in collar! I find it kind of odd that they still make them in two pieces. They make vest/collars with Velcro and plenty of overlap but in my opinion nothing matches up to the built in collar. When a hogs cutter slides off the chest it naturally tends to go in an upward motion as the hog slashes and if it finds that separation between collar and vest the cutter falls right in place to slit your dogs throat. That gap between a two piece collar and vest is like a guide encouraging the cutter to find the crease! If you do use a two piece vest/collar put the collar on first, with the vest going OVER the collar. The collar needs to be loose enough that with normal motion of the dog's head the collar slides on the neck instead of staying put and opening up the gap.

One night, long ago, I ran into a bay to a terrible sight. The bulldog was wearing a 2 piece vest and the boar had a cutter between the collar and vest. In fact, it was stuck! The bulldog was getting thrashed, and that is putting it lightly. The hog wanted rid of the dog, but it just wasn't happening, and the dog, despite the thrashing was trying to get a grip but couldn't. The old boar had resorted to chewing on the dog best he could. In reality it was probably only a minute, but it seemed an hour as I tried to leg this boar that wasn't anchored. After some time the bulldog came loose of the tusk and got an ear. With the aid of the baydogs we caught the hog but the bulldog was in pretty bad shape! The vest that was meant to protect the dog had in reality done the opposite!

It seems like a no-brainer to vest your bulldog but that is not always the case, sometimes the safest thing to do is send them in with just their god given skin. Our decisions as dog owners effect our dogs. A couple years ago I made the combination of a couple lapses in judgment that my dog, and the dog a friend had to pay the price for.

I was laying on the couch watching tv. The phone rang and it was my friend Kolby. He spouted out some slurs while telling me we needed to turn some dogs out. It was around 85 degrees at 2 pm, in early August a cool spell for sure. Usually I stand my ground about hunting in the day during summer, but the cool air had me thinking of fall so I loaded a couple dogs and headed out. (mistake number one)

We drove down an old road we could barely make out, on the ridge of a deep holler. When we got to where we could no longer make educated guesses at where the road used to be, we stopped and kicked a couple cur dogs out. They dropped to our left and sounded off a time or two at barely 60 yards on the x axis, and about 100 yards on the y axis. It was a good ways down! We could hear a very large group of hogs; grunting, charging dogs, and just generally being fussy. I grabbed a video camera, told Kolby and Tanner I would text them when to send bulldogs, and started down.

When I got to the bottom of the holler there was a clearing and a wad of around 50 hogs just 20 feet in front of me. The dogs were circling, barking now and then but not 'bayed.' It seems our dogs will bark less on large sounders of hogs, concentrating more on wadding them up with their movement rather than by baying. I climbed a tree, and started the video. To my right about 100 yards I could hear another wad of probably around 20 hogs.

I sent that text to the boys telling them to send bulldogs. (mistake number 2) I waited, ears cocked to the summer air, for the sound of those two bulldogs crashing down the mountain. I never heard it. Shortly I could hear voices down in the holler to my right, closer to where I had heard the sounder of maybe 20 hogs. The big wad was still right in front of me, and the two dogs were darting around and really doing a fine job of putting just the right amount of pressure on the hogs, it was good dog work and I was happy to get to witness it.   Finally I thought to look at my Garmin. My heart sank when I saw my bulldog "treed" at 650 yards to my right. Immediately I recognized just how hot these mid-80's temperatures were.

The boys had sent the bulldogs towards me, but before they could get there they heard the fussing of the smaller sounder and went to them instead of the group I was watching. The dogs weren't hammering hard enough to draw the bulldogs to them.

I climbed down from my perch and took off in the direction my Garmin was pointing to my dog. Along the way I ran into Kolby, we were both gasping for air in the windless bottom. We kept up the pace, "Backup is caught...... or stroked out," I got the pessimistic words through the thick spit in my mouth. Kolby cursed a bit, at a run.

When we got to the dogs, Tanner had a boar legged. Backup was laying on his belly in tall grass about 5 feet from the pig, and he is not that kind of laid back dog. Tanner's catchdog, Red, was caught, but staggering and I could tell he was in rough shape. I took the hog from Tanner so he could tend to his dog. The truck was a good half mile away. We had no water! (mistake number 3)

Red was in pretty bad shape so I told Kolby to cut his ears. We striped the vests off both dogs and Kolby took an inch off the tip of each ear. The ears bleed a lot, for whatever reason they take a long time to clot. The idea with ear clipping is that the blood loss cools the body. It is a last resort approach though, so use that little nugget with caution and be ready to combat the shock it will probably cause.

Backup

Red

Kolby said he knew about where a little mud hole was so he and I took off at a run. When we found it we stripped our shirts off and filed them with the thick wet mud and took back off towards the dogs. Red had already died when we arrived, and Backup looked a little worse so we clipped his ears. We rang the little bit of water we could get from the mud in our shirts onto his groin. The mud was cool so we coated him in it and then scrapped it off. I got him up on my back and Kolby and I hustled back towards the mud hole. After a little wallowing he seemed to be getting along better. By this time Kolby had taken off topside to get a 4 wheeler and when he got back we loaded the dog and he took off at breakneck speed for the house while Tanner and I led the bay dogs back towards the truck.

At the house we slowly put water on Backups groin and backside, careful to not put the ice cold well water too close to his head. I got a syringe and injected 5cc at a time under the skin on his back. He didn't want to drink any water but I got small amounts of Coke down his throat. I always like to get pop, or some sweet liquid in a dog, I think it tends to help ward off shock. After a couple hours of little bits of water, and laying in the cool grass under a tree, Backup looked a whole lot better and I figured he probably had a 75% chance of pulling it out. The next day the dog was coming around, drinking and eating but he passed on the next day due to kidney failure.

Both of these dogs were very well conditioned and not fat at all. Backup had better wind than Red, just genetically, and that probably accounts for him holding on longer. These two bulldogs caught hogs all summer, in night temperatures that were often hotter than the 83 or so it was on the day they overheated. It was a humid 83, and I have to believe that played a role in things going south.

I am responsible for the death of these two dogs. I have been at this game long enough to know better. I guess after a long summer of very hot days, 83 degrees seemed like an oasis. It is not that you cannot hunt in that weather, but I know to hunt around very wet areas. This was a dry bottom. I know to only send bulldogs from very close and only to those kind of bays that have that set-in-stone sound to them. We also should have been packing at least a little water with us, and we should have left the catchvests at home!

So with two catchdogs gone, we started a couple newbies and that brings up my second point - keeping your mind right when dealing with green dogs.

Saturday morning, me and Tanner Herr loaded a couple dollar store curs and hit a plot of land where the hogs were buffaloing all that yellow corn. The dogs hit a track and dropped into a deep holler to the north. Tanners dogs came up bayed at about a mile so we drove to 600 yards and got a green bulldog ready. At 40 yards we could see 10 or 12 hogs. The two dogs were working good. We sent my new bulldog. This was the dogs first attempt at a catch in the woods. It was not the best case because in a wad like that the hog is not really bayed tight to hold him for a catchdog, but it was trial by fire because he was all we had. Well, we saw him hit about a 100lb hog, and he missed. The dog looped around and came to our right and hit another much larger hog, and missed again, and that hog put his running sneakers on! The bulldog stuck with him for 1.6 miles before he started to get home sick and came back to us. It happens, and that is the only way to get dogs some experience. It was starting to heat up so we called it a day and planned to meet up later that evening for another go.

Saturday night we met up and cast dogs at a new place where the deer hunters were mad at corn stealing hogs. The dogs dropped into a draw and we got some barking immediately. They ran to the east, into some of the thickest stuff I have seen in a good while. At 250 yards they sat down bayed so we jumped in the truck and got to within 130yds. At 100 yards we unclipped the same bulldog that had missed two hogs earlier that morning and pretty soon we heard the tell tale squealing that told us we had a caught hog. The dogs bayed within 5 minutes of casting them, and by the time we got the darn hog dragged out of the tangle of briers and back to the truck an hour and a half had passed. Our arms and legs were striped with blood and it looked like we had fought three or four wildcats, yet our faces were adorned with those upwards facing corners of the mouths.

Sunday at daylight we hit yet another piece of land where deer hunters were tired of feeding hogs. The dogs again dropped into a deep holler to the north that held a spring fed creek. It was a perfect place for a hogs lazy day - thick, thick, thick, water, and they knew no deer hunter was going to walk up on them and ruin their napping, though the dogs interrupted their siesta. We were still up top, listening to the dogs work, and black hogs were pouring up out of the holler all around us, getting away from them pesky hog dogs. We counted at least a dozen. After we got done watching hogs run across the hay meadow we took off on foot 600 yards downhill, to where the dogs were bayed. As we were making the trek into the bottom, hogs continued to pass us heading for higher ground. The dogs were bayed in the creek. We sent the green bulldog again, and again he did a fair enough job of getting the hog caught.

Some folks will probably think to themselves, "Why would this dude write a story about his dog missing hogs?" Well, it happens, and great dogs are not born - they are made. Like most folks, a dog learns by making mistakes. You have to give your dog a chance to screw up.

There was a time when I would have retired that dog for missing two hogs like that, young or not. I know many men would have. Years back, I would have just moved onto another prospect and started over. Maybe it's a bit of age on me, but I take a little less hard approach to young dogs now. I don't believe in making excuses for dogs, and if I find myself doing it, I will stop and do some thinking. That said, when you are evaluating a dog, you have to take a good look at the big picture and see if there are factors involved that set the dog up for failure. Sometimes we stack the odds against a dog succeeding, and then get mad at him for failing. I know I have lost my temper with a dog, and then after cooling down realized that I was really mad at myself for doing something stupid, and I took it out on the dog.

Sometimes with young dogs you just have to look for the positive things, even when everything looks bad. When my catchdog missed twice I was disappointed, no doubt, but I was not mad, because I understood he was young, and really I had thrown him into a situation where he had a good possibility of failing. When the dog got out 1.6 miles I was glued to my tracker... I was hoping he would show me something good. When 'Outlaw' started heading back to me I was tickled pink. Yeah, he had messed up on the catch, but he showed me some brains and handle when he came back. Strangely I was pretty happy, even on that day.

(Gumbo)

CHAPTER 12
CATFISH PONDS

Late May in Northeast Oklahoma should be about 85 degrees, it wasn't, it was in the mid-nineties and we were coming off a late winter with almost no spring to get ourselves and our dogs acclimated to the warmer temperatures. We needed to clear that dog spit up! (If your dogs spit is cloudy, and full of bubbles then your dog is not in good enough shape for running in the summer.) Myself and a few friends met up about 9pm to make a few drops. We had plans to hit a ranch we call "Rocky Ford." It is a large ranch stocked with bucking cows. The top is pastures dotted with ponds but it falls off in all directions into large, deep hollers. We hadn't been there in a few months and the night before I had hit about eight of our regular spots just to get a couple of out of state friends on hogs, so we were head scratching a place to go. As we were getting dogs loaded and trading back stolen dog leads from each other and getting collars arranged, my buddy Tanner comes in with an idea, "What if we check out the catfish ponds on the way?" I had forgotten about the place but it was a perfect fit to our weather, "Hell yeah."

In the winter we had gotten permission to hunt the catfish ponds, they backed up on the east side of a place we already hunted, it was only about 160 acres but it increased our block of hunting land in that area. The land owner used to raise catfish in large ponds on the land. Whether by design or accident, the pond dikes had broke and now for the most part it just held small areas of shallow water. We hadn't hunted it, or even walked it out since we had gotten permission, we figured it would be a summer spot. We knew it was a thick mess though.

We pulled just inside the gate and parked. To our left were the ponds, and to the right a good hay meadow with about 20 inches of seeded out grass. It was flat, something we are not used to. Tanner casts two dogs ahead of us on the trail and we all start loading down on bug spray, getting leads over our shoulders, digging out hobbles and the such. Within a minute we get a few barks. We traded glances with raised eyebrows. The dogs headed to the left into the thick stuff then circled out with an occasional bark as they high-tailed it into the hay meadow. Our buddy Slim cut a young dog in to them and we waited. It didn't take long and they were bayed at 540 yards. We could hear the grunting of a large sounder. There was no wind to speak of so we just made a straight line to the bay with two catchdogs. At 140 yards we cut the bulldogs, giving them about 10 seconds head start on us and then we took off running. Hogs were running everywhere as we went to the deep grunting of a 220lb boar anchored by Samsquanch, an ugly-as-hell crossed up bulldog. The three bay dogs all bailed to our left giving chase to the biggest part of the herd with Slims bulldog doing his best to keep up. They were headed back to the catfish ponds. Before we got the boar hobbled Slim's bulldog returned and we had another bay back towards the trucks. Tanner, and Sha took Slims bulldog and headed that way, while Slim and I stayed back to get the hog in the field taken care of.

We met back up at the trucks and after a good look at the maps figured it best to go back down the county road and come in from that way. The fence row was covered in honeysuckle, briers, poison ivy and it was about 7 foot tall. We picked what looked like a good spot and started to climb our way in. Sha, Tanners girlfriend stated in very concrete fashion she wasn't going in, so we told her to just wait. Once through the fence row and about 40 yards of thick brush it opened up and wasn't too bad, except for the boot-high water. We all had our headlamps pointed down on the lookout for water moccasins, it was perfect habitat! We sent bulldogs, this time from just a touch over 40 yards in case we got caught up in the jungle between us and the bay. The dogs hit and the squeal told us it was small before we even got there. It was about a 60lb red boar. Again the dogs rolled out as we hastily made our way in to the caught hog. Almost immediately we had another bay to our right about 100 yards so Slim stayed back to deal with the red hog and Tanner and I took off with a bulldog. It got thick. Slim's Maytag dog was by herself and holding a good bay. We sent a catchdog from about 50 yards and as we came out of the thick stuff and crested a small dike we could see him caught on the other side of a deeper slough. He wasn't huge, but he was staying quiet even with a dog on his ear. We got around and I gathered up his tail and then a leg. Tanner broke the bulldog off while watching his Garmin and as soon as he got Samsquanch on a lead he said, "I'm headed to another bay." I told him to go on, as I gasped and wrestled the boar in a mud hole. He tossed me a set of hobbles and disappeared into the jungle. The hog wasn't huge, only about 180lb but he was a stud and could kick like a mule! About the time I got him hobbled and dragged to a tree where I could tie him out Tanner showed back up, "Broke." We stood and listened and watched our Garmins. The race was on. Slim showed back up and we all caught our breath. Chic, Tanners old dog was on the run to the south so we started the trip back to the trucks.

As we trudged on towards the trucks, overland and not by the road we had come in on, we got a glimpse of just how "piggy" the land was. There were trails beat down like cows had been using them, there were rubs on trees 18" in diameter dead from hogs whittling away at them like beavers, wallers were everywhere. Over the 250 yards back to the trucks we heard multiple hogs in brier thickets as we passed. This place was a sure enough summer time honey hole.

The second we climbed out into the open Sha started, "I got charged! I was standing in the dirt road and about 10 hogs came out into the road, at first I thought they were dogs. They looked at me and came running!" She went on to tell us of having to climb up the wall of vines and honeysuckle to shimmy up a little tree. "Which way did they go?" I asked. So far that night the hogs acted like they didn't want to leave their safe home, even with us and dogs running around harassing them, kind of like a corn field. With a raised voice Sha said, "Back in there!" That made me happy.

After Sha finished her story we all loaded up in the trucks. Chic was bayed 1.05 miles to the south at another property we had all hunted before, but long ago. As we got closer I watched the Garmin and we came to a stop that put us as close as we could get. It was only 250 yards to the bay and clear walking in another hay field. We turned two of Chic's pups in to give her a hand and get them some more experience. They went to her and started singing.

The hog had bayed right at the wood line. It was going to be thick but he wasn't in there too deep. We cut two bulldogs right where the land transitioned from field to jungle, maybe 30 yards in, so we stood and listened. The hog broke bay before the bulldogs got there, but he didn't seem to want to run. We could hear him, the hog went to our left about 20 yards. Chic and her pups followed and bayed for just a second and he broke again this time coming right back to where he had been when we turned in the bulldogs, straight in front of us. We could hear the catchdogs coming in hot and then WHAM! And he was caught. It wasn't an easy 30 yards for us, and the dogs earned their feed as they waited on us. Once in we started snapping dogs as fast as we could lay hands on them. We were almost done, now all we had to do was go back and gather up all the other boar hogs! We were wet from the knee down from the sloughs, and from the knee up we were wet from sweat. We were covered in ticks, muddy, wet, and tired but that's all in a nights hog hunt.

After a couple beers on the tailgate and after the sweat had started to dry and our breath was back, Tanner says jokingly, "Wanna turn a couple more in there?" We didn't, but we could have, there were still plenty of hogs in that 160 acres. We laughed and all agreed to lay off the place for at least a month.

I tell that story because there are a few gems of knowledge in it about hog habitat, hog habits, and hog hunting strategy. I will start with habitat. If you want to be a successful hog hunter you have to know habitat, and how it changes with the seasons. I mentioned that we had hunted an adjoining property in the winter, and in fact our dogs had drifted over into the Catfish Ponds property without striking - on more than a few occasions. In the winter that property holds very little interest to a hog. There is almost no hardwood, so no acorns. It would still be good and thick, but thick doesn't matter if deer hunters are stomping around! In the summer months though it is a paradise for hogs; thick cover, water, snakes to eat and on three sides there is good grassland to graze. The night before this hunt I caught a few hogs. We killed two hogs to cook. When we gutted them we took a look inside their stomachs and both hogs were plum full of grass. Their stomachs looked like a cows stomach. Just like with fishing, always take a look in the stomach. After years of hunting and understanding hog movement and eating patterns a lot of guys stop looking, but I say if it's right there you might as well take a look. I have cut a stomach, knowing it was going to be full of grass and found it full of creep feed, and after a little thinking and talking found who close by was feeding out cows and who was having a hog problem. We hunt hogs by looking for the trifecta of food, cover and water. If you know what they are eating all you have to find are the closest or best of the other two.

The second lesson is on hog habits. Many folks will load up after catching a hog thinking that all the barking dogs, squealing hogs, cussing men and trucks have run them off. It does depend on the terrain, but in my experience most hogs main line of defense is not running, but rather it is in hunkering down. The property I talked about above is surrounded by fairly open country. The hogs know they have a better chance in the thick stuff so they stay put. We all deal with running hogs, and it is easy to get a mindset that hogs just almost always bust out 100 miles an hour, but they don't unless it is necessary. In our country we bay large sounders and it is fairly common to have hogs that don't have dogs on them stand right around and watch us tie a hog! In fact a favorite strategy of the older, large boars is to stay put after the catchdogs get there. The largest part of the sounder will scatter with baydogs running them down, but the old smart boars will stand just barely out of sight until all the dogs have taken a track, then just walk off at a leisure pace.

I was talking with a friend a while back, he had gotten a grown dog off another friend of mine and it was a sure enough good dog, "Crackhead" was his name. I had hunted with the dog a bunch. The fella tells me they bayed a sow the other night and while they were tying it Crackhead had his back to them and was just baying up a storm. Chase says he thought the dog had taken a hard blow and lost his mind. We laughed. After a bit he shined his light to look the crazy dog over and there was a big ole boar hog standing right there! It had been there the whole time they were tying the other hog. Crackhead wasn't crazy, just a hog dog.

A couple months ago we were hunting in the day. We bayed a hog and myself and Tanner took the dogs and started walking to the truck. Slim was dragging up the rear, slow as usual and we heard a pig squealing. We looked at each other and then the dogs. We had all the dogs? Shortly Slim came walking up holding a 40lb gilt, "It was laying right there by that log on the trail," Slim said. Me and Tanner had walked right past it. It couldn't have been 20 feet from where we bayed. Hiding isn't just a strategy of shoats though!

A few years ago I went down to Louisiana to spend some time with Pat Lewing and run pups in his 40 acre pen. Pat has roads cut criss-crossing the pen and you can get a truck or buggy close to just about anywhere. The hogs in his pen will make a good dog look worthless, they are wise and get dogged often and hard. We had some young pups out and they were sure enough pushing a good hog. We would listen then drive fast to get to a crossing to watch the race. We did just that and stopped on the top of a little hill, hoping to see the hog cross and see which pup was in front and how close they were. Here came the pups, lined up and scooting. "Guess we missed the hog," I hollered and Pat hollered, "No way they THAT far behind!" After the dogs crossed the road they ran it out about 30 yards then started zig-zagging. They had lost the track and were trying to pick it back up. I watched one pup on the Garmin coming straight back to us and I figured we had messed her up and she was quitting, but she crossed the road and opened up "BUAAGGGH," and lit out when the hog - within eyesight of us - jumped up from his hiding spot and took off in the direction he had come. He had used that road, knowing the dogs would overshoot him and give him even just 10 or 12 feet of poor track conditions to fumble them! Now that tactic wouldn't work as well on a seasoned dog, but it still might just give him a couple seconds advantage. Point being -we SEE running as a strategy used by hogs, it's easy to recognize, but that is not the only trick in their book, sometimes a well placed hidey hole works too.

On a big patch of government land I hunt once a year or so the hogs also use the roads as a tactic. The wise old hogs, when putting on a race will hit the road but not cross, they will run the gravel road for 50 yards or so then duck back the direction they came or continue on across. The dogs will trail him to the road, shoot straight across then realize they no longer have his scent in their nose. By the time these dogs get back to the road and figure the trick out it is usually too late! A dog can track dry dirt, like the road, but it is tougher and takes a different strategy in the dog. The dog cannot switch instantly from good track conditions to poor track conditions in a matter of seconds, at a full run.

While I am on the topic of hog tricks I have to tell this one before I forget, and you probably won't believe me. I wouldn't believe it except I saw it with my own two eyes. One Sunday evening me, Tanner and Kolby went for a quick drop with some young dogs. We cast them to the north but they made a wide loop and headed south across the county road. We were a little ticked off but we drove around to them and when we shut the trucks off we could hear them barking on the run. Shortly they went to baying but it just didn't sound right, they weren't blowing any leaves off the trees, just a bark about every 5 seconds and not all the dogs barking together. We figured it was some trash but took a bulldog and walked in anyway. We came to a shallow pond in the woods. The pups were circling around it, sounding off every now and then. One would jump off in the pond and swim around aimlessly, barking, then come out, shake off and go to circling the pond again. We were standing there, a bit dumbfounded. Kolby says, "There's gotta be a hog in them cat-tails or something." He no more than got the words out and I see something shooting towards us, like a torpedo, underwater! It was a small boar and he came up the bank between the two of us and the dogs were on his tail, talking the whole way! We started looking around closer and there were hog noses poking out of the water about 2 inches! The hogs were underwater, sitting on their hind ends breathing through their noses just barely above the water line. Beat all I have ever seen. We are up against a very smart animal!

The last lesson in my story about the Catfish Ponds came at the very end, when I said we all agreed to not hit the property for at least a month. What we are really talking about is pressure. This is a tough one and it takes self control. If we went back there in a few days and then started hitting it every week, before too long it would dry up, not because we caught all the hogs, but because we took one large part of the trifecta I mentioned out of the equation. Food, cover, water. Cover is not cover if men are there all the time. Hunting pressure moves hogs. It seems simple enough, but I have seen it over and over - a guy hunts one spot until he can't catch a hog there to save his life.

There are times we will hunt an area hard to purposely move hogs - when a land owner is having a hard go of it with hogs. This is not the case in the area I mentioned earlier, those hogs weren't hurting anything. If you don't want to pressure your hogs you obviously need a lot of hunting ground. They way we do it is to have a circuit. We rotate where we hunt. We are generally in and out, not hunting one spot for 9 hours at a time unless we just can't help it.

Let's say a guy has 12 spots to hunt, some will say, "Dang! We all ain't that lucky!" But it isn't a matter of luck, it is about work. He rotates where he hunts and can hunt those 12 spots for YEARS! Another guy only has one spot to hunt at a time. He over hunts that spot until he has to go find another spot, then he over hunts that spot and the cycle repeats. At the end of a year he has ruined 12 spots, and is still looking for a place to hunt. If instead he would continue to gather land to hunt so that he could rotate, at some point he would be set. Go knock on doors! As hog hunters we have an advantage because we are dealing with an animal that is hated. A hog hunter is more likely to get permission to hunt over a squirrel hunter simply because most people don't hate squirrels.

CHAPTER 13
LAND ACCESS

There is an on-going fight for land access. As large blocks of private land are carved into smaller and smaller tracts every day, hunters of every persuasion are seeking a place they can live out our distant past: hunting and providing meat for our tables in a way that nourishes us much deeper that just our bellies. The big game houndsmen need large areas of land to pursue their game. There are only two options for gaining access to land in large enough tracts to do this: public hunting grounds or piecing together permission on enough adjoining private properties to in effect, make a large property.

Problems arise when a dog, or a dog hunter, ends up outside of these man made boundaries. For man, there are few excuses for trespassing in this digital age of Google Maps and GPS tracking. For hound, there is excuse. That excuse is tens of thousands of years of breeding and training by man to aid in taking game. That excuse is predicated on the notion that canines helped secure a future for primitive man and his place in this world. They helped feed us! The gray wolf was the first animal primitive man domesticated, between 20,000 and 40,000 years ago, and that union is one of the most important in human history. Short of being a physical threat to man or livestock, no hunting dog should have to give his life for crossing a boundary that he has no means of understanding.

By-in-large dog hunters are an ethical and moral bunch, despite often giving the appearance of being vagabonds - following our hounds through hill and holler often leaves us dirty, bleeding and tired. - homeless looking. Hunting dogs are very valuable, their health and ability are the keystone to a dog hunters enjoyment of the great outdoors. Hunting dogs require commitment from a man- the care, training and conditioning of these animals is not only expensive in finance but costly in time. This commitment weeds out many of the lesser men. The vast majority of dog hunters are intentionally hunting in a fashion as to limit the chances that hounds venture onto private property without permission. To do otherwise would be foolish, not unlike a still hunter tossing his Weatherby Mark V with a Leupold 5HD scope in the bed of his truck and taking off down a dirt road. Chances are high in both cases that future hunts are not going to be successful. A highly trained hound is more valuable than any rifle and care is taken to protect these hounds from the likes of the general public found today.

The still hunter is also fighting to carve out his block of hunting land in an ever shrinking natural world. Sixty years ago even most urban hunters had access to family farming and ranching land, which helped keep the land access battle to a minimum. Now, many do not and are forced to hunt public lands. While public managed lands have regulations to limit the interaction between still hunters and houndsmen, problems do still occur.

It is no big secret that the hog dog community has a bad reputation. The very nature of hog hunting with dogs often forces us into a corner where we must choose between wrongs. It is wrong to trespass, and it is wrong to stand at a fence and listen to your dogs get a thrashing from a hog without doing everything within your power to help them. No matter which action you choose you are in the wrong. Most all of us do our darndest to hunt in a way so that we aren't faced with this conundrum, but it is going to happen, especially the way these hogs run nowadays, and the land being cut into ever growing smaller and smaller parcels.

Not too long ago I found myself in that situation. We had 4 dogs out - two were on a hog to the west and two were on a hog to the east. The dogs to the west were bayed so we made our way to them at around a mile. About an hour and a half after we got that hog caught and taken care of we made it back to the other dogs. They were bayed 200 yards across the road on property we didn't have permission on. Now it was about midnight on a Saturday night so knocking on a door at that time, in this area is not even an option. We went to the dogs, and we were glad we did - it was a big sucker!

After all the excitement had whined down we made plans to contact the land owner the next morning - the age old thinking that asking for forgiveness is better than asking for permission. We just wanted to be up front, as we have many land owners in the area that let us hunt and we didn't need or want bad feelings. The next day we knocked on his door, introduced ourselves and said, "Sir, we just wanted you to know that we trespassed on your land last night..." The man took it very well and was understanding. "We noticed walking across that pasture that the hogs have you pretty tore up." He agreed and cussed them a bit. In a matter of minutes we had added his 500 acres to our 2000 or so right in that area. With us coming to him and admitting our trespassing, I figure that showed him our character. Now all men don't react the same way, but I would venture to say that 90% of them respect the forwardness, if done in the correct manner.

Since that had went so well, we headed over to a property that bordered on the northwest of our block of land. We had not trespassed on it, but it was just a matter of time so we thought we'd head it off at the pass, if nothing else we would find out how we stood with the man, the family was new to area. Pulling up to the grand gate, and seeing the huge, high-dollar house I figured we had no chance. The workers in the yard let us in after we told them our business but didn't give us any hope of acquiring the land. In fact they told us we were wasting our time. The owner met us in the driveway and we name dropped all the neighbors that we had permission on, showed him some pictures of hogs we had caught right in his area and then asked him about his hog problem. We knew they were tearing him up. The key to getting land is to get them talking. People like to talk, LET THEM! After listening and agreeing with his theory that the hogs were hurting his deer population we simply asked for permission to retrieve our dogs if they got on him. He said, "Of course," then of his own accord gave us permission to turn out on him anytime, no phone call necessary, and handed us a map of gates and gate combinations that he scratched out on a piece of paper. We traded phone numbers, and told him to call if he ever wanted to tag along, or if he ever wanted a butcher hog. We were in and out in about an hour and added 1062 acres more to our patch.

After that, we headed over to the first landowner in the area that had allowed us in. His land is kind of the anchor for our hunting in the area. He is an older gentleman and doesn't get out or get visitors very often and he is always happy when we stop by and he can't help but tell us all the same hunting stories he has told us over and over. We showed the man pictures of recent hogs, relayed details of the hunts and you could see the excitement on his face- he was living those hunts right with us.

Getting land is just half of the battle though, keeping it is the other half. Many times I have had a landowner call, invite us out, then after a bit of homework I find out that I know the hog hunter who is hunting it. I will tell the landowner that so-n-so is already hunting it and I would prefer not to back door him. The landowner always says to, "Come on," and that ole so-n-so "Hasn't been here in 6 months, he won't return a phone call and even when he was coming wasn't doing his job of catching hogs!" Many times so-n-so IS hunting it, and IS catching hogs, but he is not relaying the information to the land owner so he just assumes there is nothing going on. We like to keep our property owners up to date on how things are going, especially the older men. We are preforming a service for landowners, they need to know what is getting done or they will find someone else. That said, we do have land owners that have told us, "Don't call me, come and go as you want. I don't want to be bothered!" And of course we go by their rules, but if we pass them on the road or bump into them at the store we give them a progress report.

With laws all over the country getting out of hand, private land is a great way to avoid at least some of the mess on public lands. Respect is the key in all hunting, but even more so when you are hunting on private land. Don't be afraid to ask, the worst they can say is "No."

Most times when we are knocking on doors it is because we already have adjoining property. We approach the new landowner from the angle of getting permission to just retrieve our dogs if they get on them. Almost everyone is OK with that. Usually after a little time they go ahead and consent to us hunting their place.

Hunting private land I have come across large wildfires that we helped put out, found gates that had been left opened and helped get cows back in the right pasture, pulled calves from cattle guards, alerted ranchers of downed cattle, mended fence and even showed up to make a hand working cows or baling hay. Most ranchers keep a good eye on their cattle, but they can't be there all the time, and they don't make it to every corner of their property - being an extra set of eyes is just common courtesy. Having folks coming and going at odd hours is also a good deterrent for thieves.

Conducting yourself in the right way, and lending a hand when you can beats knocking on doors any day of the week. Often these landowners will talk to neighbors at the road, or at the sale barn and they will get us permission on other ranches. This network of neighbors can work to your favor, but screw up and it will work against you just as fast, or faster!

(Jarrett Martin and Ed Barnes)

108

CHAPTER 14
BEING A DOGMAN

Some time ago Danny Meadows called me from Florida and we had a good conversation as we usually do. Danny has a way of saying very large ideas in very few words. In person I get to see that little glint in his eye, and it makes me feel like he has more in mind than he is letting on to. "I want to ask if you have noticed something, or if it is just me getting old and cranky," Danny started off. "Does it seem like there are more people who own dogs nowadays and less dogmen?" I have to admit, I didn't have much of an answer. After we got finished with our talk of dogs past and a few present, and 'kids,' I got back to his question in my mind.

We all throw the term "dogman" around, myself included, but what does it mean? All too often, it is just used in place of an old man that has had dogs a long time, but that isn't it. I know some old guys that have owned dogs for 50 years and I wouldn't refer to all of them as dogmen. I asked some friends what they thought made a dogman. I got mostly names of men - we know a dogman when we meet one, but it is a hard thing to put your finger on. Dogmen are a lot like dogs, it takes both the right breeding and learning - nature and nurture. Not everyone can become a dogman, you have to be born with the gift. The gift alone will not make you a dogman though, you have to take that gift and build on it. We have all seen a man that just had a way with horses, a man that could communicate with a horses' soul through his eyes. I think it's not much different with a dogman. Some men just have the gift of being able to understand a dog and make dogs understand them. Most Dogmen are old, probably because it takes close to a lifetime to gather the learning end of the equation - but being old is not the key.

A trait of the dogman I have witnessed over my years is that most of them are a bit 'off,' weird or quirky - whatever you want to call it. While these men can inherently communicate with a dog, they have a hard time communicating or relating to other humans. This trait sometimes makes recognizing the dogman harder, because they are generally hard to get close to.

But back to Danny's question, "Are there more men with dogs and fewer dogmen nowadays?" That day on the phone Danny and I had decided that there were fewer dogmen. Then it was, "Why?" Partly we figured it was because there were just fewer guys around hunting with dogs. I mean really hunting hard and putting in the kind of time it takes to know dogs. But we also figured it was more than that. Danny and I have both noticed a disturbing trend; Sometimes younger people, just getting into dogs, will come to an older, wiser man with a question, but when that sage starts to talk you can see their face start going blank like they aren't listening to anything being said. Now, I am not a dogman, Danny is, but in general, when someone doesn't listen I stop talking because I find talking painful anyway and why bother? Some folks talk just to hear themselves, and these people should be avaoided at all cost and expense! Danny relayed that he does the same, and he said that many old dogmen just don't bother to try to teach people anything because so many have a know-it-all attitude. He's probably right, and it's a damn shame. "Most of us rednecks have to learn things the hard way," Danny said. We also gathered that a lot of it had to do with a kind of disposable attitude many have with dogs today. If the dog doesn't work out right away, many don't train or work on the behavior, they just throw the dog away and try another. Working through a problem with a dog doesn't just fix the dog, it fixes you. Know-how comes from doing, not talking and not reading!

I consider myself blessed that in this life so far I have found myself in the company of real dogmen many times. When the opportunity arises I cannot listen enough! I go into full 'record' mode in my brain when I get a good sit-down with these old men, and often, as soon as it is over I rush off to a quiet place and scratch out notes. Dogmen run in tight circles, they know other dogmen, and when you get to meet one, and conduct yourself right they will introduce you to many more.

My wife often makes fun of me for having so many old men as close friends. I have a knack for finding the old dog hunter no matter the situation, be it a ball game or a trip to Wal-Mart - I can find those old men and make friends in a way I cannot do with my generation. I see old men as an opportunity to veiw the past and glean it's knowledge - I seldom pass the chance.

Yet another trait of the true dogman I have noted is an over abundance of humility. A few years back I had the opportunity to sit down with arguably the greatest living dogman. He was the truest meaning of the word 'gentleman.' He spoke soft, not needing to scream his ideas into your head, he was generous with information and patient with questions. He also scoffed when referred to as a dogman! The dog is a humble creature, as is the dogman.

The dogman is also open to ideas. Shutting the doors to your brain because you already know everything is the fasted way to not reach 'dogman' status. That does not mean you believe everything you are told, but it does mean you are at least open to new ideas.

Now we can't all be blessed with the gift and natural ability to command dogs and understand them, but everyone can get darn close if they put their mind to it. Being a respected dogmen should be the goal of everyone that hunts with dogs. If we as the younger generation will take that knowledge from the dogmen around us, we can take over where they left off. If we don't, we have to learn lessons by making mistakes that could otherwise be avoided if we shut our mouths and opened our ears.

Don't EVER call yourself a dogman! I have never heard a real dogman call himself a dogman. It is almost an unwritten law that you don't. More times than not the man that calls himself a dogman is not. If you are a dogman others will use that term. To be called a dogman is a HUGE compliment, don't bestow it upon yourself, no matter how much you think it fits. It is similar to not talking too good of your dogs, if your dogs are good others will do the talking about them.

CHAPTER 15
READINESS

I have got to be about the worlds worst when it comes to being prepared. I rarely have a hunting knife on me when I am hog hunting, never a gun, seldom a set of hobbles or even rope. I do usually remember to get two dog leads before I go into a bay though. It might be that I rely on the young men I hunt with, they always seem to have 5 dog leads a piece, two large knives, and three or four sets of hobbles. I have hunted with guys that carry a backpack full of everything imaginable, and while that is a good idea, it just doesn't suit me, but I would encourage folks to be more prepared than I generally am.

I will tell a story on myself. A few years back myself and a couple other guys went to central Oklahoma to hunt a good piece of property that by all accounts shouldn't have ever seen a hog dog's foot on it before. Shortly after sun up we sent three dogs and they were on hogs instantly. One dog split off from the other two after a brief bay and they were running hogs. The dog by himself bayed pretty fast and wasn't too far off, around 500 yards if my memory serves. We caught that hog and then pulled two dogs from the box to pair with him and sent the brace of dogs. The two dogs from earlier were still running to the north so we figured we'd get another set of dogs on a track. Sure enough, those dogs started a track and we had two sets going, in opposite directions. The fresh dogs caught another hog and rolled out. Before too much longer they were bayed again. After that hog we loaded them so that we could get back on the county road and track down the two dogs from earlier.

It wasn't long and we had them picked up on the tracker - bayed. They were about 2 miles from where we had kicked them out. We got as close to the dogs as we could and went in. We were in a hardwood bottom and it was pretty easy going. Going in we all agreed, "Catch the dogs at the bay and lets go to the house." The catchdog was sent and we scooped up one of the baydogs before he could roll out. Now my big dog, a 'stop-dog' on the rougher side wasn't ready to go to the house. Pluto scooted out.

The hog had picked him a good spot, on the steep edge of a creek, it was straight up and down. The bank was about 5 feet tall and dropped into waist high water. A young man had gone down to the cold water to get the hog and another man was coaching him along, trying to keep his own pants dry! They had everything under control so I was watching my dog on the Garmin. He was on the road. I hollered at the two men that I was going to go get Pluto off the road. "He's going the way we come in," I yelled as I went to get my side by side. He was running the county road. I stepped it up to get to the buggy then high-tailed it up the road after him. The dog liked to run a road! I rounded a bend and caught sight of him hauling butt. I hollered. I tried to run him down. I cussed him up and down! Then he made a sharp right and hit the woods, there was a wagon trail so I darted down it after him in my side by side. 100 yards off the road a tree blocked my way so I stopped. When I cut the motor I could hear Pluto's big deep bawl just a little ahead. I rounded the back of my dog box only to remember instantly that my bulldog was back with the other guys. I took off on foot anyway, Pluto could hold most hogs anyway. and he would catch when I got there. As I got closer I heard Pluto switch from baying to catching, so I ran in and gave him a hand. It was about a 160lb boar hog with some decent ivory. I legged him and gave him the ole twist-n-flop and landed with my right knee right where his head met his body on his left side. Pluto was still on his ear when my hand went to my belt looking for a piece of rope. It wasn't there! And I then remembered using it on one of the first hogs of the day. I had meant to grab another piece off the dog box, but there were three of us after all - someone else would have some, or hobbles. I knew I didn't have a knife but I still searched my pockets hoping, no luck. The hog I could manage, if not for Pluto stirring him up and pulling - I was fighting the hog and the dog. I got my phone out to give a call for help but there was no signal. I went to pull a lead off my back when I devised a plan. I'd tie Pluto up and just let the darn hog go! Yeah, you guessed it, no lead. After catching my breath Pluto had let go and went about 20 yards and got himself a seat in a mud hole where he could keep an eye on me and the hog. I should have grabbed Pluto when he was caught and just taken my chances letting the hog go - but now it was too late. I contemplated just getting up, but this dude had some cutters and he was the size hog that could use them, I wasn't going to do that to Pluto, besides the dog would run him even deeper into the woods. I'd just have to wait and hope the other guys saw my tracks in the road. This went on for about 30 minutes and then I heard a buggy rapped out heading up the road. I hollered but it was pointless, and as the sound got past me I knew they hadn't seen by tracks. They were heading back to the trucks expecting to see me drinking a pop waiting on them. I knew they'd be back after they saw I wasn't there.

Fifteen minutes later I heard them coming back, and they passed me up! At this point, through no fault of their own, I was getting pissed. But I heard them stop about where the wagon trail was, I could hear them muttering but couldn't understand them. I hollered and was greeted with a holler back, "Ed?" There was confusion in the voice. "Hurry!" I came back and shortly I could hear the men crashing through the brush. When they got close they stopped, "What the hell are you doing?" "Kill this damn pig!" I said. I was whooped, and it was all my fault! Many a laugh was had, with re-enactments of my expression when they showed up. In the weeks that followed everyone gave me a checklist of supplies when we headed to a bay, and I just had to take the ribbing.

While I still don't carry a backpack, I do make a point to always have dog leads and rope and sometimes a knife. It is easy to run out on the good days where dogs keep rolling out and you just relay from one bay to the next. Each hog is one less set of hobbles or length of mule tape, and each hog needs a dog lead to secure him to a tree.

If I was to carry a back here's what I would put in it: An extra dog lead, a few pieces of mule tape, a bottle of water, Benadril, aspirin, extra batteries, a lighter or matches in a waterproof container, a syringe of Dexamethazone, a syringe of Xylazine, a small flashlight, sutures, a staple gun, a cheap pocket knife, blood powder or flour, a small bit of wax, bottle of rubbing alcohol and one of those little thermal blankets. It's easily discernible what each item is for, and you noticed the fire-starting items and blanket. I will tell why those items hit my list.

One February in Arkansas we were out hunting. The day before an ice storm had hit, kind of out of character for the area, and everything was either frozen or wet, and it was cold! We had been on a binge of a hunt with close to 30 hours of non-stop hunting. We were hog hunting so of course we were wet. We had followed dogs from hog to hog and crossed the same steep-banked creek 100 times! Smackover Creek is a snake of a creek. We had long ago abandoned our side by side and went ahead on foot. The side by side was useless because of the web of creeks it had no chance of crossing. 1 am rolled around and we were flat give out, dogs included. The dogs had given us all they had but they were done. We forded the creek yet again to get to a trail. At the trail we started looking at the maps and figured the buggy we had abandoned was about a mile away and the trucks were about a mile and a half away. We hadn't marked the buggy on our Garmins so we were just going off our tracks. We had a kid with us that was around 12 years old, he was beat so it was decided that I would stay put with him while my partner walked back to the buggy and drove in to get us, we'd head back to cabin and the wood stove, eat something and get some sleep. It sounded great! As my buddy started off he instructed us, "Stay right here. I marked it on my Garmin." "Yep," I said and eased up against a tree trunk, happy he had volunteered for the hike. The young man did the same and the dogs kicked around scratching up beds around us. I was ready for a nap.

It didn't take long of sitting around for the cold to set in. We had been miserable walking, chasing dogs, but all the walking had kept us fairly warm. The kid chimed in, and from the sound of his voice I could hear he was shivering, "Cold." That's all he said. I told him the buggy ought to be back in 30-40 minutes tops and reminded him of the cabin, while reminding myself. 30 minutes came and went, and the boys questions lengthened. "It's thick country, shouldn't be much longer," I told him in my now shivering voice. Both our ears were perked on the night air, waiting to hear that machine whirling towards us. A few times we conjured it up and convinced ourselves we could hear it off in the distance, but our ears lied to us, little more than wishful thinking.

By 2:30 the kid was beyond worried, and I was starting to get that way but I kept it to myself. I told him to get up and we paced around our little camp to get body heat going. I could keep myself warm by moving but the kid just wouldn't stay at it, so I found a set of cane close by and cut a couple arms full. Back at our outpost I laid the cane on the ground criss-crossing the direction it lay to get it up off the ground. The boy laid on the bed of cane and I covered him up in the somewhat dry leaves I could find. Then I got the dogs and laid them on top of him, a dog pile. I continued to pace.

The sun was just starting to peak out when I finally heard the sound of a buggy coming our way. It was after 6am, and 5 hours of extreme cold was enough for me. As cold as I was, I think I was more curious to find out what in God's green earth had taken so long! "What the hell..." my words were cut short by a rebuttal I am quite sure had been planned and rehearsed, "Aghhh, shit! I couldn't find the buggy. The batteries in the Garmin died. I finally found it though, then I went back to the truck 'cause I thought I could drive around and get closer. I'm going down the road and the buggy came off the trailer and went in the ditch!" "Tell us later! Let's get out of here," I was climbing in the side-by-side, my body curved down huddling close to the motor and a truck heater never felt so good!

A well placed lighter or matches could have saved us a lot of discomfort. If you have ever been seriously cold, dangerously cold, you know what I am talking about! Logic goes out the window when you are that cold, your mind gets foggy, and your motor skills go with it. It isn't a good feeling and one that should be avoided at all cost - carry matches.

CHAPTER 16
HOG DOG BREEDS

One of the hardest, or most interesting parts of hog dogging - depending on how you look at it - is the dogs. Obviously the dog is at the center of our sport, yet we do not have a true "boar hound" in America, yet. In the race to create a true boar dog the Australians in my view are ahead of us Americans. In part I attribute that to their more uniform way of hog hunting. That said, I have never been to Australia, but from what I gather they do not have the varying terrain on a scale with America. They seem to all hunt, in large part, the same way. This uniformity allows them to more easily define what they want in a hog dog breed.

Recently a friend posed a question : "Describe the perfect hog dog." The answers were all over the map, making it clear that there was not one set of attributes of the "perfect hog dog." Therein lies the problem with creating a "Boar Hound breed." This diversity is also a part of what makes hog hunting with dogs such a great sport.

In America what most consider to be hog dogs are in fact repurposed stock dogs - the Catahoula and Black mouth curs. These are very capable breeds and make good hog dogs, but they are not at the point yet where they could be considered a hog dog breed. What I mean is that these dogs are not on par with Beagles for rabbit, Walkers for coon, and so on, they have not been specialized, as a whole. There are strains of these dogs that get close to being specialized enough to be considered hog dog breeds, but they are just that - strains, and until hog dog traits can be isolated and bred with stability and reliability they will remain strains or families. When the specialization does happen then they will be considered a breed, if they come far enough away from the stock that originally produced them. The Plott also gets very close, but again, the specialization is not there. In hog hunting we don't have a go to breed. While hog hunting with dogs has a history that stretches back around the globe literally thousands of years, one breed has not popped up and set a standard. It really is kind of amazing.

Over the years I have owned and watched guys catch hogs with Catahoulas, Blackmouth, Plott, Treeing Walker, Running Walker, Bluetick, English, Black and Tan, Redbone, Leopard Cur, Airedale, Labrador, Blue Heeler, Beagle, Kelpie, Australian Shepperd, Patterdale, Jagd Terrier, Rat Terrier, July, Staghound, Wolfhound, Greyhound, Mountain Cur, Lacy, Feist, German Shorthair and German Wirehair - not to mention the countless crosses within those groups. I am quite sure I have left some breeds off, and have without a doubt left off the individual strains and sub-breeds from most all of the ones I mentioned. I also did not count in the breeds that are largely used to catch or more often used to run and catch, and some today have forgone the track dog and hunt the catchdog alone - yet more, some just use the sighthounds mentioned.

Our lack of a "hog dog breed" sits in our diversity of hunting methods. It would be very tough to start a breed that alone could handle all of our needs - from rough to loose, from bay to catch, from open to silent - a dog that could produce pork in the swamp, the mountain, the prairie, the cropland and everything in between. The lack of a secure base is one big factor in making hog hunting with dogs a tough nut to crack. If a man wants to start coon hunting he easily picks the breed he wants from the list of coondogs and gives it a go. These coondog breeds have their slight differences in speed, drive, grit and track ability but any will likely tree you coons. The same goes for fox hunting, rabbit hunting, squirrel hunting and the list continues - but not so for hog hunting.

The big three hog dog breeds, especially for folks just

starting out has to be the Catahoula, the Blackmouth, and the Plott. These three make a good foundation. Inevitably, as most hog dog men mature and move from simply wanting to catch pigs into wanting to catch pigs in a way that they find pleasing; crosses are made. Sometimes these are full blown crosses outside of breed and sometimes they are outcrosses inside of a breed for certain characteristics. Either way, it is a fine tuning of style, and something we should all strive towards.

I am not going to go into depth of all these breeds, I am no expert and there are books aplenty dealing with each breed, written by men that know more than I ever will. Instead I will just give a brief description of some of the more major breeds and their traits as they relate to hog hunting. These are broad strokes that I am about to paint. There will be exceptions to the rule, but we are not after exceptions. On a weekly basis I get phone calls from men just getting started, it usually goes like this:

"Do you think Blue Heelers make good hog dogs?"
"Well, not really."
"Why's that?"
"They tend to push, as their name suggest."
"Well, my buddy has a Blue Heeler that is the best hog dog in the world!"

The exception does not make the rule. I have seen amazing hog dogs of nearly all breeds, but it didn't make me run out and buy a Wolfhound or a Blue Heeler. They were anomalies, freaks of nature. Now if you hear of 200 Wolfhounds making top notch hog dogs then there might be something to it, but one alone is not enough, two is not enough, twenty is not enough. What we are after as houndsmen is repeatability, not freaks of nature. If we stumble across the best beagle hogdog in the world what good is it? We might get 5 of his best years of hunting, but if we cannot take that and duplicate it, or better yet expand on it, the whole experience is a wash and we are left looking to start over. Having dogs that catch hogs regular is a good feeling, but it pales in comparison to having a lineage of dogs that regularly catch hogs. The continunity has a more full and purposeful feel to it. That lineage is our relation to the future.

There is a continuity that comes from keeping a strain or line going, you get more understanding, traits and faults are not always so obvious that you can see them in one breeding or even two, the trick is in not getting so invested that you purposely overlook faults just because the thought of starting over, or heavily influencing your dogs in a new direction is overwhelming or seems like admitting defeat.

The Catahoula has medium hunt, trails silent, and tends to be more loose. These are not solid traits of course, and are not set in concrete with history. The Catahoulas of the past tended to be larger dogs, with a larger, more bull-type head and were usually rough. Over the last 20 years I have watched their head narrow, their overall size shrink, and seen them soften up on grit. With these changes I also saw their rise in the bay pen, and watched their hunt drive trail-off. The characteristics of dogs are not static in history, thankfully!

The Blackmouth has medium hunt, trails silent, and tends to be rough. The BMC, more so than the Catahoula has long existing lines of dogs that are more stable in their traits - as those traits deviate from the breed as a whole. There are even BMC lines that sit heavy on the treedog end of the spectrum, just how this line of BMC ended up as treedogs while maintaining 'pure' BMC blood is up for debate, and I am not going to get into that! What is the point anyway - every dog alive today is a product of crossing at some point in his ancestry.

One has to understand the name "Cur" to get a full understanding of dogs that carry that name. From the dawn of time until probably the 1960's "cur" was used as an insult to a dog. It denoted a mongrel dog. A cur was a do-it-all type dog, one you tossed in the yard to do general dog duties. Somewhere along the line the importance of a multipurpose dog was noted, long existing family lines were seen as having value and those lines were preserved and improved. What we are seeking to do now is to deviate from origin - to deviate from the do-it-all nature and specialize the line.

The Plott has plenty of hunt, trails open to semi-open - though there are lines that tend to be silent. The Plott tends to be on the rough side. Plotts, more than any other dog are comfortable treeing or baying. The Plott was original a cur-type dog, doing it all, and in my opinion - doing it in a silent fashion. Like many dogs, the Plott deviated from its origin and in the 1950's and 60's gained popularity with the hound men. The dogs direction changed as is clearly evidenced in the longer ears, loose skin and open mouth. Von Plott, in large part, is responsible for not only bringing the Plott dogs into popularity but also breeding bloodhound into them and drastically altering their purposes. The Plott does have the fierce temperament necessary in a hog dog. Some of the best hog dogs I have ever seen were F1 Plott crosses, yet again, we will get to crosses later.

The Treeing Walker has plenty of hunt and drive, trails open and tends to be less gritty. These dogs can and do make great hog dogs, but we are diverting hundreds of years of selective breedings. With the cur type, do-it-all breeds we are not diverting breeding, we are trying to narrow or focus the dog, this is a much easier task. Treeing Walkers are still deep down treedogs, though their past is all directly rooted in running dogs. The hound head is hard and when you couple the stubbornness with deep seated instincts that you need to change - breaking them can be a long road. When I say stubbornness I really am misusing the word though, what I am describing are instincts so ingrained in the breed that to get the dog to turn it's back on them is very hard. That is what we should all be striving for though, but with hog hunting instincts so much a part of the dog that to try to change them in a dog is almost impossible. What I am describing there is the result of hundreds of years of breeding for purpose. You cannot duplicate that in 25 years, or 50 years. Pursuits like that take multiple human lifetimes all the while staying true to the original course.

I called out the Treeing Walker but of course all of the coon hounds are somewhat popular in hog hunting. The Bluetick, Redtick, Redbone, and Black and Tan. Where I am from, probably 50% of hog hunters are converts from coon hunting, and at least in the beginning, most converted hunters also convert their coonhounds over to hog, or stick with the breed they are familiar with.

With the nature of hogs, and the evolution we have all

witnessed in respects to running, it comes as no surprise that the running hounds are seeing an insurgence in hog hunting, the Running Walker; Trigg and July. These dogs have plenty of hunt, seemingly endless bottom and stamina that dwarfs most breeds. While some folks are hunting them pure bred, they seem best suited in a cross. Most run more open, and grit is all over the place. Many of these dogs are lacking in the 'bay' department though. A solid F1 cross with a running hound and a baying, or cowdog can throw a couple pups that pick up the "bay."

I will also bring up the Airedale, not because it is popular, but because it is to my liking. The Airedale is an amazing animal, although a terrier, like it's cur cousins, it has a great ability as a do-it-all type dog. The Airedale has plenty of hunt, runs silent, and runs to catch. I have had my hands in these dogs since about 2012, and they hold my attention and respect. In the 1960's they gained popularity with the coondog crowd, shortly thereafter largely being discarded because of a proneness for fighting at the tree. In the 1980's they were a staple of the yuppie pet market - yuppies that wanted an edge I guess you could say. They also had a short stint as protection dogs - a task that fit them to a tee. The history of the Airedale is marked with disposal, most probably due to their terrier brain - they are ADHD. That brain wiring can be seen as a detraction, or an attraction if you take the time and inclination! Again, F1 crosses of an Airedale and a loose hound tend to throw a minority in the litter that are quite content to sit back and bay.

Cross bred dogs are another game! As with pure bred dogs, if you get them from an established breeder, you should have a very good idea of the traits and qualities the dogs will have. There should be an established pattern. Of course there will still be cull dogs, and there will be varying degrees of talent inside the same line, and even litter of pups. With crossed dogs it is not cut and plain!

CHAPTER 17
PICKING PUPS

Earlier I talked about all of the different ways or styles that folks can hog hunt. Those styles of hog hunting are the outward appearance of how we train our dogs, they also are dependent on the pups we choose to start. We can train hog dogs to hunt close, long, rough, loose, catch and even to a degree to be open or silent. Of course the dog is an important part of the process and we cannot train a wiener dog to run like a greyhound. We also might have limited success in quieting a treeing walker down on track, or backing a pitbull up to bay, but unless you are just up for the challenge to check your ability, why bother?

When we start pups we try to set them up to succeed, we need to do the same for ourselves! We need to pick a pup to start that has or should have the appropriate tool box for the job we want it to do. If we are wanting to train a loose baying dog then picking a full blood Airedale for example, is not a good choice. We might be able to train it to bay, but it will be a long hard road, and after 2 years we will likely end up with nothing of the sorts. If we are wanting a track dog that can take very old tracks and put a hog at the end we shouldn't start with a Staghound - not to say they can't do it, but again the exception does not make the rule. Play the odds, pick a breed that is known to have exceptional nose and track sense if you are wanting a track dog. When we pair a dogs' job with it's natural instincts we are taking advantage of the hundreds of years, in some cases, of breeding to that end. Take the

Stag for example, they have been bred for speed, endurance, and sight, if we try to get a Stag to take a track we are working against all of the selective breeding before us, but if we use the Stag as it was intended we are working with it.

At the heart of what we are dealing with here is nature (breeding) verses nurture (training.) Many of the "breed" guys will land solely on the nature side of the argument, and others solely on the nurture side, when it is in reality a complex mashing of both. I tend to lean towards the nurture side, but I also understand we can't nurture that wiener dog I mentioned earlier into growing longer legs and a deeper chest. Nature may give us the traits in a dog but it takes nurture to bring them out. I often hear of lines of dogs that just throw 100% automatic hog dogs. Of course I don't believe that. Show me a man with a 100% success rate and I will show you a man that needs to increase his standards! Aim small - miss small, aim big - miss big, as the old shooting saying goes.

If a man got one of these 'born hog dogs' as a pup and put it in a little sweater, had it live in the house and never exposed it to any hunting training do you think at 15 months you could just take it to the woods and it would run and bay you hogs? We all know the answer. The pup may have the best nature (breeding) but without the nurture (training) the traits will not be exhibited, they will not be realized or expressed. Nature and nurture interact! On the other side - If we take a Yorkipoo that hasn't had a hunting ancestor in 300 years of it's pedigree and pull out all the nurturing stops and train constantly and correctly we aren't going to see much. Every dog that is to be a successful hunting dog needs nature and nurture. If you disagree with that statement you might as well lay this book down and walk away.

PICKING A PURE BRED PUP

There are a million theories on picking a pup from a litter, most of them are pure garbage, simple quackery! If you have one of these theories that you use and it works every time then my advice for you is to go to Las Vegas, because you haven't cracked the code, you are lucky. I've heard them all I reckon; Get the pup that comes to you first. Get the pup that stays in the back. Get the pup that wonders off by itself. Get the pup that wags his tail the most. Get the pup that holds his head the highest. Get the pup that puts his nose down. Get the biggest dog. Get the runt. The list goes on and on. My theory is get the last pup left, that way all the people before have made their misjudgments and left the best pup with his mother.

Many people like the runt, and while I am a sucker for an underdog, I won't take a runt. A runt is natures loser, and I will not start with a loser! There of course have been some outstanding dogs made from runts - but yet again, we are not after the exception, we are after the rule. Runts often have a fight in them, necessary for their survival I reckon, yet I still don't like starting from behind.

I will describe an old indian method of picking a pup, not because I believe it, but because it is entertaining and there could be something to it. You make a pile of leaves and push out the edges of the pile to make a large donut shape. Then you set the leaves on fire and place all the pups inside the ring. When you let the dam loose she will go to save the pups; picking them up one by one and taking them to a safe spot. The tale says you want the first pup the bitch gets. The reasoning is that the momma dog knows the best dogs in a litter and will save them in the order she ranks them. The mother does know, just as she knows to eat the pups that have developmental problems. (On a side note - the mother eating pups can also be a vitamin deficiency.) She probably has more natural understanding than we do.

Similarly, his method of understanding goes back to an old California bear and lion dogman. He had a large dog pen and when a gyp was in heat he would turn her into the pen with all the dogs. His thinking, and probably correctly, was that the gyp would pick the correct dog to breed her. Nature is predominate, don't overlook it! We don't always know better, sometimes we must place faith in nature. (Dominant males probably bred most of his bitches, and dominance is not a substitute for ability)

Aside from indian tricks and hair-brainery, at 6 or 8

weeks old there is just no way of knowing, other than the obvious large indications. You might be able to get a sense of an overly shy pup or a dominant pup, but I say that is about the upper limit. At 6 or 8 weeks old these characteristics are fluid, they are not set for life, their environment has not had time to shape them yet. Patterns of dominance are about the pack (litter of pups) and will often change when a dog joins a new pack. A dominant Bluetick pup will not likely be dominant if you throw him in a Catahoula litter.

A good friend offered his theory on picking pups a few years back, and I have to say it was the most scientific of all the theories I have heard. He said to take a stethoscope and check the resting heart rate of all the puppies and take the pup with the highest heart rate. The blood pumps blood and air to the muscles and it is as simple as more air to the muscles - more strength and stamina (in a group of similarly built dogs.) While this makes sense, it does of course leave out other factors in making a great hog dog. It should come as no great surprise that my friend came from a background of running hounds. I have seen great dogs that lacked speed but had excellent brains and track ability, conversely I have seen great dogs that had the speed and stamina but fell short on the track side. It is never as clear a choice as one single trait. There are a whole lot of ingredients in a great cake, leave one out and it will probably not be a cake you want to eat.

It really comes down to a high percentage of luck when you are picking a pup from a litter. If you want to increase those odds though, before you even get a chance to see the pups you can. Instead of pulling out your bag of tricks when the pups are running around your feet, pull that bag of tricks out to pick a breeder, and then pick a whole litter to choose from, now all you have to pick is a healthy, large pup with no glaring faults. The group tells you more than looking at individuals. If you see faults in littermates you must know that those faults are very likely to show up in your future breedings even if they are not outwardly seen in the pup you take home. Almost any pup from a reputable breeder will likely suit you, while the best pup from a poorly bred litter will probably not suit you!

Picking a breeder is not as simple as it sounds though.

That green paper corrupts, and in todays world the hunting dog is a valuable commodity. Where there is money to be made there will be men willing to lie, cheat and steal to get it. Talk to folks, not people trying to sell you a pup, talk to folks that know them, or have bought a pup from them. The Ford dealership will tell you Fords are best, the Dodge dealership will tell you Dodges are the best, and the Chevy dealership will tell do the same; heck, Volkswagen will probably tell you their truck is the best and they don't even make one. Their opinion doesn't matter! In fact, be weary of the dog seller that starts every sentence with "I". If a man has good dogs you will hear OTHERS tell you about it. Social media can be a good tool in picking a breeder - IF you dig very deep. Watch out for the dog peddler! The dog peddler has THE dog for everyone. Dog trading, like horse trading can be a fun game to play with a trader, but it is not for the beginner.

Below are a few examples of how conversations might go when you make calls to breeders with a litter on the ground:

Example 1

"So what kinda hog dog you looking for?"
"Well, I want a medium range dog, loose baying, with tons of bottom, silent, put teeth on a runner, medium nose and catch with the catchdog."
"I got 'em. These pups oughta be JUST like that."
"Really?" You come back, surprised at the luck you have found.
"Oh yeah, that's how I like 'em too. Only way to hunt"
"How much you asking?" He's got you on the line.
"Well now, dogs like THAT aren't cheap!" He's fighting back a smile, and already planning how to spend your money.
"Where can we meet?"
"Well I live in Barnsdall, but I got problems at home so I'll have to meet you in town somewhere."
"Can we hunt the parents, or I mean the sire?"
"Oh, I just lost my lease, besides it's too damn hot. Hey! If you don't like 'em you just bring 'em back and I'll give ya your money back, makes no difference to me."

This is a dog peddler! He has just what you told him you needed. He will seldom let you come to his house, and NEVER show you a dog in the woods. Yeah, he gave you a guarantee, but all that is behind it is his word, no FDIC here. These men prey on folks starting out. In all likelihood you are about to buy a pup that he has no idea about! He might be stretching the truth or even flat out lying through his teeth, the pups may just look like hog dogs. In the age of the internet, if you have doubts about a man, type his phone number into Google with the word "dog" and if he is a peddler you ought to find a long list of his unsatisfied customers. Often you will see a list of fake names he uses too, trying to stay ahead of his bad reputation. At this point you run, you don't pass GO, you delete the phone number and consider getting yourself a new phone number too!

Buying a dog from a stranger is like playing poker, don't let him see your hand, it makes it too easy for an unscrupulous dog seller to get over on you. Let him talk, after all he is the one that has something to sell, let him tell you what he has and don't give him the easy road of telling you he has what you just told him you wanted.

Example 2

"So what kinda hog dog you looking for?"
"Well sir, I'm not really sure, (you really are, but a little white lie won't be the worst thing you do that day). Tell me about the parents of the pups."
"Well, they damn sure fine hounds! Best hog dogs I have ever seen... EVER!"
"How do they hunt?" You chime in.
"OOOHHH, good, real good!"
"Are they close range dogs? Medium?"
"Sometimes they are close, sometimes they are long, well last night they ran one 3 mile!"
Now you are having to pull all the words out of his mouth, "They pretty rough?"
Mr. Dogman comes back with his middle of the road answer, "They can be..."
"Think we could make a hunt sometime so I can see the sire?"

"Well I just had back surgery... so I can't."

"Well they sound like some fine dogs, thank you for your time sir."

This guy might be just an opportunist, he saw an easy target and needed the money, hence the non-answers that leave him open to change them based on your response. He might be straight as an arrow and just a little slow in the head. Either way, he wouldn't show the sire in the woods, and in most cases that is a dead giveaway. In reality, most times a guy isn't going to need to see the parents (or just the sire) hunt, but it shows you something if they offer. If I just had back surgery, or even lost my places to hunt, I could, and would make a few phone calls and have a buddy take my dog to show a guy if I thought he was serious and was really coming from a place where I could see he was trying to do things the right way. Aside from hunting the sire, a quick once over of the dog can tell you something. Is the sire to the pups fat? If so, you know he's either not hunting or not hunting hard, more than likely the first. Pick up a foot. How do his pads look? Are his nails overly long? Again, if so he isn't doing much hunting. We want pups out of dogs that are hunting. A sire that is not presently hunting is not a definite deal breaker, but it is a hint and gives way for more questions. Maybe the sire is retired? Maybe the owner doesn't hunt year round? Either way, if the dog isn't hunting you need to know why and be satisfied with the answer, proof of past performance is what you really want. I will say it now in case I forget later — pictures of hogs are not proof of a dogs performance!

Example 3

"I heard you had a good litter of pups for sale?" You break the ice.

"Well, they oughta be. What are you looking for son?"

"I don't really know, I'm just getting started hog hunting."

"Well my family has been raising this line of dogs a long time. They good dogs."

"How do they hunt?"

"They are fairly close dogs, 200, 300, get pretty rough. Kinda one man dogs though."

"Do the parents hunt?"

"Wouldn't breed 'em if they didn't. Where you at? Wanna come hunt?" He throws it out there.

"Sure!"

"OK, we will go make a round and you can take a look at the pups after."

After 3 calls we finally have one that is worth digging into, but let's not get ahead of ourselves! The fella seems honest, and that is a start but we still have to see if he has the dogs he thinks he does, or more accurately if they suit us. Go on the hunt with him. If you have a Garmin take it and add his collars and watch the dogs. If he is raising a line of dogs you can learn about the pups by watching his dogs work. Ask questions about the various dogs and how they relate to the pups. If the dogs please you take a look at the pups and let your gut feeling do most of the work. If you have any inkling that things aren't right thank him and tell him you will be in contact. Do some digging on his dogs and reputation. It's easy to cast off a bad feeling and buy a pup because you are already there, but it is ALWAYS best to do your homework and return if everything checks out after. If you are just starting out hog hunting, and you are worried about a little gas, get ready because you are going to put thousands of gallons of gasoline into your dogs, put that gas money into the very best dogs you can find, not the first you find.

You have picked a breed that suits you, you found a breeder that you respect and it is time to go see these pups. Look the whole litter over - are they standing right? Are they all pretty much the same size, save for maybe a runt? Are they all pretty much uniform in appearance and do they ALL fit the breed they are attributed to? If you are looking at a litter of BMC pups and one or two have long hair and a flag-tail it might be time to run back to the truck. If one has hound ears it might be time to ask some questions.

Do the pups looks wormy, with overly large stomachs? Keeping pups worm free is not an easy thing, and an 8 week old pup that is wormy is not rare or a deal breaker but it is something to consider into the general equation. What we are really judging is the care and attention given to the pups, dam and ALL of the other dogs on site. This is not a judgment on the mans income, it is a judgment on the worth he places on his dogs! The fanciest kennel setup does not guarantee the best pups, and on the other side - a rag-tag kennel setup does not mean the pups are no good. If a man doesn't value his stock enough to take good care of them then chances are you don't want one! Are pens clean? Do all dogs have access to plenty of clean water? Is there adequate shelter? If you can see without asking, look to see what kind of feed the dogs are getting. If the feed is cheap trash then that gives you pretty good idea of what the man thinks of his dogs. Some will say that not everyone can afford high quality feed, and that is true, but if you can't afford gas then don't buy a car. A great dog with a poor diet is not a great dog so why bother? There are other hobbies that are cheaper, take up whittling - all you need is a pocket knife and if you neglect that knife at least it won't suffer.

Does the dam look healthy and is she built right? The dam is responsible for in the neighborhood of 70% of the traits you will see come out in the pups - the mother is more important than the father. Science tells us it is a straight down the line 50/50 on genes between mother and father, but old school dogmen and life experience tells me it's not that even, while the mother and father of a litter may be a 50/50 split on transfer of genes, the mother will play a larger role in their life, having a greater influence on which of these genes get "turned on." If you don't like the dam, chances are very high you won't like the pups. When we breed we breed the female! Our lifes work is a hunt for exceptional bitches. In the coondog world it is all about the stud dog, but I have my theory that is because there is less work in studding a dog out than raising pups off an outstanding gyp.

Is the sire on site, and how is his confirmation? Just like with pictures of hogs, scars a hogdog do not make, but they can be indications of performance. Ask about the scars on a dog to get a feel for the roughness of a dog. Is the dog suicidal, or is it a loose dog that just got in a tough spot a few times?

Never be afraid to get in your truck and go home empty handed! If something doesn't seem right it probably isn't. Trust your gut and don't let that puppy breath or your cooing wife cloud your best judgment. This choice will set your path for the next few years to come, and if you plan on breeding this choice could determine the rest of your life in large part. I make it sound dramatic, but it is.

Years ago, when I was starting out I had a Catahoula gyp given to me by my sister. The dogs name was "Oleo" and she was a pretty good hog dog, better than I give her credit for honestly. She was rough as a cob and the definition of a "one-man-dog." But she wasn't just rough, she was mean; she would eat a man up for just getting close, and she was a dog fighting hussy! I wore myself out thumping on that dog to get her back down to earth, but, like I mentioned earlier I was trying to go against her nature. She was the very old school type Catahoula - ranch dogs you don't see much of today; partly, because to say they are a handful is a gross understatement.

One night about 2 in the morning an old cowboy was awoken from his sleep by a knocking at his door. He got up to find a young man standing on the porch asking to use the phone. The cowboy agreed then stopped the man and pointing at the dog laying on the porch asked, "Did that dog not offer to bite you?" The guest gracefully said, "Oh NO, he was real nice, just wagged his tail." The cowboy gave direction to the phone and then pulled the lever gun out from behind the door and shot the dog.

I liked Oleos' hunt and she became a solid part of my foundation stock. I saw the fault of her meanness, but I was in a hurry. I fell into the trap of 'best-to-best' breeding, and she was the best gyp I had at the time. I knew I shouldn't have used her, but I did. For the following 7 years I chased that fault around my breeding program. I did everything right, after the fact, ruling my kennels with an iron fist - setting myself as the leader, making the pecking order of the pack clear to everyone. I kept an eye and tried to cut off dominant coup d'etats I saw on the rise. I couldn't hunt with other men and their dogs. I had to put dogs in the box one-up or carefully thought out doubles. I couldn't kennel certain dogs together or even next to each other. Then one day I had enough. I stopped lying to myself and admitted that I had flawed my program right out of the gate. I had so much time involved it was sickening. I started over completely and never looked back. Starting over isn't a good feeling, but that was probably the best thing I have ever done in my dog career. I bring my mistake up to hammer home the importance of starting right. There is no such thing as a perfect dog, they all have their faults, make sure the faults you start with aren't dead-end faults. If you don't like what you see in the first litter of pups pass them up, even if it takes you a year to find what you want, you might just save yourself 7 years of wasted time.

I mentioned that best-to-best breeding was a trap and I know many now think I am a fool. Let me explain. The vast majority of great dogs cannot duplicate themselves, unless the whole litter turned out to be great dogs. If the whole litter were great dogs then you and I likely have a differing opinion of "great." In either account, if the whole litter was great then breed. A great dog is an out-lier - they defy the norm. While they defy the norm they are also genetically full of the norm! Great dogs should be bred to very solid dogs that are consistent in performance and consistently produce solid litters full of average dogs. Great to average. When at all possible go back to the dam of the great dog - here in lies your best chances of repeating the great dog. When we return to the dam we know all the pieces are there, all that is left to do is hope. Lines should also be tightened off the dam when we find a truly great dog! Using the great dog as a starting point will be less likely to lead to success than stepping back to his origin and focusing there.

We have to talk about papers. Papers can be a valuable tool, but you have to understand the inherent fault in them - they are filled out by men, and sometimes greedy and dishonest men! Papers can give us a good idea of the traits or genes that we have at least a chance of getting in a pup. They can show us a track record. Papers are not always correct though, so they can be used but your eyes and your mind have to be used in conjunction with the papers. We all know cases of hung-papers. Do not discount the owners own book of papers, they hold just as much weight as the fancy certificates with embossed seals, possibly more! I have seen men breed paper, I guess with their eyes closed, and what in theory should have been litter after litter of great dogs was one flop after another. Even the 'flop' pups had very impressive papers, some of course going on to be bred by paper yet again. In the gamedog world papers are regularly hung, in a playful game of cat and mouse. In the hunting dog world hung papers tend to not be so 'playful' as I put it, but sometimes down right rotten, dishonest and greedy. Never buy a pup just off paper! Great papers lead to great questions.

Picking a crossbred pup is a little different than picking a purebred pup. We are still going to avoid the dog peddler, and we are still going to check references though. We don't have the clear confirmation guidelines we do with purebred dogs so you are going to have to know what you want, and what it looks like. This litter of pups will not likely be uniform, in appearance or in ability. As a good friend told me many years ago, crossing dogs is not like mixing paint; one part white and one part red doesn't necessarily make pink, instead it makes white, red, whitish red, reddish white, white with red spots, red with white spots, red with white stripes, white with red stripes and if you are very very lucky there might be one pink one in the bunch, but you're also blind in this example so you have to hunt the fire out of the dogs to see what color they are. If crossing dogs was as simple as mixing paint there wouldn't be a pelt of fur left in America! You hear it all the time, " Think I will breed some hound in to up the nose in these dogs." All you can do is laugh! If it were only that simple. Don't think you are going to show up to look at a litter of cross bred pups and SEE the right one, you aren't! The only way to tell is to take the whole litter, raise them up, hunt them all and evaluate - though that is not usually an option.

So in lew of buying the whole litter we ask questions. We need to know what kind of cross this is. Are we talking about an F1 cross, where the breeding is of a full blood sire of one breed and a full blood dam of a different breed? If so, this is an F1 cross and will give us the highest level of hybrid-vigor, but also the highest level of non-uniformity in the pups within the litter. Hybrid-vigor, or Heterosis in a very limited definition is an increased vigor or other superior qualities arising from the crossbreeding of genetically different animals, or the tendency of outbred strains to exceed both inbred parents in fitness and health. The pups can be better than the parents. The future breedings of the crossbred dog result in F2 when an F1 dog is bred to another F1 dog, or an F2b when an F1 dog is bred back to a parent, uncle or aunt. I am not going to get too deep into all this though, there are entire books dealing with these ideas and they can become very complicated, fast. Each passing generation sees a leveling off in hybrid-vigor but also sees a concreting of traits becoming more stable with each breeding, in theory. (Heavy linebred dogs can also be crossed inside the same breed but to a different line and get a lesser degree of hybrid-vigor)

Mr. Dogbreeder tells us this is an F1 cross of a Plott gyp and a BMC dog. Next we want to know if this is the first breeding of this cross using the same gyp and dog. If it is the first cross then his opinion of how the pups will turn out does not carry much weight. He might have made the same cross with different dogs, but that is little more than a hope when it comes to these pups. Hopefully he has made this cross with the same dam and sire before and we can add weight to any insight he might give us from the last litter. With that said, we still can only guess at what we are getting in a pup. The F1 pups are a crap shoot, but they are also our greatest chance for 'freak-of-nature' unreal hog dogs - whether they can reproduce is up for debate and in most cases it's a "No!" Even more so with crossbred dogs than with purebred dogs.

What we are trying to get at is the reason for his cross. There are three main reasons folks cross dogs;

1. An accidental breeding. This sounds bad, and it can be but it doesn't always have to be. The second best dog in my kennels today is the result of an accidental breeding of an Airedale bitch and a Treeing Walker coonhound. The parents weren't even hog dogs, yet I wouldn't sell mine for any amount of money and I know her full sister from the same breeding that has also made a good hog dog. (While writing this I have acquired her sister and she is a also a grade hog dog) If both sire and dam were hunting dogs in the accidental breeding and the cross seems to make sense it might be worth going for. Now if it is some dudes jam-up Plott dog over his wife's yorkie...? Maybe, maybe not! Or even if it is his Plott dog over a 9 month old unproven BMC? Maybe, maybe not, it just depends on the time and dog food you are willing to gamble.

Crosses with solid hunting dogs top and bottom will give us the best odds at making a dog and also at duplicating the dog. Let's say the Plott over the Yorkie mentioned above throws a pup that makes a once in a lifetime dog. It is not unheard of. We really have something, but it will most usually end there. That pup won the genetic lottery and wound up with the right genes coming from the Plott, but the Yorkie genes are still there. Those Yorkie genes didn't get expressed in that first cross but if we breed that dog they could pop up in mass. Future breedings of the dog will be wild gambles with very un-uniform outcomes. In that case, the cross makes no sense. If we have to HOPE that the majority of genes expressed come from one dog - the Plott, then why not just breed the Plott dog to a Plott gyp? If you want a drink of water you don't pour in Kool-Aid without stirring and hope it all falls to the bottom so you can drink straight water. We cross dogs to get the benefit of the stirring of the Kool-Aid, if you want water just drink water.

In the second case of the Plott over the unproven BMC - we have a little better odds but not by too incredibly much. If we know the breeding of the BMC and everything looks solid then we can breath a little easier, but in the reverse to our Plott x Yorkie, the BMC may have lost the genetic lottery and got all the worst genes, leaving him just a slightly better bet than the Yorkie. We cross proven dogs to proven dogs so we are not playing a life and death game of chance, hoping for a lions share of genes from one dog. When we cross right we have 'dream dogs' in mind but we lay it out so that practically any mix-matching of genes from dam or sire should make solid dogs, while keeping an eye out for the exceptional dogs. We mix fire with fire and not fire with water.

2. The second reason for a cross is a planned cross for a pup or two. Ole' Jimmy used to have a Cat x BMC that was an unreal hog dog... so Jimmy is going to make some more. It's like making a cake right? And he has the recipe! Once again, not necessarily bad, but a crap shoot, and it really goes back in large part to the parents of the pups. We ALWAYS want to see that the parents hunt, even if they are not the best dogs, we at a bare minimum want to see something good in both parents and especially in momma. We aren't even looking for stars, we want good, solid, dependable dogs - middle of the road - meat and potatoes! These type dogs will produce better overall litters over the superstars most times. I know that flies in the face of what most say but I believe it to be true. I won't ruffle feathers by mentioning dog names but how many truly great coondogs have you seen studded out until they just can't walk, hundreds of breedings and yet no pups seem to ever get to the level the stud was at? The reason is they are trying to get lightning to strike the same place twice. There's money in it. In reality the more

likely pairing is in the superstars brother or sister that made a consistent but not exceptional coondog. An even better pairing is one back to the mother of the superstar. I would say 75% of truly GREAT dogs can't reproduce solidly consistent pups, hence my slight at best -to-best breeding. Most of the great dogs are freaks of nature and cannot duplicate themselves - go back to the paring at least on one side in order to have a shot at reproducing them. The gyp is the key!

      3. Next is a planned cross out of a program with a plan. This is the one we want and the hardest one to get! These are pups with a purpose. A man has a program and he is aiming at something. This really is an attempt at the start of a new breed, in some cases intentionally in most unintentionally. There is a catch 22 here though - if the man is doing things right you won't get a pup, unless you are in very tight with him. Men with long term crosses like this rarely sell pups, because like I said earlier about the paint mixing - they keep the whole litter so they can observe and see what 'color' things are. A master chef isn't going to make a new dish and not taste it. If he did, he has no proof that it was good, he might have an educated guess, but guesses won't get you very far in this game. Due to the sheer number of dogs that a program like this produces it is common for the breeder to 'place' pups with folks he knows will hunt hard and can give him insight as a third party though. Often these arrangements come with the string attached that he can draw the dog back at any time and breeding is not allowed. If a man proposes to have a program like this, and he is selling pups? Well, they might be good pups but the chances his program will pan out are pretty low, but it still might be a better deal than the planned cross for a couple pups explained in example number 2.

      Picking a crossbred dog is not an easy task, and even with all the knowledge in the world it is still left to chance in large part. Really it is not all that different than in the purebred world, just the arch in the swing of traits is much larger and a little more wild. We can use our brains to increase our odds though, or we can close our eyes and swing for the fence, nothing is wrong with either approach, but I am going to think about it. For the man newer to hog hunting the pure bred pup holds more certainty though and would be my recommendation in most cases.

CHAPTER 18
CYCLES

Over the years of hog hunting I have gone through the cycles many times of losing interest and being ate up with hunting. I have found it best to go with that natural flow and not fight it. When I find myself in an ebb I just roll with it and know that the flow will come again.

An ebb I was definitely in on a Saturday in June. One of our hunting buddies had taken a job on the island of St Croix and since his departure I just hadn't hunted much. Though I didn't much feel like going, I agreed when Slim called me, as a sort of concession to him and the dogs sitting in my kennels. Normally we hunt out of trucks but we made plans to load buggies and do something different for a change of pace. That simple change of vehicle gave me a jolt of 'want to.'

I unloaded my Ranger while Slim winched his four-wheeler down off the trailer. We were loaded for bear with dogs spilling out of each box and rack. Rather than casting dogs, we instead eased along the wood line that pushed into the vast pastures of the property; looking for a hot track to drop on, looking to see a hog, or better yet get an opening dog in the box. With none of the such we turned to the south of the property and made our way along an old overgrown road that snaked along a spine with very deep fingers of hollers peeling off to both sides. As we approached a small muddy pond that sat in the woods, Slim's brake lights came on and in an instant he was off holding two pups. "Hog," he whispered, barely more than making the motion of the word with his mouth. I hadn't seen the hog but I knew what was up from his response. Slim was dropping his pups as I hurried to get a collar on a dog, something I should have done already. I dropped my old Shuugs dog from the back of the buggie and she headed straight to the pond and was on the run with a bawl. As I came around the back of my Ranger I saw Bo, a pup of Slim's off my old Gyp I had turned loose. Bo had come off the four wheeler rack in the excitement and was hanging by his collar. I was on my way to him as he thrashed around then he slipped his collar, hit the ground at a run and was giving his strange bawl scream as he hurried to catch up to the race.

We froze, with heads cocked in that weird sideways angle that makes no sense I guess, but is a deep ingrained habit. My lips were held welded together from the hot air but if they had broken free they would have naturally fell into a smile, pulled at the corners from the barks that lit up the dusky sky. Slim made a few gentle steps my direction and held his hand flat to earth about mid-thigh. I nodded my head in approval though I wasn't concerned with size as I ate the sounds out of the air. The barking fell faint into the distance and I knew they had went into the holler to the south, the big one of course. We both dropped our silence and stillness as we went for Garmins and talked. They were bayed at 600 yards. We agreed to drive to 300 yards. Once there we gave everything a good listen then grabbed Slim's bulldog, Buffalo Hump, and headed into the holler.

As we slid, tripped and fell down and down and down, the bay had broken and come back a couple times, with only small gaps - breaking only twenty or thirty yards each time. Finally at the bottom we landed in a small spring fed stream. The heat was evident at that point. While it was only about 72 degrees it was muggy as all get out and there was no breeze - it seemed as if there wasn't even any oxygen to breath. For those not familiar with hunting in hills, going down is in a way harder than going up. Climbing is a cardiovascular exercise, while going down in an exercise in agility and dexterity - you use every muscle in your body to keep on your feet. In the type of hills we are used to hunting, going down may not necessarily be life or death but keeping square to the world is definitely the difference between just being tired and being in the hospital! Slim and I were both gathering the information from the air and the Garmins and it was glaringly obvious they were across another hill and holler. Although just 320 yards it was disheartening to think of climbing back up and dropping off again. We had a hard bay going so we went at it but not at all eagerly. As we climbed I couldn't help but keep pushing that Garmin in my face and I was watching the bay break over and over. At the top we got words pushed out between the panting. We were both completely soaked with sweat. "He's walking on us Slim." Slim spoke in his normal slow draw, "Yeah."

We had a hard decision in front of us, one every hog hunter knows all too well. We could climb down and back up, down and back up yet again to buggies and sit it out and see where a hard bay ended up, hopefully in a place we could get closer to on wheels, or we could keep moving forward on foot. On flat ground we would have returned to the buggies without question, but the thought of climbing back out was heart breaking, and the chances the bay was going to end up somewhere we could drive close to was looking pretty bleak. We discussed the options and landed on a plan based on some guesswork and some knowledge of the area - we would try to flank the hog and send the bulldog in from far to put an end to the walking bay. A walking bay always makes me mad, the hog in essentially disrespecting the dogs! As I thought about it I knew it was a big boar because we had two dogs on him that were not pushovers, they were going to sink teeth to get respect, but they were not bay busters!

For the next 30 or 40 minutes we climbed and sank trying to get ahead and get within a reasonable distance to send Buffalo Hump without signing his death warrant. Finally we were 120 yards and had a good bay. I told Slim to send him, followed by the disclaimer that I could not run and he would be on his own for a spell before I got there. I am twice as old as Slim, and I felt it that night! Buffalo trotted off towards the bay, already tired and panting heavily. Slim stepped his pace up as I walked, relieved we were finally doing something. Slim hollered back, "He's got 'em." With rough words, pushed with frustration and exhaustion I told him to get there, as I continued to walk, knowing well if I tried to hurry I would be spent up by the time I got there. As I got within earshot I could hear Slim's words but they were jumbled up, but I didn't need words, I knew the picture. Slim had both hands on a single back leg of the boar, and it was a stud. I eased in beside him, and seeing all the blood on the ground I took the leg from Slim and told him to stick the boar. Buffalo was hanging on the ear and the boar was thrashing. The bay dogs were coming in for a quick nip then backing out and baying. As Slim stabbed him I was scanning all the bay dogs and it was clear the blood was from Buffalo. Slims knife found the heart and I held on to the leg feeling the last of life leave the hog in shakes. I dropped the leg and Slim and I both dropped down to the cool dirt, exhausted. The hog had found a clump of three large trees that had fallen and brought up the big root ball. The bare dirt felt like ice. The dogs did the same.

After a good bit of studying Garmins we came to the hard truth that there was no easy way back to the wheelers. Buffalo was cut in four spots but nothing major, "If anything the blood letting is helping him to cool off," I tried to reassure Slim, but I didn't believe it myself. Further inspection told us both he was in bad shape but not from the hog. For a few months before this his breathing had slowly become more and more labored. We had landed on the conclusion that he had a bad case of heart worms. Slim had got the dog as about a three year old from a pet home. Buffalo was a crossed up Pit mix, he had a short snout and in prime physical condition he didn't have great air, but the dog was having a hard time getting air at rest! In my amateur diagnosis, I figured he had a bad case of heartworms, and his lungs just weren't getting enough oxygen in his blood.

We gave Buffalo, and ourselves, plenty of time to recuperate then we started the trudge back to the buggies, our bodies depleted of the adrenaline that had gotten us to where we were. It wasn't long before Buffalo refused, or was unable to walk. Carrying him simply wasn't an option because of the terrain, so we gave him rest in the bottom of each holler wet with spring water and forced him to move on. Each time getting him back on his feet was harder and harder. He was a fighter and made it all the way back to the top road where we had parked, then he went down and his breathing was shallow and mechanical. There was nothing we could do. I told Slim he was dying and he nodded and mumbled something. I am hard of hearing and Slim is a soft talker. We watched Buffalo Hump go in the cool grass knowing there was nothing we could do.

Buffalo hump was all heart and he really should have died long before. He had caught a 260lb boar with no help and had done it in style, as he was on deaths door! We owed many hogs to that ugly mutt. Just a couple months before Buffalo had went 1.63 miles on a busted bay and caught the hog, in the hills, a shining example of heart, and gameness. Buffalo Hump needs no tears, only our respect and admiration - an example for man and dog to emulate!

CHAPTER 19
A Christmas to Remember

About a week before Christmas Pat Lewing called me, "Hey, what you doing for Christmas?" "Not much," was my reply. "I might come up." My attention perked up. I had been telling Pat for some time he needed to come and and hunt. "I'll call you next week and we will make plans." We hung up. A couple days later I was laying on the couch and my phone rang, it was about 8 at night, Pat was on the other end. I asked him what he was up to and he said, "Driving. What's the best way to get to your place from Hwy 20?" We went over directions for a while and I figured he ought to make it here by 3am. When I got up at 5am my shop lights were on and Pat Lewing and Kolby Ingram had a fire in the wood stove. Pat had picked up Kolby on the way.

I had hunted with Pat at his places in Louisiana, and we had a good time and caught hogs - but it was very different from home. Long races were the order of the day, miles... and miles. Pat told me of 15 and 20 mile races, relaying fresh dogs and cutting tracks at roads. That is what had spurred me to hound Pat about coming and hunting with me in Oklahoma. We have spots where the hogs are like the ones Pat is used to, mainly on public land that is dogged very hard, but I stay away from those spots unless I just want to see how some young dogs are measuring up in the bottom department. For the most part, on our private lands we have very short races, 300 - 500 yards being our norm and constantly bay very large sounders of hogs. I was excited to show Pat the small time capsule we had carved out in our neck of the woods! Without a doubt most folks reading this will mumble, "Lucky sucker" under their breath about now, but luck has very little to do with it. Me and my hunting buddies have worked very hard to replicate the days of old. There is a bit of luck involved though. We are lucky to not have a hog hunter on every corner, and we are lucky in that the few hog hunters we do have around hunt in a very similar style to us, and with a similar mindset.

The first night out we cut a couple mutts towards a creek and they were struck in a matter of minutes. Two donkeys started some braying and headed west in front of us. To be honest my heart sank. I thought, "These darn dogs are gonna make me look like a jackass tonight?" In an instant though I gathered the information from the sound of the dogs that they weren't messing with stock and were indeed on hogs. The bawl mouth of a young dog trailing was reverberating off the hillside and mixing with the fussing of what sounded to be 10 or so hogs. The dogs ran the hogs 100 yards to the east, then back west and bayed at the base of a mountain. We were about 350 yards from the dogs and we could hear the sounder. Pat looked at me, eyes wide. I shrugged, glad it had gone the way I had assured him it would. We forded the creek in my truck and got within 200 yards of the bay and sent the catchdogs. It couldn't have been any more beautiful. The dogs were bayed in a deep horseshoe holler and had them backed up to a rock face with a dripping spring. We peeled a sow for the table out of the wad and another small boar that was ridded of his nuts.

We loaded and headed to our second turnout. At this spot we have races every so often. There is a huge boar that has given us the slip many a night, and we know because he always runs the same track. Sure enough we struck him. After a few miles we managed to catch the dogs on the road, this wasn't what Pat had come for so we changed spots.

At our third turnout, after kicking dogs out we learned that gun hunters had shot at a big wad of hogs just an hour or so before we got there. We figured this spot wasn't going to be very fruitful but the dogs were already out making big strides so we waited. Shortly we had a bay and drove in closer and then set off on foot. The dogs were bayed in an open pasture. We could hear the woofing of what sounded like big hogs. The catchdog was sent and we took off. The sounder was about 25 strong and held some very big hogs, we were looking at them. I knew my bulldog was there, but running in I couldn't see him and didn't hear any squealing or grunting? The hogs were bunched up very tight and it became apparent my bulldog was in the middle getting worked over! They had rallied. As we got right up on top of the wad, the hogs rolled to our left like a school of fish - they were moving as one unit, and I assumed my catchdog was in there with them. The group dropped into a small gully and then we got some squealing. It was time to take off! We were running down in some pretty rocky ground and I heard something go bump in the night behind me, I went on. The catchdog, Gumbo had a very nice and fat sow - a blooded hog. I was looking around for Pat when Tanner tells me Pat took a fall. Shortly Pat comes stumbling up, breathless and recalling the tale of the hogs running every direction. We took the sow for the table - there was going to be a lot of cooking the next couple weeks and she was prime table fare, a much better hog than the rooter we had caught earlier that night.

We didn't have time to talk though. Pat tapped, his knee was already swelling and he told us to go on. We did. The bay dogs took the hogs into the finger of a large draw and we had bays everywhere. It was getting late and we were done hog hunting, just trying to catch dogs at the bay. We ended up catching two more hogs and Pat showed up, attracted by the barking of hounds, bum knee or not he couldn't resist his breeding. We managed to get all the dogs caught, except one - Digger. He was not done hunting, despite our sentiments on the subject. After an hour, and a mile, Digger had one bayed. We drove around and started getting gear together. Pat stayed at the truck, his right knee was twice as big as a knee is supposed to be.

Me, Tanner and Sha made our way 800 yards and sent Gumbo to a bay on the edge of a pond. It was a sow around 250 and fat. She was bayed on the edge of the pond, barely in the water but on a steep pond bank. There was a barbed wire fence right at the waters edge. When we went in to leg her the pond bank slid us down to the barb wire and a mess of green briers. We were trying to get her handled while we were standing at a strange angle, fighting briers, and this hussy was all there and none to happy about it! We finally got her flipped but because of that darn fence we couldn't get to the correct side of her. We were on her leg side instead of her back side, and that hill was constantly trying to throw us down on top of her and her swinging head - mouth agape and snapping like a turtle. After a good while of fighting physics we decided to drag her to the top of the pond bank. About the time we hatched the plan Tanners girlfriend let us know, "Gumbo's guts are hanging out!" Now that is all we needed. Tanner looks at me and says, "Kill her!" "You got a knife?" I came back at him. "No." I fished in my pocket and came out with my two and a half inch Old Timer. This wasn't going to be easy. Seeing my little frog sticker Tanner reasserts, "Let's get her to the top." We gave it a gallant attempt but we just couldn't. We were wet, the bank was steep and muddy, the hog was fighting us and the bulldog was working against us pulling down as we were trying to go up. Exhausted we gave up and I started carving on the sow. I managed to get her killed and we were ready to take off to the truck to see if we could save the bulldog. At this point I realize I had lost my Garmin, of course. I scooped Gumbo up and we started to the trucks, tired beyond belief. On the way we switched off carrying Gumbo, taking turns running. Back at the truck we saw Gumbo wasn't going to make it. He had a great life, full of satisfying work that suited his nature and breeding though. He died doing what he loved and he never backed down - even though his innards were outwards. Gumbo had come to me from Pat, and it was fitting that he was there on Gumbo's last hunt.

Digger had rolled out in all the commotion with the big sow. At the truck we could faintly hear him baying in a deep draw so we went home and got another catchdog. It ended up being a long night, the sun was coming up when we finally got in our beds, but I guess we broke Pat in proper. These hills are no joke, you learn to be half billygoat.

The next day we dined on some of Pats cooking and were planning our hunt with bellies full of pork and rice. Pat had told me he was going to sit this one out, and I had agreed, but Seth Cobb showed up at my house and started twisting arms. "I guess we could go for one turnout?" I knew deep down how that usually goes. Pat and I both ended up going and I am glad we did!

We met Tanner at the store and headed to a place that the last time Tanner and I hit the hogs had rallied on us good. It had also been an all night affair of catching hogs and tackling dogs just to go home. We came in the gate and headed to the fields at the bottom. Tanners dogs struck and worked a hog to the top of the mountain and bayed. At the top it had broke and was coming back down. We knew it was a good hog. They made it almost all the way back down and fell bayed. We all slipped in and sent Tanners catchdog, Samuel D. Sqwuanch. We then KNEW it was good one from the sounds as we busted brush. When I got there the hog and Samuel D. were easing around, sliding down the hill and spinning. Tanner was yelling at me to "Catch him!" Samuel D. had him by the snout, with about a 2.5" tusk pressed snuggly against his side and all I could think was, "Two dead catchdogs in two days and oh heck we are screwed if he dies!" Seth came in with his K-Bar and ended that. We were home by 10pm. Samuel D. didn't even get a scratch.

Pat stayed for a couple weeks. He killed a good buck and we caught hogs almost every night he was here. Pat said he saw more hogs than he had seen in the last 5 years. We bayed wad after wad and all with short races and great dog work. It was one of the best Christmas' I can remember. We hunted until we were wore smooth out. Sometimes I get nostalgic for the days when I hunted alone, but then times like these remind me how great it is to be surrounded by folks you want to be around, where conversations aren't forced and knowledge is shared and discussed.

Seth Cobb, Pat Lewing and Ed Barnes

CHAPTER 20
SPOILING DOGS

I'm a bit nostalgic I guess. When faced with a decision where my veternarian and the old timers have differing views I almost always ride with the old timers. I will always take the advice learned by doing over the advise gained from a book. (So... figure this out yourself.)

We've all heard the old men tell us not to let the kids play with a pup, or bring it inside. Most old timers anyways. And like I just said, I usually go with the old advise, and I do here, somewhat. There is a fine line to balance. I want a dog that handles, and to get that pup there you have to spend some time with them, but I try to limit it.

I like an independent dog, not skidish, or timid, but independent - some folks intermix those words incorrectly. There are three types of hunting dogs

- dogs that don't hunt.
- dogs that hunt for you.
- dogs that hunt for themselves.

I prefer the later. These type of dogs start faster. This is where I take the old time view. I limit my interaction with the dog to feeding, cleaning kennels, and maybe the occassional yard time. When I feed I call the dogs name each time and in just a few times they know their name, and that is the basis of general commands. Once they know their name is "NoGood SOB" I work on a "Back," making them get back before I pour their feed. All the basic commands can easily be taught at feeding time. Now I don't want my dogs to be afraid of me, so when deserved, a quick rub under the chin or ear lets them know I am not the boogie man without them thinking their job is to give my hand a thing to rub on. It can be rough listening to that darn pup bawl an cry, even tougher to keep the kids away from the kennel latch and I don't always win, but I try.

When it's time for the woods the dog that isn't focused on you is almost always going to start easier and out perform the dog that thinks you are the center of the universe. That pup that latched onto you after momma was gone and sleeps at the foot of your bed, looks to you for fun and food and comfort is now expected to go hunt... without you? A lot of guys walk their dogs, so maybe that would work? I expect my dogs to GO! And a pup raised that way just isn't likely to do it. Some think it cruel, cold-hearted to treat a pup this way - at arms length, but that's how I look at it. All that said, I like to have a bond with my dogs, I just choose to wait to make that strong bond until after the dog is hunting the way I want them to. After the dog is where I want them, then we become friends. Every so often I'll bring a dog in the house, let them lick plates and lay on the couch, get petted, all that good stuff. If I'm in the mood, sometimes I'll even let a dog ride in the cab of the truck on the way to hunt. I have never had a problem with it spoiling a dog as long as it isn't done too often. And that is where I stray from the hard line old timers who would never pamper a hunting dog. I see no harm if done right, at the right time - when "pup" no longer suits them and we refer to them as a dog.

(Splinter - staghound)

CHAPTER 21
BEGINNER MISTAKES

We all start somewhere and we all make mistakes and we all do some downright stupid things! I know I did, and I know I still do sometimes. Mistakes are important, if you learn from them, but avoided mistakes are golden. I want to talk about some of the most common beginner mistakes in hopes it might save a few from having to make them. There is no shame in starting out and making the mistakes many of us make though.

The single biggest, and most common mistake I see is folks start breeding hog dogs way too soon after starting hog hunting. I would say it takes the average man about three years of hog hunting to really get a grasp of the sport and the dogs needed. It also takes some time to feel out what your style of dog is. In the beginning catching a hog is such a thrill that little else matters, as things progress many want to catch a hog in a certain way. This is style, and the type of dog used is at the heart of it. Why breed dogs before you have reached that level?

All too often I see a young man starting out, he's looking for people to hunt with, looking for a 'good' dog to buy and he has two litters of hog dogs for sale. Most folks just got a smile across their face, and most people could name a couple guys that fit that description too. It's ridiculous, and true - the best sort of comedy. There are a couple problems with breeding trash hog dogs, or even just generic hog dogs. For starters there is already enough trash out there! There are also enough mediocre dogs out there. If you are of the mind you are going to breed top-notch hog dogs before you have a real grasp of hog hunting then you are mistaken! Secondly, if you are just starting off hunting and also haphazardly starting your 'line' of dogs then you are not just hurting yourself in the present day, you may very well be boxing in the next ten or twenty years of your life. What I mean is that when you have so much time invested it is hard to make the sometimes necessary decision to start over. Wait to make that large commitment. It is not unlike starting a 100 foot mural as soon as you decide to start learning to paint. At some point you will likely look back at the time, energy and money you wasted, shake your head and sigh, I have. Breeding dogs is such a jumbled, complicated science that to throw your hat into the ring, even by the most seasoned dog hunter, takes a pretty large pair. The three or so litters of dogs that I have purposely bred in the last ten years were merely an attempt to save blood - a more simple task, yet still a riddled venture.

I have had this same conversation with a couple coon hunters that switched to hog hunting and started breeding right out of the gate. Both guys defended their breeding with the argument that they knew dogs. They did, they knew dogs in general and knew breeding as much as anyone can, but they didn't know hog dogs, at least not yet! Before you can breed hog dogs you must know hog dogs in the most intimate manner. Most people that start hog hunting will end up changing their dog style in the first five years anyway, or quiting! So wait, cuss me today and thank me in five years.

The second most common mistake I see in beginners is having a yard, and I mean a yard FULL of dogs! A few years ago I was sitting on the couch at home and my phone rang. I answered, for some reason - I usually don't. The accent on the other end was that heavy northern rolling question mark at the end of every sentence - Wisconsin, North Dakota type accent. "Ed Barnes?" I was already smiling, thinking of that "Fargo" movie, "Yeah." "Hey, yeah, I heard you got hog dogs?" "I do," I said, "Sometimes." We meandered around talking about hog hunting for a bit. The man had been on a few guided hog dog hunts in the south somewhere. Finally he got around to what he had been after the whole time, "How many hog dogs you got?" "Well... HOG DOGS... I'd say 4 and a few coming close," I told him. "Sell me one?" I knew it was coming. "Oh, I don't sell dogs. Don't have none to spare." I could tell he wasn't going to take my answer. "You just said you got four!" He laughed a bit and urged more. "Sell me Such-n-Such dog," he knew the name of one of my better dogs. "Naw, can't." A more observant person would have known I wasn't going to budge. I went on to tell him about how hog hunting wasn't coon hunting, and that we had to keep an A Team, B Team, and somewhat of a C Team because we sometimes lost dogs fast. "$1000," he blurted out. "No." I laughed. "$2000!" He said fast, with a force like he was slapping hundred dollar bills on a table. "Nope, can't," I told him. The man chuckled, thinking I was playing hardball, "AAGHHH....OK, final offer... $3000! And I will be down there tomorrow." I kept my cool but I was getting a bit aggravated, "Can't." We ended the call with each of us a little testy. My son, Eddie was beside me on the couch and he had heard the conversation as I always use the speaker-phone because I don't like my ear sweating. "You turned down $3000 for ole So-n-So?" "Yeah." He had hunted plenty with the dog and as a young man he already knew hog dogs better than most grown men. "What you think she's worth?" He said it with that youthful misunderstanding of money. "About $1000," I remarked and laughed at myself. Eddies face contorted into a question mark and I left it at that, for him to think about. The best things in life cannot be bought! Good dogs are one of the best things. You won't buy them! The funny part is that the dog was just a good dog, not great, and not the best in my kennels. Good dogs are rarely for sale and I will go out on a limb and say great dogs are NEVER for sale! Beware of the malarky, great dogs go to friends, they don't go up for sale to the public.

Buying a good dog is a slight in your face anyway. The pleasure is the journey. If you miss the journey you have missed the best part. You cannot buy your way into hog hunting, and that is one thing I love about hog hunting. Successful hog hunting takes work, there are no shortcuts. More than any other dog hunting sport - hog hunting requires work and that is why it has stayed true - a blue collar endeavor. Good dogs that are bought usually end up mediocre at best in the hands of beginners in just a short time anyway.

As I told the man from up north, hog hunting takes an eye for the future, sometimes in a fast way. It might seem like I am making an argument for a yard of 20 or 30 dogs but quantity has little to do with it. Average, or below average dogs are easily replaced and there is no reason to horde sub-par dogs. One man, who hunts alone even, cannot hunt 20 dogs enough, even if he hunts every single day. He cannot hunt enough to evaluate dogs and he for sure cannot hunt enough to push young dogs into becoming great dogs! Chances are good that a yard of 20 dogs has one or two that have potential, but they usually get lost in the crowd.

I was talking with a friend and we were talking about the dogs that we each started out with. The young man went back to a great dog that I had hunted with plenty and I can attest to the fact that the dog was a great dog, her name was Shiloh. Those first dogs often reach legend status in our minds, sometimes it is rose colored glasses - sometimes it is the truth. My buddy and I came to the conclusion that those dogs were great because they were hunted, and pushed and relied upon EVERY time we went hunting because it was all we had. Chances are very high that if this young man would have had ten dogs when he started that not a single one would have reached legend status, not because they lacked the potential, because they were from a good line of dogs, but because each would have lacked all that exposure. I could see the gears in the young mans head spinning as we had the conversation, he was understanding - not me, but his own understanding, "Think I'm gonna thin my yard." I agreed with him.

I think it best to focus on a few dogs, with heavy hunting you will see the cream rise. On the chain you just see four legs and a color. As the bottom becomes apparent add one dog at a time to your yard, bringing the count up and then cull that lowest spot after a fair shake. After much boot leather the dogs will continue to rise higher and higher! With that said, culling can easily get ahead of itself. Many times I have culled the lowest end of my kennels and then in a couple weeks I found myself wishing I had them back due to the top end getting killed. It is a tight rope, walk it with care and thinking. Culling is not to be taken lightly, it is a great responsibility and should be shown great respect. A dog's life is not a small thing!

Some equate a large yard of dogs to success, and many of the great dog hunters have had very large yards but they didn't start that way. To me the large yard is for the breeder, the ones trying to push dogs in a new direction. The hunter needs a much smaller yard. Master squeezing the greatest potential out of dogs and everything else will fall into place, one day maybe leading to a large yard. Keep the cart and the horse in order.

The third biggest mistake I see new hog hunters make is not thinking in the long term. Hogs are not limitless! Pressure moves hogs faster than feed. Hogs need to feel safe, harass them and they will move. Ease off places where you know there are hogs. It is hard to do, but your future and the future of your dogs depends on it. That is not a widely popular idea, I know. In almost every other hunting sport management is a popular word, in hog hunting it is a polarizing word. We have to remember that we did not bring hogs to America, we are not by default tasked with removing them. If I catch a hog and release him I have not created a hog, it is a null point. Deer hunters and farmers may moan all they want, but until someone pays me to kill hogs it is not in my best interest. We have to assign a value to our hunting. The "right" to hunt a land alone is not enough to force me to kill hogs, and limit my future. There is value to our hunting and if others do not see that then there is no sense in us playing against ourself just to satisfy the short term. Manage hogs. Killing boars is not hurting our future, killing sows is. Sows WILL be bred, either by a 320lb stud with 3 inches of cutters or a six month old shoat. We will not save this world from the "onslaught" of wild hogs, don't buy their propaganda. "Eradication" is a dirty word. Some just got angry at me, I am fine with that, the truth isn't often politically correct, and I will not be running for political office anytime soon. Don't work yourself out of a job.

As a new hog hunter the best thing you can do is to hunt with as many people as will put up with you. Hunt a million ways, keep your shit-eaters at home and broaden your horizons. You will eventually wind up hunting in a way that perks your ears up, decide what type of hunting style is most enjoyable for you and then have at it on your own. I limited myself when I started out by hunting alone, but if I had it to do all over again I would spend one or two years hunting with others to determine my style.

A man new to dog hunting emailed me with a very concise question that was large in scope, "What is the most important thing to focus on to become a top dog hunter." At first I thought the question was kind of ridiculous, but as I went over it I soon saw the beauty in it's simplicity. A few days later I had my response, although it was not as focused as the question, I could not narrow it down to one focal point, but I did rank my points in order of importance.

1. Make an effort to continually hunt with guys that have better dogs than yourself! There are two prongs to this idea. First, by exposing yourself to better dogs your own bar is moved higher. Secondly, dogs are like people - we mimick what we surround ourselves with - like when your mom told you to find new pals to hang around because you were running with trash. There will always be someone with better dogs, seek them out! Some men are content to be a big fish in a small pond, yet the small fish in a big pond often outweighs the big fish in a small pond. Accepting knowledge is a humbling idea, it usually comes from above and you have to admit your lower position to benefit from it but it is needed to move up. Surround yourself with men that can broaden your horizons, humble yourself.

2. Strive for the future. We have to remember that we are only guardians of these dogs, and their history is deeper than our meager life. We have to leave 'dogs' better than we found them. Dogs have been in mans camp for over ten thousand years, our 60 or 80 years is trivial. Striving for the future is not about our own legacy. Striving for the future is not maintaining, it is bettering. Complacency does not move dogs forward.

3. Measure dogs. All the great dogmen were great evaluators of a dogs ability. A cook must have a good sense of taste, a good dog hunter must have a good sense of a dogs ability. Ability is not always skill, it is potential! If we cannot see this we will cull the greats and feed mediocre dogs. This seems simple, yet many men I have hunted with wouldn't know a great dog if it bit them. Go get bit.

CHAPTER 22
LAWYERS GUNS AND MONEY

I learned long ago that money and dogs didn't mix for me. Dog hunting is in large part a release from modern society, and mixing money with it taints the whole picture. Here is a run down of the last hunt I guided.

The guy showed up three hours late, falling down DRUNK! He then wouldn't shut up about how rich he was. At the first turnout I see him practicing his "drunken lunging stabbing motion" with his spear. A little while later I'm sitting in my ranger and this dude drops his pants and takes a shit in the road right in the beam of my headlights! Later the dogs are trailing open and I ask him to shut up, he wouldn't, so I called my dogs in. I didn't cut em loose again. We had some words and I made it clear I had no interest in him or his money and that is why I don't guide hunts for money! A pile of money is pointless deep in the woods after we turn hounds loose, except to take away from the peace.

I also will not sell a dog, for many of the same reasons. You can sell a good dog to an idiot, he will ruin it and then run down your name. If I respect you and your work ethic I will give you a pup, but I'm not mixing money and my release from this money driven world.

I really have nothing against lawyers, but I like the Hank Jr song so it was a fitting chapter title. Hank might have asked to send lawyers, guns and money, but I have no need for any of the such when it comes to my hounds.

I have never been a fan of having guns around when hog hunting with dogs. I carried one when I hunted by myself, simply because I had no one to help me if I got in a sticky situation, and I think that is a good idea for anyone that hunts alone, if for no other reason than personal protection. There have of course been situations since when I wished I had a gun, but not frequently enough to justify carrying one.

The .22LR has probably killed more deer and hogs than all the other calibers combined. Often you see beginner hog hunters, more on the gun hunting side, pulling out guns looking like they are going on safari in Africa to kill a Cape Buffalo, but it really isn't necessary. With that said, I am not a fan of the .22LR for hog hunting, a .22Mag suits me better and I will tell a story to show you my point.

I had an old friend who was retired and he hunted with dogs probably 5 days a week; hogs, rabbit and squirrel. Me, being much younger and having the burden of a job over my head didn't let me go every time with him. One snowy day the old man called me in the afternoon, I could tell by his voice something was wrong. He went on to tell me the goings-on of the day. He had bayed up and he slipped in. He had a little black bulldog that was a cracker-jack, and when he got there sure enough, Dude was stuck on the hogs ear. The man got up close, almost point blank and shot the hog between the eyes with his .22LR. As soon as he pulled the trigger the bulldog went slack. He gave the boar another round and it took the hogs feet out, so he focused on his dog. The dog was junk yard dead! His first thought was that the dog had a heart attack but upon closer inspection he noted he had a bullet hole in his neck. The jugular had been hit. After getting the situation under control - tying back the other dogs and such, he went to figuring. After peeling the hide on the hogs head back he found that the bullet hadn't made it through the sows skull, it had ricocheted and rolled around the top of the hogs skull and came out on the side the bulldog was latched on to. In all the excitement he must not of got a very good blunt angle on the shot. The low velocity of the .22LR is what makes it deadly, it usually breaks the skull then rattles around inside turning the brains to scrambled eggs, but that low velocity can come back to bite you too.

Lee and myself argued back and forth about guns for our whole hunting career. I seldom had a gun and Lee always had one. We'd be unloading mules and getting our gear gathered and every time Lee would ask me if I had a gun, I'd nod my head "no" and he'd give me a hard talking to, for the two-hundredth time. One morning I brought my new bulldog and I was ready for him, I couldn't wait for him to ask me if I brought a gun. I had named my new dog "Pistol." "Ya got plenty leads?" I came back, "Yeah," waiting. "Gun?" I fought the smile back, "Oh dang I almost forgot, still in the truck!" Lee cocked his head, I'm sure he thought hell had froze over. I pulled the dog out of the box and he was more confused than ever. "Lee, meet Pistol." We laughed, and he lectured me yet again.

As hog hunters most all of us find ourselves taking people hunting that are first-timers. They usually show up dressed in head to toe camouflage, a 15" knife on their left hip, a boot knife sticking out of their right boot, and a .44 Mag on their right hip. They look like they are going on a mission in Faluga, Iraq. They deflate when I tell them to leave the hog-leg in the truck. First off, I don't want someone I don't know shooting a gun around me in the woods. Hog hunting can get pretty crazy, with hogs running all around, guys and dogs split up going different directions and then there is the adrenaline. Some folks lose it in pressurized situations. I don't need to dodge bullets and hogs. Then there are the dogs. I don't shoot around my dogs, and I will be damned if someone I don't know is going to shoot around my dogs!

The new guy undoubtedly usually gives a bit of attitude about having to disarm, "What if I get CHARGED!?" Climb a tree, side-step, run, hell fight him off with that 15" knife, I don't care, but you ain't shooting with dogs and men scrambling everywhere. It's a hard rule!

In or around 1999 I had a buddy in central Oklahoma, his name was Carl. He had some good Russian hogs in his pen and I used to go over to his place about once a month to practice some dogs and we'd make a hunt in the evening. Carl always carried a .357. He had been a coon hunter but the hogs had gotten so bad around him that he switched over to hog dogs after spending the better part of a night up a tree surrounded by hogs while out coon hunting one night. Carl hated hogs, and was a wee bit scared of them too!.

So this day we worked the dogs in the pen. His wife, Lisa had some yard dogs that were yorkie poos or some such and Carl always had exotics around. Lisa's dogs started baying some prong horn sheep in the pasture and she stepped out on the porch with a 1900's .22 with no sights and shot in the direction of the dogs to get them to stop. I'll be danged if she didn't shoot one of them house dogs dead as a doornail. We laughed, as we turned from her, and pretended to be sad to her face. Why she did not aim up I will never figure.

Just before dark we went on a hunt. We had one Catahoula on the ground, a bitch named Oleo. She was a pretty decent dog and game as they come. We were roading her around and she struck with one bark and headed to the woods. We stopped the Jeep and listened. Shortly, Carl says, "You stay here, I'm gonna go check." Before he left he pulled a 30-30 lever gun out of the back of Jeep and handed it to me, "You might NEED this!" Emphasis on the "need." Carl was over the top. I laid the gun across the hood and waited. I didn't exactly know what Carl was "checking on," I figured he needed to clean out. In a few minutes the shooting began. BAM BAM BAM BAM BAM BAM. 6 shots fired so fast it sounded like an automatic! I took off down the trail he had vanished down and in about 100 yards I saw his .357 laying in the dirt. I hollered out, "Carl? Carl?" Bigfoot was surely having his way with him I figured. I got a response, shaky and kind of quiet, "Eddd." Carl was usually loud and boisterous. I followed the sound upward with my eyes. Carl was in a tree, not a little bit, but way up a tree. Now Carl was not a little man, I'd guess him every bit of 400lbs, how he got up there I have no idea, fear has a way of making men do extraordinary things I guess. "What are you doing?" I was confused, and tickled. Before we got our question and answer session finished we could hear a caught hog in front of us about 100 yards. "Big hog!" Carl says, "Charged me!" I coaxed Carl down from his perch. After we got the hog caught I had some questions and Carl relayed the details. "I was walking down that path and this HUGE boar hog come out of nowhere and was bearin' down on me! I emptied my '57 into him and then threw it at him, he never even slowed down! Oleo showed up and jumped on his head right before he got me down! That dog saved my life!" It was a good hog, a true 300lb boar hog, but there wasn't a bullet one in him. I gave Carl a hard time about that for years, and to this day I am sure he contends he hit it at least 5 times, bullet holes or not!

I had a yella dog that sure had the right kind of breeding behind him. I had earned the pup by trimming three mules for a fella. The dog had disappointed me at every turn but I kept giving him chance after chance. Lee would shake his head every time I pulled him out of the box, "You ain't culled that dog yet!" The dog was pushing two years old. There was a time when I would cull a dog fast, and usually regret it later. I had finally got to the point where I waited, and sometimes waited and waited too long. Lee and I were hunting off mules and the dogs struck and took a hog across open pasture, it was wide open and we got to see everything. At the edge of the pasture there was a ditch with a bit of water in it and the hog picked that spot to make his final stand. We had our mules at a run to get to the bay and this darned dog stopped baying and came running back to us as we approached. I was steaming mad! We jumped off and tied mules and the dog was still milling around us, with a blow 'em up bay going on just 20 yards away. I made my way to Lee's mule and pulled his .22 Mag rifle from the scabbard on his saddle. Lee looked shocked, thinking I was going to shoot a hog, instead I culled my dog. Desire is something we cannot put in a dog if it isn't already there, and there is little point wasting dog food, time and energy on a dog that has no desire.

Lee laughed and laughed. In role reversal the old man was impatient with dogs and the kid was the one with patience, damn near to a fault. While I culled this dog in anger I would suggest always waiting until you have a cool head, and have had time to consider things. Many dogs have been wrongfully culled in anger.

CHAPTER 23
PUPS AND EPIGENETICS

I get a good bit of phone calls about starting dogs, it usually is from someone just starting out hog hunting, and it usually goes like this:

> On the other end, "I just got a BMC pup and I want to know what I can do to start training the dog."
> "How old a dog are we talking about?" I already know the general answer.
> "Oh, he's 9 weeks old. I want to do everything I can to get him going!"
> "Well, if it were me I would hold off." I know that is not the answer the fella wants to hear.
> "There's gotta be something I can DO?"
> "If you must, you can drag a hot dog around and let him sniff it out and eat it, but that's about as far as I would go myself."

We have all been there I imagine, I know I have. You want to do everything right, and it stands to reason that starting that pup as early as possible can only help. It's not unlike a first time mother that reads some books about babies, buys classical music to play to it, gets the educational toys, keeps them away from junk food and then by the second and third kid she's throwing them down with a Popsicle in front of the tv.

I see it on social media- videos of a pack of 10 week old

pups baying a shoat, it is impressive and shows a background in hog dog minded breeding - it is fun to watch but be careful! I would say more pups have been ruined by too much too soon than pups it has helped. When we start training the first real hurtle is 'turning them on.' By that I mean we are getting them to understand the fun, and satisfaction in hunting. The pups that are baying at 10 and 12 weeks are already there, and that is a huge plus. That eagerness is directly from breeding and most probably is epigenetics at work. With that said, not all dogs that will go on to become first class hogdogs will show out that early, so if you don't see it don't worry. The danger in starting pups too early is in 'turning them off.' If the pup gets whomperjawed by a 20lb shoat, some pups are going to get mad and come back harder, some pups are going to turn off, done for a lifetime with a stressful and very unpleasant first experience with a pig.

Quite a few years back I got a pup from a long time friend. The dog was crossed nine ways to hell and came from a good line of dogs that worked going back generations. They were hogdogs. The pup was very smart and I had high hopes. Eagerness got the best of me and at a young age I put her in the pen. Things were going great, and I am sure I had a big smile. Then it went south, the hog had enough and put it in another gear and whooped up on the pup. In the process the pup got a toe bit off. I saw the error I had made and got her doctored back and let her be a pup, running the yard. At a good starting age she wanted nothing to do with a hog! She was a quirky dog, and that intelligence played a strong role in her saying, "Naw, I don't wanna do that!" I tried many times to get her started but she wouldn't have it. "Racket" was her name and I still have the old bitch in my yard. She did turn herself into a decent squirrel dog though. I have wondered many times what she could have been if I had held off.

I have tossed the word epigenetics around a few times already, and I figure now is a good time to explain it since it will come into play with these young pups we are discussing now.

EPIGENETICS

We have all heard the stern warnings from old dogmen to

never breed a dog that we haven't hunted and proven to be worthy of breeding, and we have all seen a fella breed a dog that wasn't proven on the grounds that, "His grandma was dang good." Or maybe ole "So-N-So" is in his papers. We've all known people that had a brood bitch that was never hunted and we watched litter after litter pop out. In theory almost everyone will agree that it isn't a good idea to breed unproven dogs. The logic is pretty simple, you don't know what you have and if you breed off that you are throwing dice, however favorable paper may make the odds look. Science has recently given us yet another stern warning against such breedings.

Everyone knows about genes, even if we don't fully understand all the science behind it. In a nutshell - mom has genes and dad has genes, the offspring will get some genes from each parent and create their own personal set of genes. That is the dice roll. Every dog has genes, or DNA and those genes stay unchanged the entire life of the dog, except in the case of mutations that express themselves in cancer or the such. The DNA is set in stone. There is good stuff in there we want and bad stuff. The pairing of these genes from the parents somewhat randomly determines if the genes will show outwardly or not. But, now it even gets more mudded up! Experiences in life can change how the DNA is used. Experiences in life can trigger switches in DNA to "turn on," or "turn off," changing how a dog uses or doesn't use those genes.

For example: Scientist gave mice a big smell of an orange and then shocked the daylights out of them. The mice produced extra neurons in their brains and noses that made them hyper aware of the smell of an orange. The offspring of these mice had the same extra neurons and were also hyper aware of the orange smell. It was not a learned response because the offspring never got shocked 'by' the smell. It wasn't memories, memories can't be passed down through DNA. The DNA their parents passed to them was not changed either, because the shocking was not written to their DNA, it can't be. But the switches that control the DNA were changed by the shocking and those switched on genes were passed on. This is the basics of a new science called Epigenetics. Learned experiences can in effect be passed on to future generations.

Now we can ditch those mice and think about dogs and breeding. If we hunt a dog we are turning switches "on" and "off" that CAN be passed to future pups. Just like with the orange, if a dog smells a stinking ole boar hog and has a positive experience with the hunt then it is possible that a switch is turned on in the genes of that dog that will make him, and his offspring, hyper sensitive to that smell and associate it with a good time. Have you ever noticed that a Plott dog that has been coon hunted for 10 generations wants to tree coons? And a Plott dog that has run bear for 10 generations wants to run bear? Not to say that they can't be switched from one game to another, or won't do both, but they definitely have a natural inclination towards what their ancestors have done. Epigenetics explains that.

On the other side, if a dog has negative experiences when they smell an armadillo then the offspring of that dog is less likely to seek that adventure out. In more broad terms, hunting in general could turn on genes that kick the nose into overdrive if the dog has good experiences linked to using his nose, and if his nose constantly got him yelled at when he barked all night because he smelled a possum then he stands the chance to pass a more turned off nose to his offspring because of his negative experiences.

I have seen pups that just about started themselves hunting. One in particular stands out, "Bell" a crossed up BMC x Catahoula x Plott. This pups first time in the woods she looked like a 2 year old dog, just plain natural, casting deep and baying with the old dogs. She came from good dogs that were hunted, that was part of it. Maybe it was just good luck that both parents had "turned on" genes that dealt with hunting and she just got a good dose of both. Which brings up another point, the genes that get passed are still random and just because a gene is "turned on" does not mean that it will get passed to pups, but if it does that pup will have an advantage. In breeding we need to increase odds at every chance we get, and this is why we only breed proven dogs.

Everyone is obsessed with genes, as we should be. Papers can be a guideline to these genes, a measuring stick to weigh the odds. Papers and history of past generations performance gives us an idea of what traits are available in a paring of dogs, but it does not guarantee anything. That is why we hunt these dogs, to see with our own eyes what traits made it and what ones ended up on the kennel floor. Without this knowledge we are doing little more than yanking the arm of a slot machine. Epigenetics tells us that genes alone cannot make a dog, we have to breed good stock that is worked! A boat load of great genes in a pup means nothing if they are all 'turned off.' Don't waste your time and energy on pups that don't come from hunting stock.

In the mock conversation earlier I told the young man to train with hot dogs. Really this is just to satisfy the desire to train in the man and make him feel he is getting started, but there is a little bit of truth to it. If you drag a hot dog through the grass just a few feet to start and let the very young pup sniff it out and get a treat at the end you are teaching him the value of using his nose. You can lengthen the distance slowly for your own amusement. It is important to say now that when we are training, with a 8 week old pup and a hot dog, or a 2 year old dog, we ALWAYS finish on a positive note! Sometimes this can be hard, but we do it every single time. We have graduated up with our little pup and we are dragging a hot dog 20 feet through the grass and he just can't seem to get it; we have to finish positive so we don't just pick him up after he has failed and take him back to his kennel. Instead we pick him up, pet him and get his mind off it then make a shorter drag that he CAN finish. Now he can go back to his kennel. When we are dealing with pups this young the main problem is their attention span is so low, they can't stay on task and this is the reason I don't like to even attempt to train pups at 8 weeks, 12weeks or so on. It might seem like the tiniest blimp, but when we allow a pup to lose interest and move on the the next exciting thing without finishing the task we could be setting a habit that will later bite us in the rear. In hog hunting quitting isn't going to being tolerated! In pups of this age you are better served to spend your training time on socializing, teaching them their name, to 'come' and such simple things. Slow down.

How we train, where we train, and when we train is largely going to be determined by our own personal situation. If you live by a busy highway and have to keep even small pups put up in a pen you are going to have to train different than the man that can just let them run free. I live pretty far back in the woods, my driveway is a touch under a half mile and we are surrounded by woods. The closest blacktop is about two miles, so I can let pups run. At any given time I seem to have at least 8 dogs running loose. A couple are older dogs that just never took to a hog, might be a grade squirrel dog or two thrown in, and various pups. I mainly keep out of it and observe. Usually at about 3 or 4 months the pups will light out with the older dogs, I can hear they are running deer so I get a seat and listen. I'm listening to see who's in the lead, who's falling back and babbling, and who already fell back and has returned. I'm taking mental notes. I see who is the last to return, or better yet which dog continues to push after everyone else has quit. It might be a deer, then a couple hours later they go tree squirrels, they might dig an armadillo or run a hog, makes no difference to me, though I don't particularly want them running hogs. I am watching that drive. I allow my pups to do this until I regularly go out to feed and see a pup is not there. When they start staying hooked in the woods all night or two or three days I put them in the kennel because I have something! Most never get a spot in the kennels. Some folks are inevitably thinking, "Dang! Ed let's them pups run trash!!?" I sure do! Those pups are training themselves, they are learning the fun of the hunt, they are learning how to trail, they are learning the tricks game throw at them to push them off a track. They will be miles ahead of a pup their age that hasn't had the schooling trash has taught them. We will get to trash braking later, so don't worry.

Now the guy that lives by the road can't use my method, so he is going to have to be taking that 10 week old pup out of the kennel EVERYDAY to let him run around the yard and get exercise so his lungs and muscles develop to their full potential. That pup needs to feel grass under his feet, chase butterflies and learn how the world looks and feels. He needs to try eating a bee and he needs his head covered in fire ants. That pup also needs to be around other dogs. If I had to kennel pups I would probably use the hot dog method until it got too easy, then a fella can switch over to dragging some hog hide around to use as practice with a good reward at the end of a successful track, but not all rewards have to be food, and shouldn't be. A good petting and praise will do better than a hot dog as a reward, but I am not going to over-do the "training." As the pup gets older, say 3 or 4 months old the yard isn't going to hack it, you are going to have to take him somewhere he can get stretched out. That doesn't mean throw him in with your hogdogs, this is purely exercise and learning the woods, maybe some trash if you're lucky. DON'T scold the dog for trashing!!! DON'T! We don't even worry about correcting trash until around 15 months, when the dog knows hogs and understands that is what we are after.

Many years ago my great uncle John was at my house witching a well for me. I had a few catahoula pups running loose and one was chasing butterflies, watching them, chasing and jumping at them to try and catch. My great uncle noted the dog and told me he was going to make a dog. The pup did make a great dog. He had game on the mind and ran to catch - even if it was just butterflies!

By the time I was 12 years old I could work like a man. Just because I could, didn't mean I should though. If we take our 12 year old son and get him a 40 or 50 hour a week job he can physically handle it, and it will teach him responsibility and a long list of cuss words. He will probably go on to become a hard working respectable man but there WILL be a hole in him from a piece of his childhood he missed. Somewhere down the line he is going to fill that hole. Dogs are no different. Pups need time to be pups, it is not wasted time. Let them chase butterflies. We all know of some kid whose parents pushed them in baseball or some other sport from the time they could walk; they eat, breath and live baseball, and they are good at it. Dad has visions of the major leagues but when little junior hits high school he's burnt out. Junior doesn't want anything to do with baseball. I've seen the same in hogdogs; dogs that had great potential and they could get it done, but you had to threaten them with violence and push them every step of the way. Usually these dogs are labeled as "lazy" and sometimes they are, sometimes they are burnouts, burnouts that could have been superstars. With an eye you can see the pups limits, don't push past, as the dog gets older we will push and make sure we don't end up with laziness, it's all timing.

You have probably noticed that I am not practicing what I'm preaching. I am telling the guy who kennels his pup to not let it run with older dogs, not pushing it and keeping it pretty low key, while I am throwing my pups headfirst in with trashy old dogs to sink or swim, and that is a fair assessment. Inevitably, I have pups that get burnt, pups that have a coon jump on their head and 'turn them off,' pups that die from snake bites, pups that just never come home and pups that drop out of the race altogether. For me that is part of the price of their free training. I am also, with very little energy, starting a good many pups when I only want to peel one off the top. I have lost some fine pups, it is just part of it, but there are more behind them. I am looking for the cream. A man can also take that hard approach to pups he keeps in a kennel but it is going to be a good bit more work, and it has to be undertaken with an understanding that out of 5 pups only 1 may make the cut out of the 'pre-hog woods training.'

(Eddie Barnes and Lee George)

CHAPTER 24
TRAINING IN THE BAY PEN

I sat down determined to tackle the large topic of training in the bay pen. I labored over the different types of dogs to be trained, and carefully side tracked with every scenario of 'what-ifs' I came to for each style of hog dog. After a long night I had eighteen pages of complicated scenarios and what to do in each case. It was confusing even to me as I went back and read, and I had written it. So I walked away for a few days and kept the topic in the back of my mind and wandered to it when mindless work presented itself or when I found myself gazing at a TV that I had no real interest in. It dawned on me one day at work; I was attacking the training scenarios like the reader was a computer or a robot. I wasn't giving the reader any credit.

As I have said before, the hog dog is not straight forward to train - like a coon dog, or a beagle, or a bird dog - there are so many styles of hog dogs, and they each require modified training. For me to attempt a case by case training regiment of each, with a 'what-to-do' for all the different outcomes was overwhelming and also was avoiding a chance to teach the undermining factors of training - so I will try to boil this down to the root so that a person can deduct the 'correct' method to deal with each case on their own; a better understanding.

Obviously before we do any training we need to know what we want in the dog. A long range loose dog, a close range rough dog, a close range loose dog, a running catch dog, a cast dog, a road dog, a rig dog and so on. We pick the style and we train accordingly, we don't just fall in love with what we get by default.

The bay pen is a great tool but needs to be used in moderation. The pen is the best tool we have to somewhat safely teach the dog about the movements and ability of a wild hog. Used too frequently though and it seems to limit a dogs hunt. Once a pup is reacting to a hog in the manner we want it is time to end the dogs career in a pen. A dog wants to bay a hog, it is the reward of a hunt, if we give it to them too much they don't want to put in the work to get the reward. The pen should be seen as preschool - keep them coloring too long and they will never read.

If you don't have access to a pen you can still use these methods with a few adjustments. Take the pig and tie one back leg and stake him out in the open, it will be tempting to do this in some brush and make it more realistic, but don't, just wait, we will get to that sort of thing later in the training. Keep the rope holding the hog very short - we don't want the pig running over the pup.

Whichever style of hog dog we want there are a few basic ideas that stay the same.

We need a dog willing and capable of being trained. The dog must be mature in body and mind, whichever method of the first stage of training we have done. We move on to the next level of training when our pup understands the world and has a general positive feeling towards the fun and trouble his nose can get him into. The pup is between 6 and 12 months old, and is moderately developed enough physically to take the extra work. There is no measurement of age to say when a pup is ready, we have to see it and the only way we can is by spending time with the pup and understanding his nature. Some dogs won't make it to this marker until they are 12 months, or even later. Sometimes these late bloomers make great dogs. I will venture to say that most great dogs come on later than average, and many would-be greats are culled prematurely. Often early starters stall out and slower starters pass them up. Patience is a virtue and dog food is cheap. When we see the pup take a whipping from an old dog and stand up and give him a talking to, instead of running back to mom then he might be ready.

When his will is determined, when his puppy feelings are gone, when he holds his head and tail high and bows his chest (and has the ass to back it up) and he is acting the part of a dog, then he is ready to see a pig, not before.

We have to understand that how we train obviously effects how the dog hunts in the real world. Years ago I read a police manual on firearms training. In the old days when cops trained at the firing range there was a strict policy of not leaving brass on the floor. A person on the range emptied their revolver down range and then ejected the spent casings into their hand and placed the cases in their pocket. The author of the book I read was a firearms instructor and one day he was investigating an officer involved shooting. At the scene of the shooting he couldn't find the officers casings. He knew the officer had fired but he couldn't find them. After some time, in conversation with the officer involved, the casings were found in his pocket. The policeman had reverted to his training without even knowing it, and in the midst of a life or death shoot out had taken the extra time to empty the spent casings into his pocket! After noting this the the firearms trainer made moves to make training closer mimic real life. Dogs are no different, our training, in every detail, needs to mimic what we want of the dog in the real hog woods.

While every dog has a born inclination to be rough or loose, the first hogs we pair the dog against will either support or refute this natural inclination. If we have a very confident dog, that wants to be aggressive, pairing him against a hog smaller than himself will drive home this inclination, while pairing him against a larger hog may back him up. What we want of the dog will determine which direction we go. We humble the over confident dog to be a loose baydog, and we build up the timid dog to catch. These are fine tunings usually, dogs are not a blank slate so we start with dogs that are close to what we want.

Dogs are like people, in that numbers often equate to courage. If we have a dog on the timid side, then adding another dog can prop him up to action. Conversely, if we are wanting a baydog, and the dog has a natural inclination to get rough then running him alone can sometimes back him up. Whichever direction we want to go, whether we are building confidence, or taking it away, we have to at some point early in training make the dog do it alone, so we can run dogs dual to build confidence or run alone to reduce it, but we have to set it up afterwards to be done alone. As pups, most times the size and aggression of the hog can do this.

Every training session ends on a high note. This is a big one. This is our job, and takes our understanding and work to make it happen. If we are after a rough dog, and only have a 200lb boar hog then we don't train, we wait until we have a small enough hog that we are fairly confident the dog will catch and we can pull him out of the bay pen after success. On the other side, we don't put a 12 month old pup that we want to be loose in a pen with 3 other dogs on a 25lb shoat. How we end, how we leave the pen is what the dog learns, usually despite you screaming your head off and throwing things. Action teaches.

Training is a setting up of scenarios that we control, and control to end in the way we want. We never put a dog back to his chain or kennel in a sour mood. Sometimes the great objective we envisioned isn't met, but we keep a level head and drop the bar. We want to set things up so that action in the pen is how we want, but if that fails and we don't have the tools to correct it then we end on a upswing of some kind. If the dog does exactly the opposite of what we wanted in terms of baying, or catching, we have to revert and possibly we end on that high note by a simple "come." It is worth noting that your emotions, despite the outcome are meaningless! As the dog needs to exit the pen on a positive note, so do you. Do not let a pup of this age range know your emotional state. You need to be content when you kennel the dog.

For those that have experience training a mule, you know that you cannot train a mule when you are mad, nothing good will come of it. While dogs do not have the sense of humor that a mule does, not much good will come of training when you are in a bad mood. A dog cannot get as much enjoyment from your displeasure as a mule but the result is in you - your attitude towards the dog will change and tint all future interaction with the dog. Train with an even tilt.

A dog will always learn from another dog much easier

than he will learn from us. It is simple "monkey see, monkey do." If you already have a dog that works in a manner you want out of a pup then by all means pair them up. If possible, before throwing them into a pen together, kennel or chain them next to each other for a couple weeks. In most cases the old dog is going to exert dominance and that dominance will be clear in the pen if the dogs have a similar nature. Of course, putting a bulldog pup with a loose older dog is not going to make a bulldog bay, we always have to work with nature. We are fine tuning, not re-wiring the entire brain.

Watching action before getting into the action is always a good idea. The bay pen is a great tool because we have control over the situation. We can control the type of hog. We can control the other dogs that might be involved. We can control the time a dog encounters a pig. We can control the time a dog exits. Every dogs' first encounter with a pig should be made from the safety of outside of the pen. By chaining a dog outside of the pen and letting another dog into the pen we can get an accurate gauge of our dog and take the appropriate means to set him up for the success we are after. I would much rather have a pup show no interest in a pig from outside the pen than to see it from inside the pen. Do not rush getting a pup in the pen, when he is ready you will know, if he is not ready no good will come from putting him in the pen.

Keep a lead or rope on the dog the first few times in a pen with a hog. This allows us further control. If things go south we can get the dog out of the pen faster, with less running and hollering, and we have a better grasp on not letting habits start that we do not want. Ten feet of mule tape, or weed-eater string that has been straightened out works really well. This also allows us to influence action in the pen without using our distracting voice. Our personality doesn't need to be in the pen. We will likely not be right on top of young dogs baying in the woods to alter their actions, so we need to mimic that in the pen.

Keep your mouth shut! I harp on this, you already know. Our voice means nothing. Chances are very high that if you are screaming at the dog then you have not done your homework well enough, and no amount of screaming and cussing is going to change the outcome anyway. When we talk we refocus the dogs attention from the task at hand back on ourselves. Nothing positive will come in a hunting scenario from re-focusing the dog on us instead of the hog. Countless times I have seen it - a young dog is baying good and the handler just has to talk, "Good boy," or "Bay 'em," whatever, and the pup takes his attention off the hog to look at Joe, and usually one of two things happen - The pup stops baying and walks over with tail wagging to say "Hi," to Joe, and all concentration has been lost - or the pup looks back at Joe and BAMM! The hog runs him smooth over. If the pup is doing a great job baying then shut up! After a few minutes pull him out and then you can talk to him and love on him if you want.

All training should be done one-on-one unless we are trying to duplicate another dogs behaviors. As I said earlier, another dog can be a great motivator for behavior, but it can also be a great distraction. Once we get the behavior we are after we should remove the other dog and get the desired behavior out of the dog by itself. Mimicking a behavior is a great start but it must be reinforced by the dog acting solo.

Action is key for a pup. Any hunting bred dog worth his salt is going to respond to action. If your pup seems content to sniff around as a hog sits in the corner then force the hogs movement. Make him run. Dogs are made to chase. If that doesn't do it then catch the hog and make him squeal. Prey drive is the catalyst. If neither of these methods is working then it is time to contemplate culling or maturing. Very young pups should react to prey drive and see the weakness, and respond in either scenario. We can use prey drive to our benefit by making the hog seem injured. Tie two of the hogs feet together loosely so that as he runs there is an obvious "limp." Even very young pups will take note of the disadvantage of the "injured" animal and they prey drive will kick in. Predators attack the weakest prey in a herd, not the strongest. Dogs understand and react to weakness.

Tease the dog with action. Dogs are pack animals, we can use this to outwardly express the habits we are after. If your pup is not reacting in the pen then we can try putting a dog in the pen that will get the action started and then tie the pup back where it can hear and maybe even see the action but not get in on it. We tease the pup, make them go insane wanting in on it, but we hold them back and they do not get in on it that day, it's back to the kennel with no participation. We want to always leave a pup wanting more, not satisfied, they need to go back to the kennel slobbering and half out of their mind. (This method works very good when getting bulldogs to catch)

How a dog views our participation in the hunt, (training in our mind) can change their behavior. For anyone that has ever been a spectator at a bay pen competition this is clear as day. More times than not, a dog or pair of dogs will bay tight without so much as a nip at the hog, for three minutes. Once 'time' is called and the pen help and usually the dog owner enter the pen and start moving the hog around to exit through the gate then that dog starts getting rough and trying to stop the hog or out right catch it. A few things are happening - the dog is reading the physical clues telling him that his owner wants to catch the hog, but the dog is also being a dog, and getting bolder because of the numbers and/or the leader of his pack being present. You can use this to move a dogs behavior the direction you want if you are careful. For the dog on the rough side that you are trying to loosen up - get out of the pen or even hide where you can see the action but the dog cannot see you. For going the other direction get in the pen with the dog you want to be rough and let him feed off of your 'help.' In both these cases this is done very early in training, to try to set a behavior but can be over-done. This can be a fix for a dog that is riding the fence but it will not make huge differences in behavior.

Training should be done in a comfortable environment for the dog with little distractions. I already went over this earlier in the "Training for Range" chapter but it belongs here too. The best case scenario is that you have a bay pen at your house, this means you don't have to move the pup to a new place, with new smells and new dogs and then throw them into an altogether new experience of baying a wild hog. If you have to use a friends pen, then haul the pup over there a couple times but don't put him in, unless everything is just looking rock solid. If the pup is fine with the other dogs there, and not slinking around with a tucked tail and booger barking at everything that moves then you might be OK to use the pen that first trip. We just don't want to pile too much on the young dog.

Training with groups of people is tempting. You want to buy a case of beer and call all your buddies to bring all of their pups and make a night of training, don't, at least not at this point in training. When possible you should be the only person there when you train. We are trying to keep the slate as clean as possible with as few 'new' things as possible. The clear brain will make associations faster.

We have all been at a bay competition and someone brings a young dog and it just won't hardly bay. The pup keeps looking around all wild eyed and hunkers low to the ground in the pen. When it is over the handler always says the same thing, "The dog bays great at the house." That person isn't lying. There is too much stimuli, too many new smells, too many strange dogs, and too many strange people. We don't want situations like that in our training scenarios.

The baypen is the best tool we have in training hog dogs. The pen allows us to see what we are working with in a dog. We get to see up close how a dog wants to handle a hog. We can also get a good sense of the dogs drive and concentration. Once we are satisfied with what the dog is doing though we have to get out of the baypen. Training, or learning, is a progression - always getting harder, if we stall in one of the steps we aren't moving forward.

(Stripes, Ruby and Racket - Squirrel & Hogdogs)

CHAPTER 25
PUPPY STARTERS

It is commonplace to keep a very old dog around primarily for the purpose of starting pups. These dogs are usually rock-solid straight hogdogs, and you really lessen the chance of getting pups on 'off game.' These pup starters are usually old, they often carry a body full of battle scars and maybe even some injuries that have just slowed them down so much so that for day-to-day hunting they aren't really practical. They also carry a head full of remedies for working out tricks hogs might throw at them.

I kept such a dog in my kennels for a few years, many years ago. "Blondie" was her name, and while she had plenty of heart and know-how she was just too slow to cut the mustard. She was pushing 13 years old. In hog hunting that has to be about 125 years old in human terms. She had given me the best years of her life and pup starter or not, she was going to live out the rest of her life eating my dog food. She started more than a few pups in her old age, and loved every minute of it, even when she had to quit the race and limp back, or when she just laid down and I had to hike in to her and carry her out. I did it many times.

Those were much different times though. The hogs were different. My dogs were different. I was different. Today I will not use an old, slow dog to start pups. I want to start pups with the fastest thing around. If I could get a Ferrari to chase a hog I'd start pups behind that! Of course some folks have already twisted their faces up and cracked their knuckles in preperation for the seething email they are going to bang out, but let me explain myself before you get hateful.

(Old man joke)   An old bull and his yearling were standing on a high ridge looking down into a valley. In the valley were a bunch of cows grazing. The yearling gets all excited and says to the old bull, "Let's run down there and screw a cow!" The old bull comes back, "No! Let's WALK down there and screw them all!" (It will be relevant later)

Some say that if you start pups behind a dog they cannot keep up with they will babble on track. They are in effect saying to the old dog, "Slow the heck down we can't keep up, and we don't want to miss the action!" And if you continue this method you may very well end up with a semi-open dog, no matter his silent nature and breeding. I think most will agree on that. So we are to believe that habit will stick with the dog, but the habit of running a track on the slow side will not? Not to say as a mature dog they will run a track as slow as the old puppy starter, but they will run it slower than their full potential. With the pup starter they will likely be very accurate on track, each step will be a step in the right direction and they will not make it until they are certain. The old dog is probably not feeling that great, and having lost that 'Let's run down there and 'screw one' attitude, will likely back up on a lost track instead of going into the hyper-speed zig zag to pick it back up. Maybe the pup will keep with the more safe method later in life when he has to do it on his own, maybe not.

Speed has to match ability! What we are really talking about is track speed, not to be confused with speed in general. A dog that runs to the fullest of his track speed is the goal. When a pup runs according to his track ability he will be running at his maximum speed. If we set that speed with another dog we can either slow him down and limit his potiential, or we can speed him up. (and possibly over run his nose) With modern GPS dog tracking we can see what is happening. If the dog is running with dogs that are too fast it is our responsibility to see that and fix it. For me, I am going to start at full speed and slow down if needed. Pups need plenty of time running at their own speed though, otherwise you are just making number 2 or 3 help dogs. Let a dog run at

THEIR speed and you will have a better chance at maximizing their track speed.

So I start dogs with a fast dog, but I don't get the habit of babbling going. How some ask? I start them at an appropriate age! An age when they are fully developed physically and have a level head on their shoulders. It is no surprise that in todays "Right Now!" world many want to see five month old pups hauled to the woods and act the part of a near-finished hogdog. That is rare, and don't get caught trying to keep up with the Jone's, chances are the Jone's are full of shit! Just last week I saw a one year old finished dog for sale. Let me say that again, a ONE year old FINISHED hogdog.

When I hear a pup babble as they bring up the rear that tells me I pushed ol' Roy too far too soon, so it is back home to mature some more. When that babbling pup can't keep up do you think he is really learning to track? Maybe he is, he is likely tracking dogs and not hogs though. Maybe that habit will set in and you will have a fast started 'me-too' dog? Maybe when the old pup starter can't seal the deal and has to quit the pup will quit too and we can go ahead and get that bottom off to a nice low level?

Want a trashy dog? Run your pup with trashy dogs. Want an open dog? Run your pup with open dogs. Want a dog with lots of range? Run your pup with rangy dogs. Want a fast dog? Run your pup with a slow dog? It doesn't make sense! Of course, breeding has a very strong say in these matters, but we are talking about learned habits, not nature. Run your pup with fast dogs if you want a fast dog!

Todays hogs are not yesterdays hogs. I am not looking to old hog hunting ways as a guiding light. I am looking for speed, I am looking at the dog sports that thrive on speed, I am turning to their knowledge., on the nature side.

Speaking of old dogs I have to tell the story of an old dog I had the pleasure of meeting. I was in Louisiana hunting with my good friend Pat Lewing. We were staying at his camp and every morning his old man, Bald Eagle would show up. Bald Eagle would get wheeled into camp in his chair, crack a fifth of V-O and hang out. He'd talk shit on our dogs and just generally give us a hard time while playing grab-ass with the women. Bald Eagle was a running dog man, so he had the right to poke fun at us and our hog dogs, as he ran the original American dogs. One evening he said he was going to the fox pen. We rolled him out to his side by side, loaded his oxygen machine and wheelchair in the back and away he went, 3 miles down the road. Out of respect, we went to the fox pen that night, watched the hounds run and listened in to the banter of the old men. After a couple hours we went hog hunting. At day break Pat and I returned to camp, and with no sight of Bald Eagle we drove to the fox pen, he was still there - sitting in his wheelchair - fighting and lying with the other old men. Two days later Bald Eagle died. A generation passed that day. Bald Eagle would cuss Pat and his crossings of fox dogs and hog dogs, but that is the future - blastphemy to the running dog men, the future for hog dog men.

In a very large part what this discussion reverts to is the question of when to start pups. I tend to start pups pretty late. Now that does not mean throw them on a chain until they are 1 or 2. Pups need to learn, and if you miss that window from 12 - 14 months then it's an uphill battle. At 12 -14 months a hunting dog needs to be doing something! If hogs are not available then get them on any trash you can find! Miss that window and you are likely dead in the water. I am not hung up on making a straight hog dog from the get-go either. My pups run loose, so they are trashy as all get-out! They are learning though. Don't be afraid of trash, it is a great tool.

I have a dog that I have always really liked the build of. She runs loose, and while I always meant to start her on hogs I just never did because I had my fill of some other pups. A buddy was over at the house and we put her in the hog pen and she bayed really nice. She didn't just bark, she was working and controlling the hogs. My buddy had been after me to take her to the hog woods for a very long time, and he brought it up yet again. Before he left I put her in a kennel. The dog was about two and had never been 'formally' hunted. That night we went hunting and I took the dog. On the first turn-out she didn't go anywhere, the other dogs sailed off and she just milled around. I wasn't concerned, I wasn't expecting much. The second cast that night she hit the hills with the other two. They got about 800 yards deep and "treed." It didn't sound right so I walked in and before I could get there they left out, a tale tell sign it was an armadillo. I walked back to the guys with the news. The dogs had moved further out then they went to singing, and it wasn't an armadillo! The dogs bayed a stud after an 800 yard race in the hills. The intensity of the baying told us. Looking back at the dogs tracks on the Garmin the next day I could tell she was hunting, she wasn't just along for the ride, all-be-it she was probably hunting ANYTHING, but she was hunting! She will keep going to the hog woods, and will likely ween herself off trash like I have had many do when paired with hogdogs. My point is a simple one - there is no race to get these dogs turned into hog dogs. The race is getting them to be hunting dogs, there is plenty of time to break them into hog dogs. The idea of a 'broke' dog is a new one, don't limit your dogs potential by mashing them into an un-natural state. We are after hunting dogs first and hog dogs second.

(Tanner Herr, Eddie Barnes, Slim and Kolby Ingram)

CHAPTER 26
NOSE AND TRACK CONDITIONS

A friend came up a couple years ago and stayed and hunted with us in Oklahoma for a spell. After about a week of hunting we were sitting around talking one day and he said, "Y'all hunt like cat hunters and not hog hunters." I wasn't quite sure what he meant but I took it as a compliment. In the absence of hog hunting books, I have spent many years reading and studying cat and bear hunting books. It is very possible that without knowing I have picked up some other big game tactics and thinking. My friend must have been noticing the attention that we pay to track conditions when figuring out where to hunt and when.

A coyote hunter told me one time that getting a dog to run a hog was easy, after all, "They are the stinkiest animal in the woods - doesn't even take a nose," he said. There is a bit of truth in that insulting statement. Possibly, that is why some hog hunters pay little attention to track condition. The hard part of hog hunting with dogs though usually isn't in the tracking, a slight oversight in Mr. Coyote Runners statement.

A hog is a stinky animal. Their wallowing in mud and water, combined with their thick hair and low stance to the ground is a great recipe for leaving a heavy scent trail. This is something they have in common with a bear, as well as the vast territory they cover, sometimes at great speeds. Some would therefore ponder that as hog hunters we do not need to concern ourselves with track condition and the such, but of course we do.

One reason we need to concern ourselves with track conditions is in the very nature of our dogs. Hog hunting for the most part is done with cur type dogs, due to their stock sense which is crucial in controlling and baying hogs. Curs do not have the nose that hounds do though, so any leg up we can give them is going to increase their success rate and make our hunts more productive and enjoyable.

Yet another reason to understand how track conditions effect the ability of our dogs is in mock hunting, and starting dogs. We want to start pups in the very best conditions we can get - to increase their chances of success. If we don't understand these concepts then we could be setting pups up for failure.

What the cur lacks in nose, most make up for with intelligence which expresses itself in track sense. Track sense is basically a dog knowing what to do with the information that his nose is sending to his brain. A great nose on a dumb dog is kinda like those lifted 2-wheel drive trucks with mud tires. Often when folks start talking about dogs and get down to traits it is common to rank the traits we want in a hogdog. "Nose" is almost always towards the top of the list. While nose is important, nose without intelligence is pretty close to useless. Other answers come in, " Bottom, speed, stamina, drive, grit," and the list goes on. For myself "Drive and intelligence" are at the top, these two traits can help a dog with any short-comings in the other departments. Drive and intelligence have also helped many a man surpass his environment.

Winding is commonly referred to as a cur trait in tracking, though most hounds do it to a lesser degree. Winding is a must in hog hunting, it is the dogs best tool at closing the distance between himself and the hog and having a shot at stopping the hog. Winding is nose and brain working together to solve a problem.

Great winding conditions are not as complex as great trailing conditions, but a dog cannot just rely on winding. A cur trails traditionally like a hound, (although his head may not be skimming the ground) and then uses his ability to wind when the occasion arises. Even with a cur, our most successful hunts will be done when trailing and winding conditions are good. In good winding conditions we will have moderate moisture, and a slight breeze. Heavy winds and swirling winds scatter scent and make the starting point of that scent hard for the dog to determine. Of course a dog running into the wind is going to be a better case than the dog running with the wind. For dogs with good winding ability, running perpendicular to a wind can be very productive and a great amount of ground can be covered without a paw landing on it. Hot and dry winds are also not going to hold scent as long as cool and wet winds, but in winding we are talking about very hot or fresh scents anyway.

There are a lot of factors that go into track conditions; moisture, temperature, humidity, wind, sun, evaporation, ground cover, terrain and barometric pressure just to name a few. While all of these play into each other, moisture seems to be the dominant one. Scent is married to moisture because scent is actually bacteria. Bacteria needs moisture and heat to live.

Take the nastiest, most rotten piece of gut you can find and freeze it solid and it has no smell until it begins to thaw and the frozen moisture begins to return to a liquid, and then a gas. Scent is carried to our dogs nose when it is in the gas form. Those dried up jerky looking dog turds don't smell that bad because most of the moisture is gone. Moisture evaporates into the air as a gas and scent goes with it and we, or dogs then get that evaporate into our noses.

MOISTURE AND EVAPORATION

Our perfect storm of moisture for tracking is right in the middle of that frozen gut, and that dehydrated dog turd. Just as with the rotten piece of gut, tracks can be 'frozen' releasing nothing for a dog to smell. In very cold temperatures winding scents can also be frozen in the air leaving only the freshest of scent able to be detected. Old scents can also thaw and appear to a dog as a fresh track when they are actually very old! Unlike cat hunting, very little hog hunting is done in climates this cold. (In America)

The pinnacle of big game hunting hounds is the "Dry ground cat and bear dogs." These are dogs that can trail in dry ground, obviously, like New Mexico and Arizona. It takes an exceptional hound to trail in conditions with little moisture. It would be fair to assume that the best track conditions would be in a rain storm then, but to further muddy the water that is not the case. Too much moisture can raise new problems. Rain can add available scent, but much of it is washing away, being pushed into the ground, and little evaporation is taking place - what we need is the scent to get into the air. Even in very accurate track trailing hounds like bloodhounds, the dogs are picking the scent from the air - however close to the ground.

TEMPERATURE

Temperature effects the rate of evaporation. The higher the temperature, the higher the rate of evaporation, so the more scent we have in the air, BUT high temperature also lessens the life of scent. Higher temperature also moves smell faster than cold temperature. Higher temperatures are going to benefit the hot nosed dog and cold temperatures are going to benefit the colder nosed dog. In the higher temperature scents there are going to be more of them, easier to detect, but with a shorter life - and conversely for the colder temperature scents.

Lets take a fresh dog turd and sit it on the table in the house. It stinks, pretty bad! Now we take it and put it next to the wood stove and as it heats up it really begins to stink a lot more. The temperature is increasing the rate of evaporation and getting more scent into the air. That was a quick experiment but now lets do one that is going to take us longer. (Don't actually do this of course, unless you just don't believe me!) We sit a fresh dog turd on the kitchen table. It stinks bad the first day, then each day it stinks a little less. Lets just say it took 4 days for us to barely be able to smell it anymore. Now we sit another next to the wood stove and it stinks worse but the smell goes away much faster, just say a day. Less severe examples of scents dissipating happen as we hunt. What we want is a temperature warm enough to bring scent into the air, but not so warm that the scent is gone fast.

At the American Hunting Terrier field trials in Tyler, Texas the dogs run a great many trials to test their hunting ability. Though I don't own any full blood terriers that qualify to compete I go every single year as I have a great time watching the dogs work a wide variety of tasks. One year I was judging the trailing competition. A hog drag is made with a live hog down the side of a hill and the path is noted with memory and tape on the trees. At the bottom the hog is placed in a cage. One by one the terriers are led to the head of the drag and then released. As the judge you move with the dog, sometimes walking and sometimes in a full on run, depending on the track speed of the dog. Accuracy of tracking, (winding is allowed if seen) speed and honesty are noted. (there are off-game drags made crossing the track)

In that one day I must have walked and ran up and down that hill 150 times, it was exhausting! I enjoyed it though, and learned a lot about tracking. It was October, probably around 70 degrees, and a sunny day. Perfect. 90 percent of the track was in the woods and shaded. Near the foot of the trail though, the dogs had to track across open grass that was in full sunlight. Every single dog that day, even the dogs that just tracked at a full run, slowed at that sunlight - Some would zigzag, some would back up, some would slow and just press on until they picked it back up, and the dogs that shined would throw their head and wind the scent up ahead. The hog was further on, under a tree and shaded. This tougher tracking was in large part due to the added heat and dissipation of the scent - though a couple others factors played in as well - there was not a thick bed of leaves to hold the scent, and increased wind in the open also aided in scent dissipating.

HUMIDITY

Higher humidity means more moisture in the air, and therefore more scent. Humidity also determines where the scent will be. Colder humid air falls, taking scent down with it, (or holding it low) while warmer humid air rises. Very accurate ground tracking dogs work better in colder humid situations because there is a concentration of scent closer to the ground, and winding dogs preform better in higher temperature humid days because the scent is lifted off the ground.

WIND

Wind effects track condition because the scent is in the air and wind is moving it around. A slight breeze aids in striking a track because it widens the scent trail. With no wind a dog has to get pretty close to a scent to pick it up. With a breeze a dog can wind a hog down in a bottom from a distance because the wind is bringing the smell to the dog. If we were able to pull a vacuum in a large woods pen, in effect get all the air out of the pen, there would be no movement of smell. When a "scent molecule" came off a hog it would stay right there without moving. If a hog didn't move there would be no smell around him, and a dog would have to see him or get right on top of him to smell anything. Of course we cannot do that- it is just to drive home the point that we need wind to move scent.

Of course 30 mile an hour wind is not optimal tracking condition. Yet again lets get out our trusty dog turd. We sit it on the kitchen table, by now our wife is getting fed up with our stinky experiments so we wait and do it when she is shopping. We get 10 feet away and we can of course smell it. Next we set a box fan up blowing across it at a slow speed and we stand in the wind of the fan. We can really smell it now. We all knew that was going to happen. Now we get the squirrel cage blower motor fan out of our shop - this thing blows air like a wind tunnel! We set it up and blast air across it and again get down wind and perk our nose up. We are going to get small hints of the smell, but not much. There is still, in both examples, the same amount of "scent molecules" but there is a difference in the volume of air. More air equates to less "smell per square inch," making it harder, and less likely to be detected by our dog's noses. (The increased air movement is also going to increase evaporation, making slightly more "scent molecules" in the air, but not enough to make up for the extra air they are spread across.)

GROUND COVER

The type of ground cover we are hunting effects our track condition a great deal, and again it goes back to evaporation. A thick ground cover can hold a track for much longer than bare dirt - that is because it insulates against heat and slows evaporation. If you have seen your dogs work a tough track you have probably noticed that the dogs work thick ground cover when at a loss. Old dogs know that cover holds moisture and therefore scent.

TERRAIN

Our terrain also effects our track condition. Differences in elevation create their own air movements, and air movement is key to tracking conditions as it is spreading the scent and can give our dogs the games location. Hot air goes uphill and cool air drops. If a predominant wind is not noted then as the sun rises the air usually goes up out of a holler, so we would hunt from the top down. As the air cools in the evening it drops into the hollers so we hunt bottom to top.

BAROMETRIC PRESSURE

Barometric pressure effects everything on earth probably more than it is given note of. As far as how barometric pressure tints tracking it is as simple or as complicated as you want to get. A dog's and a human's nose do work better at higher barometric pressures. Higher barometric pressure also pushes scent down when totally isolated - BUT rising pressure is usually accompanied with wind and weather moving in. As with all of this it is a complex mashing of factors, but if the pressure is changing go hunting, and take all the dogs to see which ones work best - it is a crap shoot. I fish by barometric pressure, but rarely hunt according to it, because of all the other factors that often play into the conditions.

When we are hog hunting we often run into large clusters of scent. The dogs might find where a sounder has spent a great amount of time bedding or feeding. This can be aggravating because we can see that the sign is fresh, yet there is just too much of it. This usually ends up with the dogs frantically running around trying to work out a single track and then the dogs continually get side tracked on another track over and over, all the while you imagine the herd getting further and further from you. Exceptional dogs can work out a single track but it often takes time. Some old dogs will start spinning larger and larger diameter circles around the cluster in an effort to get rid of the noise and find the exit. If you don't have dogs with this experience you will probably have better luck catching dogs and leading them in that large circle around the area until you notice they have picked up the track of one or the group leaving out.

Cast into the wind. Casting into the wind gives the dogs a hand up, it helps cover your scent from being detected and can help cover your noise. We often pick where we are going to hunt by wind direction. When possible, send bulldogs to a bay with this same idea in mind. It doesn't always work, but if you do it, it will help.

Hunting heavy wind is rarely fun, it's hard for the dogs and it's almost impossible to hear them if they end up doing good. Sometimes it can be productive though, especially if it is bringing in weather. In these hills we hunt the draws in a heavy wind, it lessens the wind and we often find hogs bedding down in them to get out of the wind.

EAST WIND

I'm sure you all heard old men say, "Wind from the East hunting and fishing the least, wind from the West hunting and fishing the best." I believe in the saying fully, the question is why?

More than a couple times I have been on a hunt with folks and noticed an East wind and I bring up the topic to questioning eyes. It is very much true. Usually after a crazy night of hunting the non-believers are converted, their minds tuned forever to the direction of the wind, not as a direction to cast dogs into, but weary of that odd East wind.

Dogs can't seem to take a trail in an East wind. I've seen old dogs that were fine hounds backtrack in an East wind. We can be in very hot sign and dogs just can't seem to figure it out. Wildlife also seem to hunker in an East wind. It makes little sense, because an East wind, at least in Oklahoma almost never brings in weather. The North wind brings hunting weather, the South wind brings heat and the West wind bring storms, the East wind brings dogs that you want to choke. Luckily that East wind is rare.

There have been a few times I was loading up to go hunting and noticed an East wind and just put dogs back in the kennels. Now some are probably thinking I'm crazy, but take note of the wind and I can promise you next time you hunt an East wind you will see, doesn't mean you won't catch hogs but things will be 'off.'

The Bible talks of an East wind many times, more than any other wind. In part, at least, because an East wind in Israel brought with it hot, dry and dusty conditions as it came off the Arabian desert. The mention of an East wind in the bible takes on an ominous nature. In Revelations God says, 'He will use an East wind to destroy the wicked.'

In Greek mythology the god of the East wind is Eurus - god of the "unlucky" East wind.

In 1868 George MacDonald wrote, in his book 'At the Back of the North Wind'; "One does not exactly know how much to believe of what she (the East wind) says, for she is very naughty sometimes."

Charles Dickens also uneasily noted the East wind in his book 'Bleak House'; "I am always conscious of an uncomfortable sensation now and then when the wind is blowing in the East."

My mind is not made up why an East wind seems to throw trailing conditions into chaos. If anyone has any ideas please share them with me.

CHAPTER 27
CONTINUED TRAINING

Getting young dogs started is the hardest and most fragile part of training. We have to watch our every move and what that 'says' to the dog. While we still have to be mindful of our actions in further training, it is much easier. After the young dog is hunting in a range and style that we are happy with we start looking at the bigger picture. In this stage we are evaluating our dogs.

We cannot always pair the young dog with more experienced dogs, while this is a great learning tool it cannot be our only tool. We have to grit our teeth and let them do it alone sometimes. This can be a hard one, when we know we could go catch a hog with old dogs, but we might have to settle on a hunt that doesn't end with a caught hog, but it allows for growth and independence in our young dogs. The joy that comes when we make this step and our young dogs do go bay a hog is the greatest fullfillment of our training though. We are not after 'me-too' dogs. It is also important, when you can, to not always pair a young dog with the same dogs hunt after hunt. Switching things up gives dogs a diversity and a chance to shine while not creating dependency.

Hunting young dogs by themselves gives us clues to their ability. Many times I have started a dog and they did great. The dog hunted hard and in a way I liked, but further down the road I saw that they didn't have the tools to make a great dog, despite their efforts. This is not a dead end road though. I am of the belief that desire plays a big role, and most times I will take the dog that 'wants to,' with less natural ability over the dog that has more natural ability - in nose, or track sense etc - but lacks desire. Of course, in a perfect world we want desire to spare, coupled with ability and inteligence poured all over the top. Just as in a boxing ring, I am going to bet on the man that I see has heart, over the man that has skill, everytime. Determination goes a long way, in man and dog alike.

As we further the training of young dogs in the woods much of the liability falls on you. Exposure is key. A dog full of potential sitting on a chain will not express his full potential. Hunt those young dogs as often as you can. There is a window in a dog, that age varies slightly with each dog and their maturity, but generally between 12 months and 14 months a dog needs a lot of hunting, no matter if it is hog hunting or off-game. Dogs that miss exposure in that window rarely seem to recover. It's like 1st and 2nd grade for us, if you show up to school for the first time at 3rd grade and you don't know the alphabet you are always going to be behind.

While we don't want trashy dogs we have to be careful about trash breaking in the young dog that is getting an education in the woods. Any future great dog IS going to trash! If you have a young dog that you are thinking of culling because of trash then call me, I will take the dog. Trash shows desire and desire is two-thirds of the equation. Hogs are naturally more fun for a dog with a breeding that relates back to hog dogs than off-game. Many dogs will 'break' themselves if given the time.

How we interact with the dog on trash will also guide the dog. When the dogs bay a hog we show up and participate in the hunt, that shows the young dog our approval. When a young dog trees a possum, or catches one on the ground sometimes we have to show up, to correct the action, or just to get the dog, but how we interact plays a role. If we 'participate' in that hunt then we are sending mixed signals. When possible I think it best to just stay away from off-game situations, I will wait them out in most cases. If I have to go to a dog that is digging an armadillo then I will snap the dog, swat him a time or two, and drag him back to the truck. Do not interact with the off-game animal!

In young dogs we have to do our darndest to keep them hunting in areas we know hold hogs. Trash running is often a result of nothing else to do, and it is understandable that a driven young dog will find something to run, celebrate that and take the ribbing from your buddies. Occasionally we are going to find a young dog that will turn down a bay to go run a deer. This is a situation that needs to be dealt with in a different manner, and at a different level, than a dog that chases a deer when they scare him up from his bed and he runs, and they instinctively chase. Give great thought to these dogs, and figure for yourself how much time you want to invest.

As these young dogs mature we push harder. I said earlier to keep them in areas that hold hogs, and that is sound advice, but there comes a time when it is necessary to do the opposite and set them up to have to work hard. In school many of the kids that act out are very smart and they are just board with easy work. We have to know our dogs and see their ability and constantly challenge them. If you don't know your dog you aren't going to suceede in training him.

In the age of satelite tracking there is little excuse for not knowing your dogs. When I got my first GPS tracker I was in awe of the technology. I called an old man I hunted with and tried to explain it, to no avail, for him it was like science fiction. On the very first hunt with that tracker I learned a hard truth. For many years I had my pack ranked in my head, and that was based on a lot of information of how dogs acted when I sent them, order of barking, and what things looked like when I got to a bay. The GPS quickly re-ranked my pack. A dog that I didn't think much of was doing most of the hunting. I quickly saw the dog was doing most of the striking and I also saw that one of my previous thought top dogs was little more than a me-too dog. My mind was blown!

My wife is not a hunter. In 20 or so years she has went on three hunts with me. After her first hunt she recounted to me that it was like we "Were playing a video game with our dogs." As an outsider she said we sent the dogs and then just sat around looking at screens. That outsider view troubled me, because I saw the truth in it. After that, I made an effort to limit my 'screen time.' As I said earlier the GPS tracker can give us valuable information on our dogs, and we need to be able to read that information, but it cannot, and should not, be our only tool. Coming from a time before the tracker, after my wifes soft handed and innocent commentary, I made an effort to not rely on that GPS tracker. Ears are at our core the most effective tool. Uncertainty is a troubling, and comforting part of hunting with dogs. Today I make an effort to use my primitive tools as the key, and the GPS is a safeguard. A couple times a year I grit my teeth and leave the tracker at home and turn loose old school, it is frightening, and freeing, and I encourage every dog hunter to try it. For many thousands of years dog hunters cast dogs without that technology, and it is a re-connect to our distant past, a past many new hunters have never known. Great insight is there with our past, if you seek it out you will further your journey as a dog hunter. Before you run you must walk.

When I find myself thinking back to great hunts they almost always fall to ones before satelite tracking. I can at will hear that barking trailing off in the hills until lost. I can recall the conversations of theory on where hogs might have taken dogs, where hogs might have picked to take their stand. All these years later I can conjure up the smile that came with hearing dogs baying in the distance and the ground made up by knowledge of roads and terrain and game to get closer. I hold those memories dear. A more simple time when uncertanty wasn't so scary.

The key to woods training is in mixing things up; paired dogs, terrain, track conditions and overall difficulty of the hunt. View it as a curve of always increasing adversity.

Our training will continue until the day we place the dog in the ground. "Finished dog" is not a term I agree with, we are never finished teaching and allowing the dog to learn and get better.

CHAPTERS 28 ·46
DOG HEALTH

Unless you are wealthy, as a hog hunter you are going to have to learn to do limited medical procedures for your dogs. There does come a point where you reach your limitations though, and at that time it is necessary to go to a veterinarian. It is very important to have a vet that understands hunting dogs, and doesn't apply procedures (and prices) as if your dog is a pet.

A few years back I was at the vet, and after the doctor was done he sent me to the front desk. The lady pecked around on the computer and told me the bill was $350, or there abouts. I took a deep breath and the vet poked his head around the corner, "Susie! That's a hunting dog!" After some more pecking a new price was given to me, $75, or there abouts. That is the benefit of a relationship and understanding with a good country vet that knows hunting dogs. Another benefit of having a good veterinarian is the medications that can come your way that otherwise would not dare be sold to you. As some vets learn your understanding they will sell you medications that are hard to get. Most vets know that a hog hunter with 15 dogs on his yard is not going to bring them all in, so they will help you out. Their revenue stream is in pets, and some get that.

In todays world there is yet another reason to have a relationship with a good vet. That benefit comes into play if and when you have a run-in with the animal rights "police." Records of past vet care can go a long way in showing you are a responsible dog owner. Save those receipts. Having a vet that knows you and your dogs, and might be willing to testify in court on your behalf is also invaluable!

CHAPTER 28
WORMING DOGS

Worming dogs these days can be quite a task with all the options we have and the advice all over the internet. Some of that free advice is good and some of it is just plain wrong. I am not a veterinarian, so take what I say as a broad reference and do your own research. If you have a good country vet that will shoot straight with you and not just try to sell you overpriced wormers with the same active ingredients as off label stuff you can pick up at a feed store, talk to your veterinarian.

As a general rule, there is no wormer out there that gets all worms. For this reason it is always a good idea to vary your wormers from month to month. This broadens the spectrum of parasites that you are killing, but also offsets the negative side effects. Varying your wormer can also cut down the chances of parasites becoming resistant to the chemicals we are putting in our dogs. Wormers are poison, so follow the dosages closely! Good wormers that are safe when used right kill dogs all the time when used in doses too large.

I am going to do my best to break down some of the most popular wormers that dog hunters are using and let you know what I know about them.

The most popular wormer used where I live seems to be Safe-guard horse wormer. Safe-guard, or Panacur both use the same active ingredient, -Fenbendazole. It is effective in treating round worms, hook worms, tape worms, whip worms, pin worms, and Guardia. I used

197

Safe-guard for many years, and never saw any ill-effects, although I did hear from time to time of dogs dying from it. I chalked it up to someone giving a dog too much, as it was easy to do if you squirted from the tube straight to the dogs mouth. I was talking about worming with my vet one day and he said something I had never thought of. He said, "Ed, you are assuming that the Fenbendazole is evenly mixed in the tube! It is not!" A tube of horse wormer is a single dose for most horses, so whether the top or bottom of the tube contains more active ingredients isn't a big deal when using the whole tube. I never used a horse tube to worm a dog again. I am not saying you can't, but to me, the risk is too high, even if low. If you are using Safeguard horse wormer the best solution is to empty the entire tube onto something like a paper plate and then really give it a good mixing and dose from there for dogs.

Ivomec, probably runs a close second in popularity around here in cattle country. The active ingredient in Ivomec is ivermectin. Ivomec injectable is given orally, and general only one day. DO NOT USE Ivomec Plus, it also has a drug called Clorsulon in it to kill liver flukes in cattle and it has been known to kill dogs. Ivermectin kills hook worms, tape worms, whip worms, round worms, and heart worms, so it gets everything Safe-guard gets plus heart worms. Now that last part is very important. If you switch over to Ivomec, or an Ivermectin based wormer you need to be sure that your dog doesn't have heart worms. Heart worms are in the heart, obviously, if you kill them they can block the heart up and kill a dog. This doesn't always happen, but it is a possibility. Think of it as a log jam in a river, they don't always jam up, but it's possible. It should also be noted that Ivermectin is not recommended for use in Collies, Australian Shepherds, Shelties, German Shepherds and Long Haired Whippets. For whatever reason, shepherd dogs don't react well with Ivermectin. If you have a dog that you suspect of having heart worms Ivermectin can be used in very small doses to try to kill the heart worms in small numbers at a time to reduce the chance of artery blockage. This is what vets do, and charge an arm and a leg.

I wanted to stay away from dosage numbers in this article, just so no one fire bombs my house if a dog dies, but there is so much bad information out there on Ivermectin that I think I have to. Ivermectin is powerful stuff! Correct dosage is a MUST. Treat dogs with

1/10cc per 10 pounds of weight. 1/10! Not to be confused with 1cc! So a 50 pound dog gets .5 cc's, POINT 5! 5cc's will likely shut your dogs kidneys down and kill him. After pulling the correct dosage in a syringe, I fill the remainder of it with water. Ivermectin is hot. Ivermectin will also eat through teeth enamel like acid. I had a friend that learned this the hard way when holding the syringe between his teeth as he went dog to dog, the next day he had a spot on a tooth that had a hole in the enamel!

Another popular off-label wormer used is Valbazen, active ingredient - Albendazole. Albendazole has been around for years, although it seems to have come back around here lately. It covers tape worms, whip worms, round worms, hook worms, coccidia, and giardia. Valbazen is given orally. It is usually given three days in a row and is pretty safe and effective. I have used it for a few years and have had no health issues, although I have heard of it causing a bone marrow problem and anemia. I generally use it only every other month. Valbazen can lead to sterility in males and females for up to 45 days after administering. This is not permanent though, only temporary.

Now we are going to get a little new agey, hippy-ish, so throw on a tie-dye shirt and put on a CD of ocean sounds and flutes. I have been using Diatomaceous Earth, or D.E. for a number of years. D.E. is basically ground up sea shells, no chemicals at all. D.E. doesn't poison parasites like all the wormers mentioned before, it mechanically kills them. D.E. is a fine powder, about like flour, but if you looked at it through a microscope it has sharp jagged spikes all over each grain. When it travels through the digestive system it scratches the parasite and causes them to dehydrate. D.E. is safe on puppies and it also can be used to treat external parasites like fleas and ticks. D.E. can be sprinkled around chain spots and in dog houses. When you use Diatomaceous Earth be careful not to breath in the fine powder as it can cause lung problems for humans and dogs. If you use D.E. internally on dogs make sure they have plenty of good water.

Puppies need to be worm free as much as possible so that they can reach their fullest potential. Puppies are also the hardest to keep worm free. Valbazen is puppy safe in a lower dosage. Another very mild wormer is Pyrantel Pamoate - this is even human safe and my kids got it once a year when they were young and running around barefoot and making mud-pies in the yard. Pyrantel Pamoate is effective against pin worms, roundworms, and hookworms. It does not kill tapeworms. Very recently here in Northeast Oklahoma we have seen a large upswing in hookworms. While many worms just rob the dog of energy and nutrients, Hooks will kill a dog and especially puppies, fast! In puppies it looks very similar to Parvo. Smelling the breath of the dog will tell the difference between Parvo and Hooks though. I cannot describe that Parvo smell, but anyone that has fought it knows exactly what I am talking about.

Here is what I do, and it seems to work for me, but might not work for everyone. I worm on the first of the month, it is easy to remember and doesn't take any notes. Even months are Ivomec, ("I" is a vowel and seems 'even' in my head,) and odd months are Valbazen,("V" is an 'odd' letter.) I use D.E. every couple months, though not needed for worms I use it more as a cleanse for their bowels. D.E. can be sprinkled right on the dog food and it will stick well to a greasy dog food. I've never trusted hippies so I just use it as a bonus. It can't hurt. I have used D.E. on myself, and I can attest to its 'cleansing' abilities. In winter months when there are no mosquitoes I hold off the Ivomec, unless I see a worm problem, and just worm with Valbazen every other month. Despite the best laid worming plan you have to be checking dogs, constantly. A microscope is the most accurate way to keep an eye on internal parasites - to detect them, then identify them and then pick a way to kill them.

I have many dogs that run free and something I have noticed is that while they do get worms occasionally they do not get them nearly as often as my kennel dogs. Monica Wheelus tells me that dogs often eat things intentionally to upset their gut and make an environment not suitable for worms. I think I agree.

Worming dogs is about managing risks and rewards, we each have to weigh the options and do a bit of homework. Internal parasites are a detractor we face in getting the most out of our dogs physically and the topic deserves our understanding and focus.

CHAPTER 29

CUT KITS AND COMMON PROCEDURES

***Disclaimer:

The information here is not meant to be replacement for veterinarian care. This information is intended to be used to stabilize a dog in life threatening situations so that you can get them to a professional for care.

Below is a list of basic instructions and contents for an in-field cut kit. I have spent many hours with the staff of Tuskers Magazine creating this cut kit. This kit does not include everything though - care was taken to make a kit that handled most situations in the smallest possible package. A more complete kit could be created, but if it weighs too much, or is just bulky not many people are going to carry it with them. The most complete cut kit does you no good if it is at home. A compact kit that goes to each bay is the intention here. I encourage everyone to make additions and subtractions to this kit and carry it with them every time a dog is turned loose.

Basic Sutures: There are just two types of stitching that suit most all of our needs- Simple Interrupted and Vertical Mattress. A basic understanding of how to suture is a must for hog hunters. Staples have their place but they are no substitute for stitching in some cases. You can practice these stitching methods on a banana skin, it works very well.

Prior to suturing flush the wound with clean water. Remove any debris. Scrub the inside of the wound with an Iodine swab stick. Clean the area around the wound as well. If a sedative is not used, tape the dogs mouth and have extra hands around to help you hold the dog. You can place a towel over the dogs head - the darkness seems to help calm some dogs. Some dogs will stand like a statue while you work on them and others will shoot into space like a rocket trying to kill you on the way. Either way, be prepared for the unexpected. Restrain the dog as little as you can get away with, sometimes overly restraining a dog will cause a wild response. Whichever suture method you use it is very important to allow an opening towards the bottom (as the dog is standing) to allow for drainage. The drain will allow fluids, and debris to exit. This will speed healing and reduce the chances of infection. In very deep cuts where muscle is sutured it will likely be necessary to put in an actual drain tube. A piece of a drinking straw will work in a pinch. The straw will need to be held in place superciliously with a couple stitches that you can get to and remove as needed after healing or drying of the wound.

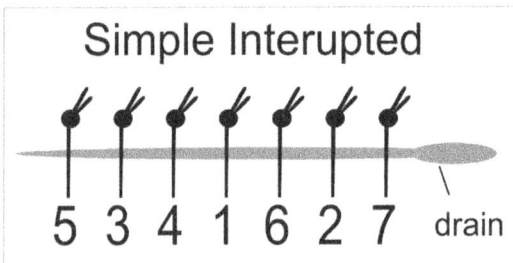

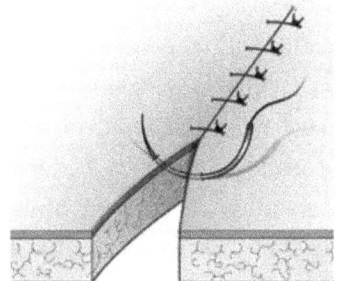

SIMPLE INTERRUPTED SUTURES

1. This is the most basic and easiest suture and is well suited for cuts that are not very deep. The Simple Interrupted stitch is best suited for cuts that are skin deep. The advantage of this stitch is that one stitch can come out or loose but the remaining stitches still hold, as opposed to a continuous suture.

2. Use hemostats to hold the needle. Grasp the needle from the middle to the back two-thirds. Stitch towards your body, not away from yourself.

3. Start in the middle of the cut with the first stitch. Insert the needle at a 90 degree angle to the skin. The bite will be as far back from the cut as you are going to go deep. When you bring the needle out the opposing side tie a surgeons knot. The knot should sit to the side of the wound and not right on top of the cut. Leave a minimum of a 1/4 inch on the end of the knot. (Stitch in the order of picture shown in the pictures - starting in the middle of the wound and working towards the edges dividing the wound in halves each time)

4. These stitches can be done with absorbable or non-absorbable sutures. Non-absorbable stitches will have to be removed after healing. If you do not have pre-packaged sutures you can buy half moon needles at most box stores in the sewing department. Un-flavored dental floss makes a pretty decent thread for sutures. Horse hair is also a favorite of old time cowboys. Light gauge fishing line works as well, but getting knots to hold is more of a challenge.

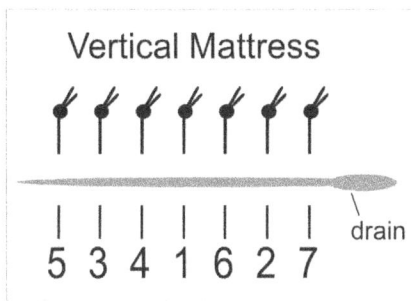

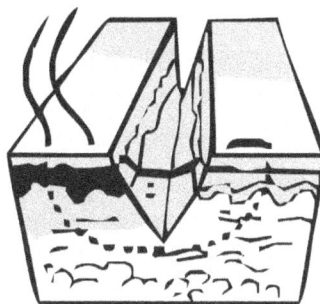

VERTICAL MATTRESS SUTURES

1. This is a slightly more technical suture but better suited for deep wounds, or in areas where there will be a lot of tension on the wound.

2. Use hemostats to hold the needle. Grasp the needle from the middle to the back two-thirds. Stitch towards your body, not away from yourself.

3. Suture placement and order is the same as in the Simple Interrupted stitch. The needle goes in deep, below the bottom edge of the cut if you are able, then back out on the other side. On the same side you exit place another stitch much shallower going the opposite direction as the first stitch. The stitch is tied and you repeat.

4. This stitch should be done with non-absorbable sutures. A deep cut will take longer to heal. Stitches will have to be removed after healing.

Surgeons Knot

MINOR CUTS. —BLOOD NOT SPURTING—

1. If the cut or poke can be reached by the dogs mouth, and is less than 2" long, attention may not be needed. Stapling or suturing will reduce the healing time though.

2. Use Providone Iodine swabs to clean the area around and inside of the cut. Alcohol will dry the area out and slow healing and should not be used unless it is the only thing available and infection is likely.

3. As a general rule, sutures will hold better than staples. Staples should be used as an emergency measure to close a would fast and allow clotting. If major blood loss is not an issue, then suture within a few hours, in a place where you have better light and more tools than in the woods. After 24 hours suturing, or stapling, is usually not effective.

4. A sedative like Xylazine can be given to make suturing easier. Follow dosages closely. If the dog has had a lot of blood loss then sedating the dog is not recommended. After sticking the needle, draw the plunger out to make sure you do not have a vein, as a vein shot of most sedatives will likely kill the dog.

5. If a sedative is not available, or there has been significant blood loss, turpentine can be used as a local anesthesia. Taping the dogs mouth is a good idea, as applying the turpentine to the area will be painful to the dog. Turpentine will also help to constrict the blood vessels and slow bleeding. ***Turpentine is toxic and may cause skin irritation so use sparingly.

6. Suture as shown earlier. Leave ½"of the wound open on the bottom side to allow for drainage.

7. A topical anti-septic such as Vetricyn applied 49 times a day will aid in healing tremendously. Flushing with water multiple times a day will also aid greatly in healing.

8. Antibiotics should be given.

9. Vitamin E supplement can be given to the dog. Vitamin E speeds healing, and is also a mild anti-inflammatory. (Vitamin E is also great for people healing wounds) If there is a lot of swelling Dexamethazone can be given to the dog but not more than couple days.

MAJOR CUTS, BLOOD SPURTING DEEP MUSCLE

(Instructions here are meant to buy you valuable time to get to a vet.)

1. Stop or slow the bleeding! A tampon can be used to insert into a deep cut or poke. Blood stop can be used to pack into the cut, you may need to apply pressure by hand for a couple minutes. Once the blood powder is working in stopping or slowing the bleeding you can then wrap the area with vet wrap. (not too tight)

2. In the case of a cut artery you can use hemostats to clamp the artery, after folding the artery over on itself. Clamp as lightly as possible to stop the flow of blood. Get to a vet pronto.

3. If you are going to a vet immediately DO NOT staple or stitch the dog unless all other methods of stopping the bleeding fail.

4. With a large amount of blood loss, shock is deadly, and likely. Force sugary drinks down the dog. Wrap the dog in a blanket or jacket to keep the body temperature up. It may sound crazy, but talk to the dog and try to keep his attention.

5. If possible transport the dog in the cab of the truck where you can keep an eye out.

6. A call to the vet to let them know you are coming can save valuable minutes when you arrive.

GUTTED DOG.

There are varying degrees of a 'gutted' dog, from a 1" cut in the underbelly where a few inches of intestines come out, all the way up to most of the insides of a dog hanging out. Obviously they are different situations, but in each they are very dangerous and take an expert hand or a professional.

1. Start treating shock first. First! I don't care how much blood and guts you see, treat for shock first. Sugary liquids down the dogs throat, a B-12 shot in the muscle, and wrap the dog in a towel, or shirt to keep body temperature up. (B-12 can also be used when hunting to get a little more "umpf" out of a dog for a few hours. It is like an energy drink for a dog, but it also comes with a crash. When you don't have an energy drink for yourself, a few cc's of B-12 down your throat will also give you a boost, but beware because it taste like hell!)

2. Check to see if there are any cuts to the intestines. If the intestines are cut, even a minor cut, get to a vet immediately! Unless your skill level of home-treating dogs is great this is a case for a professional. Infection will follow.

3. If the dogs guts are not cut, and you are going to handle it on your own you must clean inside the dog, and the exposed guts VERY good! Do NOT use alcohol or hydrogen peroxide as they will dry out and even kill tissue. Use Iodine and plenty of water.

4. Clean the exposed guts with fresh water. This helps to flush foreign objects like leaves and dirt, and also keeps everything moist. Guts will dry out very fast so pay close attention to keeping them watered down.

5. In minor cases you can re-insert the guts. This takes patience and attention to detail. Make SURE you do not have any twisted guts once they are back in place. In the case of a very small cut where just a small amount of intestines pop out, you may need to lengthen the cut slightly so that you can see what you are doing. Apply slight pressure so that you do not end up with more coming out. This is a two man job.

6. Once everything is back in place it is time to close up the wound. Staples will NOT be enough. If you are not qualified to suture then go to the vet. Use the vertical mattress stitch for strength if you are comfortable with it, if not then go ahead with a simple stitch.

7. Infection WILL likely occur. Start a heavy dose of antibiotics immediately and continue until fully healed.

If you are transporting to a vet for care:

1. Treat for shock as described above.

2. Flush guts with fresh water.

3. Gently insert the guts back inside the dog if you can.

4. Wrap the dog with a t-shirt and lightly hold in place with a couple wraps of co-flex.

5. Wet the t-shirt wrap every few minutes to keep everything moist.

6. Call your vet, and drive fast!

SNAKE BITE

1. Most snake bites occur on the face and head, so first thing to do is remove the collar. Many dogs have suffocated from a tightening collar due to swelling.

2. Give Benadryl dosed at 1mg per 1lb of body weight. This will settle the dog, slow movement of the venom, as well as counteract the swelling. Pay close attention to the dosage - ignore the instructions on the bottle - dogs take a much larger dose than humans do.

3. Get the dog still.

4. Keep the dog cool.

5. If you have Dexamethazone, inject 1cc in the muscle or under the skin. After sticking the needle, draw the plunger out to make sure you do not have a vein, as a vein shot of Dexamethazone can kill the dog.

6. Start a regiment of antibiotics immediately.

7. Most dogs will survive a copperhead bite, rattlesnake is a 50/50.

8. Get professional help.

OVER⋆HEATED DOG

1. Remove cut vest and cut collar.
2. Pour cool water (alcohol works better if you have it on hand) on the dogs back end, legs and feet. Use your fingers to work the water in past the fur so that it makes it to the skin. Rub water on the dogs belly. Do not put water on the dogs head! Do not use very cold water, room temperature is best. Very cold water can cause stroke.
3. Use alcohol pads to wipe down the pads. The alcohol evaporates fast and removes heat from the body.
4. 1cc of Dexamethazone can be injected in the muscle to stop the constriction of blood vessels.
5. In very extreme situations, where the life of the dog is in immediate jeopardy you can take a knife and cut 1/4" off the tip of each ear to bleed the dog. The loss of blood will cool the dog but it is not without risk and should only be done as a last resort. If this method is used make the dog drink pop or any sugary drink to help ward off shock from loss of blood.
6. Use a syringe to inject 2cc of water under the skin, (not in the muscle). You can do multiple injections down the dogs back. These injections will knot up, as the knots go down re-inject in different areas.
7. If you are able, an IV should be administered as soon as emergency steps have been taken.
8. Use Pedialyte packs to make a drink for the dog. Draw them into a syringe without a needle and squirt down the dogs throat.
9. Shade the dog in a cool spot and keep the dog hydrated!

BROKEN JAW

1. If you suspect a dog has a broken jaw first inspect inside the mouth to make sure there is not an object lodged in the mouth.
2. If the dog does NOT have chest injuries and seems to be breathing fine then you can secure the lower jaw with tape, light

rope, or a piece of a t-shirt cut off.

3. Keep a close eye on the dog as you transport to make sure breathing does not become labored. If so, remove the tape.

4. Bynadryl can be given to the dog to ease pain and calm them.

5. Get to the vet.

POISONED DOG

1. Measure 1cc of 3% hydrogen peroxide per pound of dog weight, using either a syringe or teaspoon. (Dosage on 40lb dog would be 40cc or ml) One teaspoon is approximately 5 cc. The maximum amount of hydrogen peroxide to be given at any one time is 45 ml, even if a dog weighs over 45 pounds. Squirt the hydrogen peroxide into the back of the dog's mouth using the syringe or a turkey baster.

2. If vomiting has not occurred within 15 minutes or so, give one more dose of hydrogen peroxide measured out as described above. This will work if the poison has been very recently ingested. Even if done very early, it will likely just limit the amount of poison that enters the dogs system.

3. Call your veterinarian.

PUNCTURED LUNG

If a dog is breathing shallow, standing with elbows spread out away from chest, acting out of breath or tongue is looking bluish, it is likely a collapsed/ punctured lung. Often a gargling sound will be heard or you may even hear air exiting through the body with each breath. Sometimes a punctured lung will be evident in blood full of air bubbles leaving a chest wound. This means that air and/or fluids are in the chest and need to be removed to stabilize the dog. This can be performed using tubing (an IV set works well) inserted into the chest cavity and slowly drawing out fluid and air with a syringe. If there is no open wound, an incision can be made approx. ¾ way down the rib cage, between two ribs at the widest part of chest. When you get through the muscling between ribs, you may even hear air escaping as you enter the cavity. You can then insert your tubing and attach a syringe. Make sure the hole is just big enough to allow tubing to slide in and makes a tight seal. If the syringe being used is small, use a hemostat to clamp the tubing as the syringe is removed to be emptied. It is important to remove air/fluids slowly and not allow the tubing to suck more back into the cavity. In the case of an open chest wound, the dog's chest should be covered with an airtight bandage as soon as possible after inserting the tubing into the deepest chest wound. Plastic wrap is often all that is needed to accomplish this. Wrap over the wounds and secure in place to seal. Once the dog is breathing easier, clamp off the tube and transport to a vet. The chest can continue to be drained if needed.

EYES

1. If a dog's eyes are watering from running through tall grasses and underbrush or have blood and possible injury you can rinse your dog's eye and eye area with simple saline solution. This can be purchased from a veterinarian, pharmacy, or made with a teaspoon of salt dissolved in a cup of warm water and carried in a squirt type bottle.

2. Carefully flush by squirting a small amount into the corner of your dog's eye and let it flush away discharge and debris from around the eye. This allows you to be able to see if there are any punctures or scratches to the eye itself and keeps dirt and debris from becoming stuck underneath the eye lid.

3. Vetericyn Eye Gel is a great product for eye irritations.

USES FOR ITEMS

Staple Gun - For shallow cuts in places where skin is not under a lot of pressure. Hold wound shut and push into the wound area with a fair amount of force while mashing the handle. Staple guns can be used on large wounds if you are looking for fast wound closure to save a dog. In such cases either a vet or yourself will likely remove the staples and suture in the immediate future.

Sutures - Wound closure for a better hold, and on more severe cuts.

Providone Iodine: swabsticks, pads and bottle - For general anti-septic cleaning. (hint, you can use one swab stick or pad and refresh with the bottle as needed in one use to save the individually wrapped swab sticks and pads for emergencies.) Iodine is a better anti-septic than alcohol or hydrogen peroxide when cleaning inside a wound because it doesn't harm tissue.

Alcohol: pads and bottle - For use on overheating dogs, (see topic Over-heated Dog)

Tampons - For use as a way to stop bleeding in pokes and cuts.

IV Administration set - For giving a dog a drip in cases of over-heating and dehydration. Also useful as a drain in the case of a punctured lung.

Co-Flex bandage - For general wound closure / coverage and compaction for broken bones.

Blood-stop - Obviously for stopping bleeding. I have flour in my kit, but you can also use corn starch, tea bags, or commercial blood stop powder.

Benadryl (diphenhydramine)- For snake bites, spider bites, and allergic reactions. It can also be used as a slight sedative. Dosage is 1mg per 1lb of body weight.

Powdered Pedialyte - For hydration and replacement of electrolytes. Useful in over-heated dogs, after a lot of blood loss, as well as a multitude of other instances when a dog is dehydrated. To check a dog pinch his skin between the shoulder blades, it should spring back fast, if it holds the shape of the pinch and slowly returns then the dog needs fluids.

Hemostats - For holding a suture needle, also useful for clamping cut arteries, and pulling porcupine quills.

BASIC CONTENTS FOR A CUT KIT SMALL ENOUGH TO CARRY HUNTING

(2) 5-0 Nylon Suture with FS needle

(2) 4-0 Sterile Nylon Suture with FS needle

(2) 3-0 Nylon Suture with FS needle

(1) #3 Scalpel Handle, Fits Blades #10-#15

(2) #10 Sterile Scalpel Blade

(2) #11 Sterile Scalpel Blade

(1) 5in Needle Holder or larger

(1) 5 1/2in Curved Forceps

(1) 5 1/2in Operating Scissors

(4) Alcohol Prep Pads, 70% Isopropyl Antiseptic

(4) Povidone Iodine Prep Pads Antiseptic

(2) 2x2in 8Ply Gauze Sponges

(2) 2in x 2.1yds Sterile Stretch Gauze Roll

(2) 3/4in Plasti-Pore Tape Rolls

(1) 35w Staple gun

(1) 2oz Bottle Povidone Iodine

(10) Povidone Iodine swab sticks

(1) 2oz Bottle Alcohol

(1) 2oz Bottle Hydrogen Peroxide

(4) 14 Guage Syringes

(1) Pack of 10 Benadryl tablets (Diphenhydramine)

(4) Tampons

(1) IV Administration set, 15dr, 78"

(1) Latex Co-Flex bandage 2" x 15'

(1) Package of blood stop (flour)

(2) Packages powdered Pedialyte

(1) Dexamethazone (an anti-inflammatory)

(1)Xylazine or Xylamed (a sedative)

(1) Bottle of water

(1) Injectable B-12

!!!!Keep a laminated scrap of paper with your vet, and alternative vets emergency contact information in your kit.

      This is just a basic kit and you should have a much more involved kit at your home for the care of dogs. This kit should stay close when hunting; in the truck, ATV, or even better yet - in a backpack that you carry on our person.

CHAPTER 30
DOG FOOD

As we push hunting dogs further and further to the limit, not unlike world class athletes, the feed they consume has to be in the top three most influential components to a great dog. The best bred and trained dog, on the worst diet, isn't going to be a great dog, just as the worst bred dog, on the best feed isn't going to be the best. Without proper nutrition we will never truly know the potential of a dog. Feed good dogs, and feed them good.

When we confine a dog to a chain or a kennel we are taking control of their diet and eliminating their choice in the matter. Responsibility comes with that confinement. We are taking control of nature and that deserves our full attention. I have dogs that run loose, and most of the year they look great on the lowest quality feed, because they are doing their own supplementing. Those dogs eat game they catch, they forage and they hit the mineral licks. Not unlike coyotes I often find seeds from berries, and usually a healthy dose of fur in their stools.

There are a few things I see when it comes to dog food that rub me in the wrong direction. It seems that in the last few years a trendiness has reared it's head in the dog food world. Every couple months a new feed comes into fashion and many jump aboard, hype or not. This trend has not gone unnoticed by dog food manufacturers! Over the years I have had dog food companies contact me, enticing me to tote and promote their feed. So far I have not had one of these feeds impress me enough to become a dog food pimp. I do feed a brand that I am extremely pleased with, but I buy my dog food. If folks contact me to ask about the brand I give them my honest opinion but I do not promote the feed because it will not suit everyone. What you feed has to suit your conditions. What the next guy feeds should have little bearing on choosing a feed that fits you and your dogs.

Dog food is a very complicated topic, folks spend four years in college to get an understanding of it. I do not know much of the science of feed, but I do know enough through life experience and common sense to recognize a good feed. The label on a feed sack doesn't really tell you much. Protein, fat, and fiber levels tell part of the story but you have to dig deeper to get a full understanding. More important than the percentage values is the source. Protein for example is a tricky one, that bag can be packed with protein but that doesn't mean it comes from a source that your dog can use. Forget that label, same as you disregard the sales pitch. The proof is in the running and you are the only judge of that.

To truly evaluate a feed in the real world we have to first get some things in line. The dogs have to be clean and free of parasites. This is a big one and many fall short. I know I have had my moments when I just wasn't holding a tight line and let my dogs down. If a dog is wormy or has fleas or ticks forget about finding a good feed until you have those problems in the rear view mirror. Parasites leach nutrients, and energy from a dog. They wreak havoc on the entire digestive system. With a digestive system in chaos you cannot judge a feed.

The other factor we have to consider, and correct, before evaluating a feed is the condition of the dog. Many hunters start searching for a new feed when a dog is either skinny or fat. That is not a bad thing, we should look for solutions when a dog is skinny or fat, but we cannot really judge a feed with a dog in poor condition. If I dropped my weight to 135lbs I could get back to 190lbs on Mountain Dew and honey buns but that would not mean it was a good diet. Conversely, if I weighed 225lbs I could get back down to weight by eating cardboard, but again that wouldn't mean cardboard was a good nutrition strategy. We want to evaluate a feed on dogs that are in prime running condition.

Truth is, most commercial dog food, when fed correctly, coupled with exercise will get a dog to a decent level, not tops, but good enough to evaluate the diet.

Full access to clean water is a must. A poorly hydrated dog cannot extract the full nutrients from any feed. Water is cheap, don't hold it back! Clean is the key word here. A dog that has clean water is going to drink more than a dog on dirty, hot water. The dog that has algae in his water is going to drink just enough to stay alive, but not as much as he needs.

We are going to judge the new feed in three parts;
1. An initial assessment.
2. How the dogs process the feed.
3. How the dogs perform on the feed.

1. Initial assessment

The first signals we will notice happen when we open the bag. Smell it. Does it smell old? Is it overly dry or overly oily? Color will also give us a clue. Is it dark or yellow? When I open a bag and the feed is yellow I can pretty accurately gauge what the dogs stools are going to look like - usually big loose mounds that stink to high heaven. I can also gauge how soon the dog will drop out of the race. Color alone does not tell the story though. Some makers of lesser quality feeds are using dyes to give their feed that dark color that we associate with a higher quality feed. The dogs stool will sniff that lie out though.

Make a mental note of the appearance of the feed and compare it in your mind when you open other bags of the same brand. We want a feed that is consistent from week to week. For many years I fed a dog food that I really liked, but it's consistency was all over the map. I had to judge rations from bag to bag. Despite my best attempts at adjusting feed, my dogs were just as inconsistent as that feed. It was a roller coaster of dogs too fat, then too skinny.

Next watch how the dogs react to the feed. Do the dogs eagerly eat it or are they picking around? A dog on a good ration of quality feed should 'wolf' it down. Not all dogs are the same here, but you know your dogs. Some scoop and swallow, some take their time and chew.

Our initial reaction to the feed is just watching for glaring faults. Now we wait.

2. How the dogs process the feed

More than a couple times I have recommended a food to someone and they have called me two days later to say they didn't like it. That is too soon after switching a feed to make a real judgment. As a general rule, it will take at least a couple weeks to see how the dogs are handling the feed. Not how the feed is performing though, just how the dogs are processing it.

The dogs stool will tell the tale. My dogs are on concrete and I try to keep them clean for many reasons, one being so that I can watch their stools. It sounds weird, but there is a lot of information in the turd itself, the timing, and the frequency. We want a hard turd. A hard stool tells us the dog is extracting most of the nutrients from the feed and that the source is compatible with a dogs gut. We want those good turds to be dark, almost black. Color is in part telling us the 'hold.' If the food doesn't stay in the gut long enough then a dog cannot get all of the nutrients out of it. If the ingredients are not in tune with a dog then the hold time will be almost nill. Not unlike us - if I go out in the yard and cut a bunch of green grass and eat it I had better be close to a place I can drop my pants because my guts are going to shoot that grass right out! We are not meant to eat grass. Dogs are no different. Some manufacturers know this and use other methods to achieve 'hold.' While faking a 'hold' does help, it is still working with ingredients that go against the dog and no amount of hold with help with full nutrient absorption.

Corn has been a staple in canine diets for probably 200 years or longer, and while corn as a major ingredient in dog food has recently gotten a black eye of sorts, it really is not a bad ingredient when given the proper 'hold.' Meat does suit a dogs nature better though, obviously. Before the 1950's bagged dog food was pretty much unheard of. Dogs ate scraps or home cooked dog food - cornmeal was a main ingredient, mixed with meat trimmings and fat and cooked in sheets. Just as today, corn was used because it was cheap. For folks that feed raw, or cook their own feed like the old-timers - mustard greens and chicken feathers are good ingredients to achieve 'hold.' When you are feeding corn based feeds often the stool is soft and yellow, this is telling us the feed is not staying in the intestines long enough - it is just passing through.

When I have my dogs 'right' they will have one turd a day. It will be hard and black. I can kick it out the back of the kennel without it leaving a spot on the concrete, or getting anything on my boot. If a dog is messing 3 or 4 times a day something is out of whack. Again, you have to know your dogs. Some dogs will do this, no matter the feed, but most will not when on a good diet and everything is fine in their digestive system. Like humans, stress can effect a dogs bowel, so you have to watch stress issues and not always throw every issue into the 'bad dog food' file.

I recently picked up a new trick for dogs that have a 'hard keep' despite an adequate ration of quality feed. We have all seen dogs that just always look poor. You can pour three times as much feed and it still seems to make no difference. of course when this happens our first task is making sure the dog is free of parasites, and this is the most common fix, but sometimes this can be due to bad bacteria in their gut. Hold the dog back from feed for 24 hours, then give him about 6 ounces of apple cider vinegar down the hatch with a large syringe. Feed them one quarter ration of their regular feed at this time. Do this three days in a row. After the three days of vinegar go back to a regular portion of their feed but add about a cup of yogurt to their feed. Feed the yogurt for 3 - 5 days in a row and then bring their diet back to normal. This will get the enzymes and bacteria in their gut back in a regular order and sometimes fix that 'hard keep' dog.

On any given day there are a thousand conversations going on in the world about what to feed a dog that is poor. Some of the recipes I have heard over the years were a bit strange to say the least. For me getting a poor dog back into shape is not a complicated concern - it is rather simple actually - raw red meat. A deer hind quarter will bring a poor dog back to normal faster than any witchcraft I have witnessed.

3. How the dogs perform on the feed

This is where the rubber meets the road. This is also very personal to your situation, conditions and style - why feed that works for one mans dogs doesn't necessarily work for the next guy. If you have 4 to 5 hour races regularly your feed is going to be different than the guy that hoods dogs and catches hogs with little running. If you hunt five nights a week you are going to feed different than the fella that hunts once every two weeks. To evaluate a feed we have to know our dogs. We have to know their bottom, speed, drive and condition. If a well conditioned dog, with bottom to spare is dropping out of a race then we have an issue with our feed. (if otherwise healthy) If a dogs drive seems lower than normal then we might have a problem with the feed. If a dog starts a hunt at 110% and then falls flat shortly after then we have an issue with feed, and it may likely be a feed full of carbohydrates. There are no parameters I can give you here, you have to know the baseline of your dogs performance, then eliminate outside factors to deduct problems in nutrition.

Some dogs will achieve great condition on many feeds, while some dogs will never get to that level of condition on ANY straight ration of kibble. You have to assess and adjust. You may have to supplement any feed with extra vitamins, fat, roughage, or protein. There is no silver bullet when it comes to dog food. There is no dog food I have found that can replicate, straight out of the bag, a dogs natural and ideal nutrition. Kibble is a starting point, don't view it as an end.

While we are on the topic of feed, skipping a meal once a week is also a good practice to get into. This suits a dog and allows them a full clean-out once a week. In the wild it is feast or famine and even when hunting very hard, skipping one day will not hurt anything.

We also need to adjust our feeding times to the seasons and our hunting schedules. It is elementary, but you don't hunt a dog on a full stomach. I primarily hunt at night, so most would assume I feed mornings, but I don't. I feed evenings most of the year. On days I am going to hunt they just eat after the hunt. This allows them to clean out and be empty by time to run. In the heat of summer feeding days creates too much body heat. A by-product of digestion is heat, and when this Oklahoma sun is burning us at 100+ degrees these dogs don't need any extra heat. For most of the winter I will continue to feed evenings, but when we get an extra cold spell I will feed a half portion mornings and evenings to use the added heat to my advantage. A dog, like a human uses more energy staying warm, so it takes more feed in the winter months - also the time most hunt more often. Summer finds me feeding a good 25% less feed than winter.

Temperature brings up yet another point. In winter these dogs are hunted hard and they need fat. Lots of fat, 24 (protein) -20 (fat) isn't even going to cut it, so it calls for extra fat in the diet, usually in the form of bacon grease or rendered hog lard, not every day but at least a couple times a week. As summer temperatures become the norm the fat needs to be reduced greatly. In winter, prime hunting season, a lean, in-shape dog is a plus, in the summer it is the difference between a breathing dog and a dead one. I generally switch to a lower fat feed in the summer and supplement with fish. Fish is low in fat and high in omega acids, it will slick a dog out and it's great for their memory. (That's a joke) I feed the skins off of catfish fillets after quickly frying them. The oil in fish is also great for joints in older dogs. For this benefit alone you can go to any drug store and buy "Fish Oil" tablets in the vitamin isle, they will limber up an old dog and make their coat shine.

MONICA WHEELUS

For many years Monica Wheelus has written dog health articles for Tuskers Magazine. While I would love to publish all of those articles in their entirety, there just isn't enough room and it could in fact be a stand alone book. So with space limitations I am going to boil down those articles that I feel are important.

CHAPTER 31
PYOMETRA ⋆ BY MONICA WHEELUS
Originally appeared in the June 2015 issue of Tuskers Magazine

Pyometra is an infection of the uterus that can be deadly if not treated quickly. The condition is most common in middle aged to older females that have not been spayed, but can develop in un-spayed dogs of any age.

Every time a dog has a heat cycle (usually once every 6 months) she undergoes changes in hormones similar to that of a pregnancy - whether she is bred or not. These hormonal changes in the uterus make possible infection more likely with age. Most often it is E. coli, found in feces, mud and standing water that is the cause of the infection. That puts hunting dogs at a higher risk because of kennels, dog boxes and exposure to infectious organisms while in the woods. Most cases of pyometra are diagnosed 4-6 weeks after a heat.

Of course, pyometra is only seen in intact females. It is most common in older females (over 6) but can happen at any age. The signs usually develop around 6 weeks after the female has finished bleeding from her last heat, but in some cases the bitch appears to have a prolonged or extremely bloody season.

Early signs you may notice:

-Licking her back end more than normal, almost obsessively
-Off color; she is pale or even grayish in her gums, eyes or belly
-Off her food
-Drinking more than normal (and will probably urinate more)

These signs will progress and you may see:

-Pus (yellow/red/brown discharge) from her vulva
-She may have a swollen abdomen

-Sudden weight loss or loss of muscling over back or hips
-Vomiting
-Collapse or no tolerance for any excercise
-If left untreated signs will worsen to the point of dehydration, collapse and death from septic shock.

Your vet will probably suspect your dog has a pyometra based on your description of the signs and from their examination. They may suggest procedures such as ultrasound and blood tests to confirm the diagnosis, rule out other possible causes and to check that your dog is well enough to undergo treatment.

The treatment of choice for pyometra is surgery to remove her uterus as soon as possible. The operation is essentially the same as a routine spay, however there is more risk involved and a higher chance of complications when the operation is being carried out on a sick animal. Your dog will also be given IV fluids, antibiotics and pain relief.

Treatment using antibiotics and prostaglandin hormone (Lutalyse) to contract the uterus is possible, but very rarely chosen. People try this in an effort to save the dog in and effort to get a litter in the future. The recurrence rate is high (around 60%) and your dog's fertility will be affected, meaning that successful breeding only occurs in a small number of dogs following treatment.

(Tenner Herr and Sha Rozel)

CHAPTER 32
COCCIDIOSIS ⋆ BY MONICA WHEELUS

Originally appeared in the December 2015 issue of Tuskers Magazine

Coccidiosis is the name of a bacterial infection of the intestinal tract caused by parasitic protozoa called coccidia. They are microscopic parasites that live within cells of the intestinal lining. Because they live in the intestinal tract and commonly cause diarrhea, they are often confused with worms.

Most dogs that are infected with coccidia do not have diarrhea or any other clinical signs. When the eggs are found in the feces of a dog without diarrhea, they are usually considered insignificant and that dog is just a carrier. However, in puppies and debilitated adult dogs, coccidia may cause severe diarrhea, dehydration, abdominal pain, fever and vomiting. In severe cases of infection, death may occur. When this is seen in puppies it is often mistaken for the corona or parvo-virus.

Oocysts (immature coccidia) is passed in the feces of an infected cat or dog. These oocysts are very resistant to environmental conditions and can survive for a long time on the ground. Under the right conditions of temperature and humidity, these oocysts "sporulate." If the sporulated oocysts are ingested by a susceptible dog, they will release "sporozoites" that invade the intestinal lining cells and set up a cycle of infection in neighboring cells.

Coccidia can be very easy to treat and usually consists of a sulfa-based antibiotic that are often found in liquid or tablet form. The antibiotic most commonly used is Albon (sulfadimethoxine), however there are others such as SMZ-TMP (sulfamethoxazole and trimethoprim) or Primor (sulfadimethoxine and ormetoprim) that are more effective on tough cases. It is usually given for ten to fourteen days. In severe infections, it may be necessary to repeat the treatment. Other drugs may be required if diarrhea and dehydration occur. If the sulfa-type drug is not effective, other treatments are available. Re-infection of susceptible dogs is common so environmental disinfection is important.

The most common coccidia found in dogs do not have any affect on humans. However, less common types of coccidia are potentially infectious to humans. One called Cryptosporidium, may be carried by dogs and can be transmitted to people. However, this parasite has also been found in the public water supply of some major cites with no confirmed source.

One thing to remember is that no matter what you do, sometimes there are diseases your dog will contract. Sometimes diseases that are very treatable can be fatal if left untreated. Coccidiosis is common in hunting dog kennels because of dogs picking up the oocysts while in the woods. Coccidiosis is carried by any type of varmint, such as squirrels, raccoon and rats. All a dog has to do is consume droppings or eat one of these and then other dogs coming in contact with the contaminated feces back at the kennel. It is strongly recommended that kennels be disinfected frequently and allowed to dry before returning dogs to their runs. The use of diluted chlorine bleach [one cup of bleach mixed in one gallon of water] is effective if the surfaces and premises can be safely treated with it.

Almost all kennels that raise pups will have an outbreak from time to time because of the difficulty of disinfecting whelping boxes and brood kennels. It is important to not let a pup with diarrhea go home with a new owner. New owners will automatically think it is either parvo or was poor living conditions of pups. If the new owner doesn't catch the illness soon enough and loses the pup it will be you they blame and talk about. It will put any other dogs they own at risk and the infection will be passed back and forth and become harder to treat.

CHAPTER 33
BAYLISASCARIS * BY MONICA WHEELUS
Originally appeared in the February 2017 issue of Tuskers Magazine

Most people are unaware that the bandit of the woods is likely also harboring a dangerous parasite. The parasite is called Baylisascaris. While most animal species have their own set of parasites. Raccoon parasites are particularly concerning because of the frequency of contact with hunters and dogs.

It's important to recognize that raccoons, like all wildlife, can carry parasites. One often overlooked is Baylisascaris procyonis, also known as the raccoon roundworm. Baylisascaris procyonis is a common, large roundworm that resides in the small intestine of the raccoon. This parasite can infect a variety of mammals including dogs and on occasion humans.

Like many intestinal parasites, infection occurs when the eggs of the worm are inadvertently ingested or when small, infected animals are eaten by raccoons. Infected raccoons can shed millions of eggs daily in their feces. These eggs become infective under proper conditions in about 10-14 days.

Baylisascaris occurs wherever raccoons live. Infected raccoons have been found throughout the United States. Prevalence of infections range to nearly 100% of all raccoons sampled in a recent study, depending on region and time of year. Baylisascaris can easily spread to hunting dogs, which increases the likelihood of human exposure. It is unknown how prevalent it is in dogs, but because it is known to be dangerous, care should be taken to avoid infection. Baylisascaris eggs look similar to eggs of dog roundworms so identification is important.

As with other roundworms, the mature worm lives in the intestines while the immature form migrates through the body of the puppy similar to any roundworm infection. There are two forms the disease can take in dogs:

* Intestinal, which is the typical adult form and like other intestinal parasites results in intestinal signs like diarrhea, with or without blood.
* Visceral, which is more common in puppies and is known to cause neurologic diseases that can mimic canine distemper, encephalitis and even rabies.

Raccoons generally defecate in concentrated areas, where fecal material accumulates for weeks or years. These are often located near dens or feeding sites. They can be used for years and because the eggs can also remain alive for years, they serve as long-term sources of infection for people and animals.

Monthly wormers that treat roundworms can provide a level of protection for your dogs and should be administered every 30-90 days, all year round. As always it is recommended to rotate wormers from time to time to prevent resistance.

(Ed Barnes and Pat Lewing)

CHAPTER 34
DEMODECTIC MANGE * BY MONICA WHEELUS
Originally appeared in the December 2014 issue of Tuskers Magazine

Demodex Canis, a mite too small to be seen with the naked eye, causes Demodectic mange. Nearly all pups acquire a small number of these mites from their mother within the first few days of life. This is considered normal and most people will never notice an outbreak. The mites only produce disease when an immune system abnormality occurs allowing their numbers to get out of control. A high incidence of mange in certain bloodlines, however, suggests that some dogs are born with an inherited immune susceptibility. Dogs that have been tightly bred to develop certain characteristics such as Beagles, Boxers, many of the Bully breeds and their offspring are more likely to have outbreaks. A correlation between dogs with a large percentage of white and demodectic mange has also been suggested.

Demodectic mange occurs in both localized and generalized forms. The initial diagnosis is made by taking multiple skin scrapings and looking for the mites. Demodectic mites are usually easy to find, however a scraping taken when the dog is in the middle of a severe flair up increases the chances of diagnosis.

Localized Demodectic Mange occurs in dogs under 1 year of age. The appearance of the skin is similar to that of ringworm. The first sign is thinning hair around the eyelids, lips and corners of the mouth. Occasionally it will be present on the ribs, legs and the feet. The thinning often progresses to round patches of ragged hair loss about 1 inch in diameter. In some cases, the skin will become red, scaly and infected. In healthy pups, localized mange usually heals spontaneously in six to eight weeks, but may linger for several months. If more than five patches are present, the disease could be progressing to the generalized form. This occurs in approximately 10% of dogs affected and are otherwise in good health with minimal stress.

Treatment: A topical ointment containing either benzoyl

peroxide gel (common trade names OxyDex or Pyoben), or a mild topical preparation used to treat ear mites can be massaged into affected areas once a day until all the hair has grown back. The medication should be rubbed with the lay of the hair to minimize any further hair loss. Treatment may cause the area to look worse for the first two to three weeks as the mites are dying and the dog's body is reacting causing a red rash. There is no evidence that treating localized mange prevents the disease from becoming generalized and ideally the dog should be checked again in four weeks by a veterinarian.

Dogs with the generalized form develop patches of hair loss on the head, legs, and body. These will begin to spread and form large areas where hair follicles become plugged with mites and skin scales. When that occurs, the skin breaks down to form sores, crusts and draining tracts, presenting much larger problems. Some generalized cases are a continuation of what started as localized mange; others develop spontaneously in older dogs.

When generalized mange develops in dogs under 1 year of age, there is a 30 to 50% chance that the puppy will recover spontaneously and not ever have another issue. It is uncertain whether medical treatment accelerates this recovery or not, but treatment is always recommended over the "wait and see" approach.

In dogs older than 1 year, a spontaneous cure is unlikely however, the outlook for improvement with medical treatment has increased dramatically in recent years. Most dogs can be cured with intense therapy and the remaining cases can be controlled if the owner is willing to commit the necessary time.

Generalized demodectic mange should be diagnosed by and treated under close veterinary supervision. The standard, recommended therapy involves the use of medicated shampoos and dips to remove surface scales and kill mites. Clipping hair from all affected areas to increase access to the skin is helpful.

The FDA protocol involves first bathing the dog with a medicated benzoyl peroxide shampoo (OxyDex or Pyoben) to remove skin scales. Allow the shampoo to remain on the dog for 10 minutes before rinsing off. Completely dry the dog. Amitraz (brand name Mitaban) currently is the only miticide approved by the FDA for use on dogs. Make up an amitraz dip by adding Mitaban to water, according to the directions on the label. Be sure to treat the dog in a well-ventilated area and wear rubber or plastic gloves to keep the chemical off your skin. Sponge on the dip over a 10-minute period, allowing the dog's feet to soak in the rinse. (A child's wading pool comes in handy for this step) Allow the dip to dry on the dog without rinsing. Repeat every two weeks, or as directed by your veterinarian. Try to keep the dog from getting his coat and feet wet between dips. Continue this protocol for 60 days beyond the day when skin scrapings first became negative.

Side effects of Mitaban include drowsiness, lethargy, vomiting, diarrhea, dizziness, and a staggering gait. Puppies are more susceptible than adults to these effects. If such a reaction occurs, immediately remove the miticide by thoroughly rinsing the coat and skin.

If the recommended FDA protocol is not completely effective, or if that treatment is not practical for your situation, there are alternative off-label treatments recommended by vets. All alternative treatments require close supervision of the dog since they are not officially approved for treating this problem.

Ivomec: One of the most frequently used treatments is ivermectin orally. A dose is given and then is repeated in 14 days. It is recommended not to exceed 4 bi-monthly treatments. Orally, the rate of 0.15mg per pound of weight is most commonly used and that same dosage can be used once monthly as maintenance against mange and as a heartworm preventative. With a calculator handy, this method allows for people to conveniently use the cattle injectable (10mg/mL) without needing to give a shot.

example dosage: Injectable given orally. 0.15mg/lb X 45lb dog = 6.75mg dose   Divide 6.7mg by 10mg/mL = 0.67 cc squirted into mouth

Small doses can also be injected under the skin daily for 7 days, then once weekly for a month or until there is significant regrowth of hair. Dogs can also be maintained on this dose once monthly as a demodex flare up and heartworm preventative. The common sub-cutaneous injection dosage of 0.1cc per 10lbs of body weight is easy to remember and allows some flexibility if an exact weight is not known.

example dosage: Injectable given sub-cutaneously. 0.1cc X 45lb dog = 0.45 cc

Ivermectin should not be given to some dogs due to possible allergic reactions. Border collies and other herding breeds in particular are highly allergic to ivermectin; a relatively low dose for another dog may be too much for collies and crosses and will cause severe side-effects such as lethargy, dehydration and even death. Many people use ivermectin based horse paste to worm monthly, however it is not an effective treatment for demodectic mange. The amount of ivermectrin from dose to dose can have tremendous variance due to all the fillers added to make the paste.

Dectomax: Fairly new to the off label treatment of demodex is injectable doramectin, trade named Dectomax. It is also an injectable cattle wormer, but is a newer drug and is highly effective against parasites that have become ivermectin resistant. It is to be injected under the skin once a week at the dose of 1 cc per 33lbs until there is significant hair regrowth, even if that is an extended period of time. This is quickly becoming some vet's first line of treatment in severe cases since long term use is proving to be safe. After hair has returned, the dog can then be maintained on a once a month dose. There are no significant studies at this time about the use of Decotomax for heartworm prevention, however it is believed useful. As with ivermectin, the use of doramectin in certain breeds is cautioned against because few studies have been conducted about allergic reactions in those breeds.

example dosage: Injectable Dectomax given sub-cutaneously at rate of 1 cc per 33lbs of body weight. 45lb dog / 33lb= 1.36 cc injection

How these treatments work: Once the drug is administered, it enters the bloodstream where the mites in the dog's skin come into contact with it. From that point on the drug does two things: First, it disables the nervous systems of the mites, effectively paralysing them. Then, it manipulates the dog's white blood cells into attacking the mites and killing them. In this way, the mites will no longer cause further skin damage. So long as the drug remains in the body, the mange will be kept under control. Often, shortly after a treatment, there is a sudden red rash caused by a massive die off of mites. With subsequent treatments this will become less noticeable since there are fewer mites.

Neither Ivomec or Dectomax affect unhatched demodex mites. That is why multiple treatments and maintanence treatments are required to eradicate the mites from the body.

Secondary skin infections should be treated with antibiotics to prevent other health issues. Most commonly recommended is cephalexin, however penicillins can be used as well. Demodex isn't extremely itchy, unlike sarcoptic mange, but it is also recommended to bathe dogs frequently and eliminate as much dry and flaky skin as possible during treatment. Topical sprays and creams containing hydrocortisone can be used to alleviate any discomfort from the infected skin. However, corticosteroids used internally, such as predisone, depo-medrol and dexamethasone that are often used to combat severe itching, will lower the dog's immunity to the mites and should not be used in treating demodex.

Because of an inherited immune susceptibility, it is not a good idea to breed dogs who recover from generalized demodectic mange. It is important to try to strengthen the immune system of the affected dog with good food, vitamins and probiotics during and after treatment. Hunting dogs are generally immunologically strong because they are often well fed and fit from the workouts they receive. It is important to remember the stress of new dogs, kenneling, traveling and hard work with little recovery time can lower immunity in an other wise healthy animal. The healthier a dog is, the better he can resist the effects of demodex mites.

Ed Barnes and Jarrett Martin

CHAPTER 35
FALSE PREGNANCY ⋆ BY MONICA WHEELUS
Originally appeared in the August 2017 issue of Tuskers Magazine

False pregnancy, or a pseudo-pregnancy, is a term used for a common condition in a non-pregnant female dog that is showing symptoms of pregnancy and lactation, without producing puppies. The female shows these symptoms about a month or two after her heat is over and a hormonal imbalance is thought to play a significant role. Depending on the severity of problem, the symptoms may last for more than a month.

Symptoms

-Behavioral changes
-Non-pregnant female dog may show symptoms of mothering activity,such as nesting and restlessness
-Abdominal distention
-Enlargement of mammary glands
-Vomiting
-Depression
-Loss of appetite
-Brownish watery or milky fluids from the teats
-Panting and other signs of labor

The exact cause for this condition is unknown. However, hormonal imbalances, especially of progesterone and prolactin, are thought to play a key role in its development. If a progesterone test is performed to time breed or AI, an imbalance may cause the optimal time to be missed. A non-ovulating female that was covered by a male can also exhibit pregnancy signs without carrying pups. There are varying thoughts on why this happens. Many think it is a hormone imbalance causing the bitch to stand too early or too late in her cycle and the

233

optimal time is missed like in a timed breeding.

Some female dogs have been found to show such abnormal symptoms within three to four days after being spayed. Many females will have false pregnancy symptoms at some time in their lives, but they are too subtle to be noticed.

You will need to give a detailed history of your dog's health, pregnancies, possible exposure to any males and the onset and nature of the current symptoms for a diagnosis. A veterinarian can perform a thorough physical exam to evaluate the overall health of your dog. Routine blood tests may include a complete blood count, biochemistry profile and urinalysis to rule out underlying disease. Diagnostic imaging such as abdominal X-rays and ultrasound is used to rule out infection of the uterus or normal pregnancy.

Unless symptoms persist, or new ones begin (foul discharge, mastitis, prolonged lack of appetite or lethargy), treatment is typically unnecessary. Otherwise, your veterinarian may recommend hormonal supplementation or spaying to prevent further episodes.

To reduce mammary gland secretions, your veterinarian will advise you on using cold or warm packs to minimize the stimulation that promotes lactation. In some patients, reducing the daily food intake can help to reduce the production of milk.

For those owners who are not planning to breed their dog, or do not want their female dogs to reproduce in the future, spaying is recommended for preventing future episodes. If an owner plans on future breedings, a change in diet and hormone therapy can essentially reset the female's natural hormones preventing future episodes. Some believe breeding on the next heat will do the same. The overall prognosis is good and most dogs improve within two to three weeks of the onset of symptoms, even without treatment.

CHAPTER 36
CANINE DISTEMPER ⋆ BY MONICA WHEELUS
Originally appeared in the August 2015 issue of Tuskers Magazine

Canine Distemper is making a comeback. According to veterinarians 2015 has seen a resurgence of the canine distemper virus, a disease that many thought was long gone. Vaccination against distemper is just as important as it ever was. Unvaccinated dogs are at risk of infection from, as well as posing a risk of infection to, raccoons and other wildlife. This means that hunting dogs are at a higher risk than your average pet.

The canine distemper virus in a dog can affect a wide range of organs including the skin, brain, eyes, intestinal and respiratory tracts. The virus can be transmitted through the air, usually through coughing by infected animals and also through body secretions such as urine and blood. Dogs of any age can be affected, however, most are puppies less than 6 months of age.

The most common signs of distemper are nasal and eye discharge, coughing, diarrhea, vomiting, fever that may come and go, and seizures. Mildly affected dogs may only cough and be misdiagnosed as having "kennel cough." Others may develop pneumonia. Puppies that recover may have severe tooth enamel damage. The nose and footpads of the young dog may become thickened, hence the nickname "hardpad disease."

Distemper is serious and can spread rapidly through a kennel, especially if unvaccinated individuals are present. Not all patients will die, however, a significant number may. Dogs of every age are susceptible, however, the very young and old have the highest death rate. Death rates may be as high as 75%. It is erroneously believed by some that all older dogs have a natural immunity. Although some may have immunity, many do not. Patients that recover from distemper may suffer permanent damage to vision as well as the nervous system. Puppies which recover often have tell tale mottled teeth due to abnormalities in the developing enamel caused by high fever.

There are several methods used to diagnose distemper in dogs and puppies. A laboratory test (called a polymerase chain reaction test) can be performed on samples of urine, cerebrospinal fluid, blood, and post mortem tissues. Skin biopsies, including the pads, can be specially examined for the presence of portions of the canine distemper virus. Depending upon the severity and time of infection, blood examined microscopically may show characteristic changes called "canine distemper inclusion bodies". With some diagnostic tests, such as antibody tests, it is difficult, if not impossible, to distinguish between infection and the changes normally seen with the canine distemper vaccination.

There is no specific treatment for canine distemper. Therapy is largely supportive. I.V. fluids are administered to prevent dehydration. Anti-seizure medications can be used if neurologic signs develop along with medications to stop vomiting and diarrhea. Unfortunately, it is simply a matter of "wait and see" if the dog survives.

Effective vaccines have been developed to prevent canine distemper in dogs. They have been widely used for many years and have made significant strides in reducing the frequency of this disease. These vaccines have minimal side effects and are available to give to puppies and dogs of every age. It must be emphasized that many older dogs will not develop a life long immunity to distemper. The vaccinations should be boostered for the life of the animal. Animals diagnosed with, or suspected of having, canine distemper should be quarantined from all other dogs until healthy and the other dogs should have vaccine boostered to prevent infection.

CHAPTER 37
LEPTOSPIROSIS * BY MONICA WHEELUS
Originally appeared in the August 2014 issue of Tuskers Magazine

Many people have heard of leptospirosis (lepto), but aren't really sure what exactly it is. Lepto is a widespread disease affecting many species of animals besides dogs. It is just one of a group of spiral shaped bacterium known as spirochetes. Most spirochetes are harmless, however there are a select few that have evolved and become problematic. Those include the bacteria that cause leptospirosis and lyme disease, both of which are zoonotic and can be spread to humans.

Lepto is a continuous threat for hunting dogs, because it is carried in rats, wildlife, and livestock. Veterinarians see more cases in the summer and fall, likely because that is when domestic animals come into contact most often with wildlife. Cases also increase after heavy rainfalls and in mild or tropical climates. That is why lepto is common in the southern region of the United States. Winter conditions in the north lower incidents since leptospira cannot tolerate the freezing and thawing of near-zero temperatures. Leptospirosis persists in standing water, dampness, muddy and alkaline conditions, but dies off during times of drought.

Most infected animals that spread leptospirosis do not appear ill. These carriers host the leptospira bacteria in their kidneys. The type of infected animals vary from area to area. In most places the most common culprits are raccoons, skunks or rats. When the animals urinate, they contaminate their environment with living leptospira. These carrier wildlife shed the bacteria intermittently. Sometimes they will shed for months and sometimes for the duration of their life.

Each species of wildlife have strains of leptospira bacteria that are not harmful to its host. We call these their "primary reservoirs hosts". Early in infection, these leptospira are found throughout the carrier animal's body. This includes their liver, spleen, kidneys, eyes and genital tract. As the animal produces antibodies, these spirochetes are cleared from most organs. However, within the kidneys of carrier species, they are hidden from the animal's antibodies and continue to live in the microscopic tubes that carry urine out to the bladder. These leptospira and their host animals have learned to live together. However, when these leptospira find their way into a new animal, such as your dog, the harmonious relationship does not occur.

Dogs can become infected by sniffing infected urine, however more often the leptospira are washed by rainfall into standing water. Dogs then develop the disease after wading, swimming or drinking the contaminated water. Although this is the way it is usually passed from animal to animal, it is also possible for contamination to enter through a bite wound or through the dog eating infected materials. Because of this working dogs that spend time in wooded or swampy areas are more likely to catch leptospirosis.

Not all dogs that are exposed to leptospirosis become visibly ill. In a 2007 study, 25% of the unvaccinated healthy adult dogs examined had antibody to leptospirosis which indicates that they had been previously exposed to without their owners noticing a problem. Although there are many causes, kidney damage can be one major outcome of leptospirosis. Chronic kidney inflammation is a leading cause of kidney failure and death in dogs.

When leptospirosis does cause sudden disease in dogs, it tends to be most severe in unvaccinated dogs that are younger than 6 months old. These are the most likely to suffer life-threatening liver and kidney damage. It takes about 4-12 days after exposure for the signs of illness to occur.

In dogs of any age the leptospira spread rapidly through the bloodstream, usually exhibiting high fever, depression and joint pain. The disease produces powerful toxins that attack the liver and kidneys, often leading to failure of these organs first. Strains of lepto vary in their intensity and in the portions of the body they attack most severely. Some varieties primarily cause liver damage, while others concentrate in the kidneys. In other dogs, blood fails to clot normally leading to persistent bleeding.

There are typical symptoms that veterinarians associate with leptospirosis, but since no two cases proceed exactly alike, not all of the typical signs are likely to be present in every animal. The most common signs are fever and depression. Fever can cause many dogs to drink excessively. Some dogs become shivery and stiff. They may carry their tummies tucked up as a result of pain. Some drool, vomit and most lose their appetite. Later in the disease, a few dogs will develop eye inflammations, nervous system abnormalities or pass red-tinged urine. As the disease progresses, they may become dehydrated due to the fever, vomiting and growing disinterest in drinking. A drop to a subnormal body temperature is common. When the liver has been damaged, the pet's skin may take on a yellowish tinge and show all the symptoms of hepatitis. When the kidneys have been severely damaged, the pet may show the signs of uremia. (high levels of urea and amino acids in bloodstream) These organ changes can be temporary or permanent. A few dogs, particularly juveniles, will die suddenly before any of these signs occur.

The symptoms discussed above, along with a history of your dog being exposed to places where leptospirosis might occur, could make your vet suspect lepto. Leptospirosis sometimes occurs in outbreaks, and your veterinarian may be aware if it is presently occurring in your community. However, because symptoms vary so much between dogs and because most veterinarians only see a few cases from time to time, it is common to miss the diagnosis on the first examination.

To confirm the diagnosis, or rule it out, your veterinarian can order blood tests. One of the typical signs found is an elevation in the number of white blood cells. However, very early in infection, white blood cell numbers can actually be lower than normal. There are often other chemical abnormalities that suggest leptospirosis, such as changes in liver enzymes, blood-clotting cells and kidney values. Damage to the kidney's would also be reflected in abnormal urine analysis results.

There are a large number of diseases that can give test results identical to that seen in cases of leptospirosis. These include ehrlichiosis (tick fever), canine brucellosis and certain poisonings. Because of this, your veterinarian may place your dog on antibiotics while another test is run. This would be the leptospirosis PCR test where both blood and urine are submitted. This test is extremely sensitive in finding the presence of leptospira and the results can be obtained rapidly. After the first ten days of infection, antibodies against leptospirosis can be detected in blood. However, antibody detection is not as valuable as a positive PCR test. The antibody test can be positive in dogs due to previous vaccinations or a prior exposure to lepto that has nothing to do with the current health problem. Occasionally the diagnosis can be made by seeing leptospira microscopically in the dog's urine.

The treatment of leptospirosis is much easier than the diagnosis. Fortunately, many common antibiotics will kill leptospira. Antibiotic resistance is not a problem so an extended regimen of ordinary penicillin and tetracycline work well. Doxycycline is probably the best since it seems most effective in preventing dogs from becoming silent carriers of the disease in their kidneys after recovery.

Control in the home environment can be achieved since lepto is very dependent on water, mud or damp clay soils to survive. It dies almost immediately on dry surfaces, even if those surfaces could be contaminated with urine from other infected animals. All common household disinfectants kill lepto quickly; as does boiling articles for 5 minutes and the liberal use of detergent. (bleaches, alcohol based products, vinegar, lemon juice etc. Porous items need to be completely submersed in solutions) Standing water can be disinfected using swimming pool chlorine tablets, with the understanding it can harm aquatic life. Common industrial chemicals are so toxic to leptospira that obviously polluted effluent water is not as much of a threat as are lakes and streams with water that appears pristine.

CHAPTER 38
TICK TALK⋆ BY MONICA WHEELUS
Originally appeared in the April 2016 issue of Tuskers Magazine

Tick season is here for most of us and I just wanted to hit the basics of tick-borne diseases for everyone hitting the woods and treating the kennels this spring.

Anaplasmosis:

• There are two variations, granulocytic anaplasmosis and infectious cyclic thrombocytopenia.
• A dog can have both infections at the same time. Granulocytic anaplasmosis is more common.
• A tick needs to be attached for a minimum of 24 hours to transmit the organism. Incubation time is 1 to 2 weeks.
• Reservoir hosts, carriers of infection and sources of possible reinfection, are usually small rodents, deer, etc.

Diagnosis

• Blood tests and a urinalysis are the main diagnostic tools for anaplasmosis. Many vets use SNAP 4DX tests that will detect heartworms, anaplasmosis, lyme disease and ehrlichia.
• If the dog is lame, x-rays are recommended to rule out injury or other physical sources for pain.

Treatment

• Treatment includes antibiotics, pain and anti-inflammatory drugs.
• Doxycycline is the most commonly used antibiotic. Most dogs respond within one to two days after they first take doxycycline.

Other antibiotic options are tetracycline or minocycline.
• Pain/anti-inflammatory drugs may be needed for joint pain. Your veterinarian will have the most appropriate medication because most human pain relievers can cause unrepairable damage to kidneys and liver, not to mention death.

Ehrlichia: There are three phases of illness with Ehrlichiosis: acute, subclinical, and chronic.

• **ACUTE PHASE:** This is generally a mild phase and occurs 1 to 3 weeks after being bitten by the tick. The Ehrlichia organism multiplies in this time period and attaches to white blood cells. During this time the platelet count will drop and platelet destruction will occur. The dog will be listless, off food, and may have enlarged lymph nodes. There may be fever as well but rarely does this phase kill a dog. Most dogs clear the organism if they are treated in this stage but those that do not receive adequate treatment will go on to the next phase.
• **SUBCLINICAL PHASE:** In this phase, the dog appears normal. The organism has settled in the spleen and is essentially hiding out.
• **CHRONIC PHASE:** In this phase the dog gets sick again. Many of dogs infected with Ehrlichia canis will have abnormal bleeding due to reduced platelet numbers. A deep inflammation in the eyes called uveitis may be present. Neurologic effects may also be seen.
• Infections with Ehrlichia lewinii tend to produce arthritis in addition to the above scenario.

Diagnosis

• A dog with fever, enlarged lymph nodes, bleeding, or arthritis in multiple joints.
• Low platelet numbers, high globulin levels, and mild anemia on blood testing.
• A positive blood test indicates that the dog has been exposed to Ehrlichia and does not imply active current infection necessarily. A negative titer does not fully rule out Ehrlichia, either, as a very sick patient will be too sick to produce antibodies and an early

case may not yet have started to produce antibodies.

Treatment

• Despite being one of the oldest antibiotics in use, tetracycline is probably the most effective against Ehrlichia. Doxycycline and minocycline have a more convenient dosing schedule and has become more popular. Expect at least a month of treatment to be needed even though improvement can begin in the first few days.

• If immune-mediated arthritis is suspected, corticosteroids such as prednisone can be used to help with inflammation and give antibiotics time to work.

• After infection, it is possible to become re-infected; immunity is not long lasting after a previous infection.

Rocky Mountain Spotted Fever:

• An infected tick has to feed on an animal for 5 to 20 hours before the organism activates and becomes infective to a susceptible animal. Transmission of the Rickettsia rickettsi can then occur due to the bite or from exposure to the parasite while handling the tick.

• Clinical signs will show up 2 to 14 days after the bite occurred. The parasite creates an inflammation of the body's small blood vessels, which results in damage to all the organs of the body.

• Common signs include fever, lethargy, inappetence, pain, eye/nose discharge, nosebleed, cough, enlarged lymph nodes, lameness, skin necrosis/sloughing, hemorrhage, and peripheral swelling.

• Up to one third of the infected dogs will have central nervous system signs (lack of voluntary coordination of muscle movements, weakness, balance problems, cranial nerve abnormalities, seizures, stupor, spinal pain, etc.). Any organ in the body may be affected and the clinical signs may be mild or severe enough to result in death.

Diagnosis

• Diagnostic tests for RMSF include blood tests looking for severely low platelet count, plus coagulation profiles, blood chemical analysis, and serology.

• Response to antibiotic therapy is suggestive, but not diagnostic. North Carolina State University is the primary testing and research facility in the United States.

Treatment/Management

• Specific treatment relies on the use of appropriate antibiotics. Response to the antibiotics usually is seen within 24 to 48 hours, although advanced cases may not respond at all to treatment.

• The most common antibiotics used are tetracycline, doxycycline, and minocycline. Chloramphenicol is usually reserved for pregnant females or young puppies. Other antibiotics such as enrofloxacin (Baytril) have shown good results, but their use is recommended for older animals. Side effects to any of the antibiotics may be seen.

Disease Prevention

Be aware of your dog's exposure, especially from March through October. Inspect your dogs closely. Appropriate tick control is critical to preventing disease, treat kennels. Preventing ticks from attaching and removing any ticks from your dog within a few hours of attachment is crucial. Wear gloves when removing ticks, as the infection can get into your body through abrasions, cuts, etc.

CHAPTER 39
TOPICAL TOXINS * BY MONICA WHEELUS
Originally appeared in the April 2015 issue of Tuskers Magazine

It is Spring and with the recent rains across the country, that means standing water and mud for dogs to trample through while on the hunt. Aside from the general mess this makes of vests, collars and dog boxes, there are other reasons to be wary of muddy dogs; topical toxins such as chemicals and stinging nettles.

Farmers will be busy preparing for the coming seasons and that means the fields are once again being sprayed with fertilizers, pesticides and herbicides that can run off and collect in standing water. That's not to mention farm equipment that may be leaking fluids. All sorts of chemicals can cause skin irritation and burns when they contact a dog's skin. They can even affect the mouth if he licks the substance. If enough of the toxin is ingested, a dog can be poisoned and his internal organs can begin to shut down.

Any substance coating the dog's fur must be quickly identified, if possible. Some substances, such as paint or motor oil, are obvious in appearance but others must be recognized by odor or checking the area where the dog has been hunting. Look for an iridescent sheen on standing water that the dog may have crossed. Also, look for areas where the vegetation has changed color due to residues such as powders, dyes and defoliants. A wet dog can run through dry chemical and essentially reactivate the effects.

If possible, identify the type of the chemical as quickly as possible and find out what possible side effects it may have. If the exact chemical can't be identified, here are a few treatment guidelines.

Motor oil, petroleum products, tar, paint or anything

with an oily appearance:

Wear rubber gloves to protect your hands. Rub large amounts of mineral or vegetable oil into the contaminated area to loosen the substance. If a small area is affected -- a paw, for example -- apply mineral or vegetable oil and rub with a stiff brush to remove the substance. A dish brush works well. This process can be repeated as many times as necessary to loosen and remove the contaminant. If the substance has already hardened, it is better to clip, cut or shave the hair away instead.

Once the substance is loosened, use lots of warm, soapy water to bathe the area. Degreasing dish-washing liquids are ideal, as they are usually gentle and do not further irritate the skin. Another option is mechanic's non-irritating hand cleanser can be used, such as Go-Jo.

Rinse the area thoroughly and repeat the process until the contaminant is completely removed. If an area is heavily contaminated, you can mix flour or powdered starch with the oil to help absorb some of the poison. This mixture should be brushed out with a comb or stiff brush before bathing the area with warm, soapy water as above.

NEVER use other chemicals to remove the substance. This includes but is not limited to paint stripper and thinner, paint brush cleaners, turpentine (and its substitutes), mineral spirits, and concentrated biological detergents.

Check the skin for burns and open sores. Topical hot spot sprays, hydrocortizone, aloe vera and antibiotic ointments work well to speed up the healing process. If the dog has been licking at the affected areas, immediately flush the mouth out with water using a hose or spray nozzle.

Do NOT point the nozzle towards the throat. Instead, rinse from the side of the mouth. If the dog may have ingested the chemical take it to a veterinarian who can treat with activated charcoal.

It is recommended to never induce vomiting when chemical poisoning is suspected.

Stinging nettles

Check for signs of shock and allergic reactions. Do not underestimate stinging nettles: dogs can die from them if they are badly stung.

Give the dog an antihistamine orally. Benadryl, or the generic forms, are always good to keep in your cut bag. The dose is easy to remember, 1mg per lb, with most hunting dogs taking 2-3 of the 25mg capsules every 6-8 hours. Once again, wash the affected areas with mild soapy water, but make sure it isn't too warm. Warm water intensifies the stinging and spreads the toxin. Keep the dog active and alert. If the dog shows signs of shock, seizures or is in extreme pain, see the vet immediately.

Don't forget to thoroughly wash the vests, collars and anything else that may have been contaminated. It is a good idea to pressure wash, or take to car wash, everything. If that isn't possible, mix a bucket full of soapy water and scrub the gear. Don't forget to rinse until the water is clear.

CHAPTER 40
PSEUDORABIES * SUID HERPESVIRUS * BY MONICA WHEELUS
originally appeared in the August 2016 issue of Tuskers Magazine

Symptoms of Pseudorabies in Dogs:

Dogs can be hosts for Aujesky's disease, but will survive, at most, two to three days after infection. A dog that has been infected with the pseudorabies virus will show the following signs:

-Fever
-Respiratory distress
-Seizures
-Intense itching ('Mad Itch')
-Neurological signs like odd behavior, circling, charging blindly and paralysis
-Sensitivity of the skin
-Sudden death

The signs in dogs CAN mimic the rabies virus, so vaccinate and have proof.

Causes of Pseudorabies in Dogs:

Transmission of this virus from swine to canines was considered rare due to efforts to eradicate the disease, however that may no longer be the case. Increasing numbers of hog dogs are being reported lost to possible infection and not just from being in the woods. They are being infected in bay and training pens as well because no one thinks to test the hogs. It just doesn't cross folks minds, pen owners or dog owners.

Pseudorabies is most often transmitted from nose to nose contact, essentially because the virus is very evident in nasal secretions. Contaminated drinking water and feed buckets will contribute to the spread in swine and is seen after only two to five days after infection. People can carry the virus on their footwear, skin, or clothing after contact with pigs. In the right conditions, the virus can survive for a few days in the grass, soil, feed and feces. It is an aerosolized virus meaning it can be passed through droplets in the air that can persist up to seven hours. Inhalation of the virus is possible form of infection.

Diagnosis in Dogs:

If your dog is exhibiting signs for pseudorabies, immediate veterinary care is essential. Though there is no cure, you do not want to see unnecessary suffering. Be as proactive as you can in relaying important information to the vet, such as past medical history, illnesses, and for certain, let the veterinarian know if your dog has been in contact with pigs or whether you have visited a holding facility recently. The veterinarian will consider other illnesses similar to pseudorabies. These could be a reaction to a drug, toxicity to a substance, canine distemper encephalitis, or rabies. A blood test to look for antibodies against the virus could be done, as well as tests to identify the virus in the tissues, such as nasal or tonsils. However, some studies show that dogs will succumb to the virus before antibodies are evident. Therefore, these diagnostic tools may be able to give a positive diagnosis, but this is not for certain.

CHAPTER 41
WATER ⋆ BY MONICA WHEELUS
Originally appeared in the April 2017 issue of Tuskers Magazine

Being an observant dog hunter, you are used to your dog panting and salivating when he has been running, or is excited. As that saliva evaporates, it cools his body temperature, but all the water must be replaced. So how do you know how much water you should give your dog? It depends on several factors. Here's what you need to know to keep him well hydrated:

Like humans, water makes up most of your dog's body. (About 60% for an adult dog and more for a puppy.) Water keeps organs healthy and helps the kidneys flush toxins from the blood. Water also promotes a healthy cardiovascular system, keeping electrolytes in balance. So, most dogs need a good amount of water every day. When dogs become dehydrated, they can quickly die. Dehydration occurs in certain illnesses, such as kidney failure, bladder infections, vomiting and diarrhea. (The latter most often in cases of giardia, coccidia, leptospirosis, parvo and poisoning) In hot weather, a dog can die within hours if he doesn't drink.

How Much Water Does Your Dog Need?

Here are the various factors you may consider:

Dog Size - If given ample amounts of fresh water, your dog will quench his thirst when he's thirsty. But one guide to go by is size. Per some experts, a dog should drink about one ounce of water per pound of body weight each day when resting. So, if your dog weighs in at 50 pounds, your dog should drink 50 ounces. That comes out to a little over six eight-ounce cups of water per day.

Amount and Type of Food Consumed -If your dog eats wet food, he'll generally require less water. But if he eats dry food, he needs more water. How much? Here's one general rule: Your dog should drink 2.5 times the amount of dry food he eats. If your dog eats two pounds of dry food, he should drink five pounds of water or more than half a gallon daily.

Nursing Dogs - During lactation, your dog often needs three to four times the amount of water she normally drinks to provide enough milk to her pups and keep up with her own water requirements.

Hot Weather - In the summer or a hot climate, your dog needs three to four times the amount he would normally drink. Don't forget about the water bowl in the kennel. Make sure it won't tip or spill by attaching it to a solid structure or secure it to the ground. Wash the bowl and fill it regularly—and keep it out of the sun.

Cold Weather - If your dog stays outside in the winter, make sure to provide him with thawed water and not just ice. The importance of water in the winter is often overlooked, but it is needed to help the body break down stored up energy to keep your dog warm.

Exercise and Working - Studies show that dogs perform better when given water while active because they utilize glucose more efficiently. This makes them better able to process energy reserves and build stamina. Drinking also prevents overheating. So before, after, and during a hunt, offer your dog a drink when you can.

Here are some ways to tell if your dog is drinking enough:

You observe your dog drinking several times a day from his water bowl.

The water level goes down in the bowl over the day. If you're aware of a sudden decrease or increase in water consumption, your dog may be ill. (Excessive thirst and urinating large amounts may indicate diabetes, kidney failure or other illnesses or diseases.)

Dogs as you know, especially males, love to pee. Although all dogs are different, your dog is probably drinking enough if he urinates several times a day. You'll notice your dog urinates around the same amount on most days. If you notice a significant change in amount and color, you might want to consult veterinarian to determine why. It could be anything from a urinary or kidney infection to reaction to a toxin.

Your dog is active and doesn't seem lethargic or ill after exercise or in warm temperatures. His hair is shiny and there isn't a lot of dryness or flakiness. His skin doesn't stay tented when pinched and stretched over the shoulder blades.

Bad Sources of Water

You know dogs. If your dog is thirsty while out hunting, he'll find water one way or another. Here are some of the less desirable sources your dog may choose if there isn't a better alternative:

Dirty puddles - These often collect runoff of chemicals

Lakes, ponds or streams - As clean as it might look, this water can harbor many harmful parasites. One of them is called Giardia which can cause severe illness.

Communal bowl - Bowls of warm stagnant water used by all the dogs on your last trip can carry viruses and bacteria that may be harmful to their health. Always carry a fresh source of water and clean bowl for your dogs when you are on the hunt.

Good Sources of Water

It's not difficult to supply your dogs with good water. Here are some tips:

Fresh, clean water every day. You must clean the bowl, as you would any dish and replace water at least once a day. Especially if you house more than one dog together. It's not enough to add fresh water to the bowl; you must rinse the bowl of food bits, hair, dust and other matter that collects daily in the water.Also, refill if the water level gets too low. Use stainless steel bowls, stoneware, and high quality plastic dishes. They resist scratches that can encourage bacteria growth, and are easy to clean. When a bowl starts to look worn and scratched, replace it.

Wash out and allow the bottles, jugs and tanks that you use on hunts to dry between trips. Occasional bleaching, rinsing and drying is helpful to stop bacterial and fungal growth.

Most of us carry an ice chest with ice. Give them a handful and let them lick it as it melts when they are hot. It keeps them from drinking too much too fast and getting an upset stomach, but it cools them down at an acceptable rate. This also aids in preventing water intoxication that can result in death.

If you would have to think twice about drinking it, don't let your dog drink it. I am not saying to drink after your dog, but unless you have strep, he can drink after you. We all know it is impossible to keep a hot dog from drinking out of cow troughs, creeks and stock tanks. If given a choice, most dogs will drink from a clean, cool source over a green, slimy and warm puddle.

CHAPTER 42
TOP INJURIES IN THE FIELD * BY MONICA WHEELUS
Originally appeared in the June 2018 issue of Tuskers Magazine

Take your dog into the woods enough, and eventually he is going to get injured. Dogs can't care for themselves beyond a quick lick of a wound, so you need to be prepared to manage injuries and emergencies in the field.

Prevention and preparedness should be your goal, know what's 'normal' for your dog, all his lumps, bumps and quirks. Always be sure that you dog has identification. A name plate with the right phone number and name on a sturdy collar, a tattoo, a brand and/or a microchip. There are more and more stories of dogs being joined at a bay by coyotes or getting attacked while trailing a hog. A current rabies vaccine is essential for your dog's safety, your safety, and the safety of anyone that might find your dog.

If you think something is wrong with your dog, but you're not sure what it is, do a quick nose to tail examination; you can diagnose most problems if you take the time to look.

I've compiled 10 of the most common injuries and how to treat them in the woods. Remember, if your dog is in serious pain or what you need to do to treat him is going to hurt, make some kind of muzzle. Even the best dog can bite when injured.

PORCUPINE QUILLS/CACTUS THORNS in face:

Grasp as close to your dog's skin as you can with a pair of pliers and pull. Do not wiggle or rock a quill or any other foreign body you are attempting to remove from your dog. Place your fingers around the base and hold the skin tight for leverage. Look for quills on the roof of your dog's mouth, as well as under the tongue and around the teeth. Brace your dog's mouth in such a way that he can't bite. If your dog does not have quills in its mouth, muzzle him with a piece of webbing or a lead. (A piece of broomstick with mule tape attached to the ends tied in your dog's mouth crossways is a handy tool) Dogs in pain will often bite, even someone they know well. Clean the spots where you've removed quills with alcohol or iodine. If the dog is in excessive discomfort, administer a pain medication prescribed by or previously discussed with your vet.

CUT PAD OR FOREIGN OBJECT IN FOOT:

Remove a thorn, piece of glass or other foreign object in the foot swiftly and firmly. Clean the wound with antiseptic and apply antibiotic salve, then bandage the foot if you deem necessary. Because dogs don't have thumbs, it can be hard to get a bandage to stay on. Push up on the bottom of the foot and wrap with a gauzy bandage from the joint above the ankle down to the pad and then back up the leg. If you wrap too tight, you'll cut off circulation and your dog's foot will swell. Apply a white tape wrap loose over the bandages for extra durability. "Vet Wrap" is also good choice, but will tighten down if you are not careful, especially if it gets wet.

BLEEDING OR BADLY BROKEN NAIL:

Apply a styptic pencil on the wound to stop bleeding. Use pliers to pull off a nail that is hanging. Grasp the end of the nail, being careful not to grasp the soft quick that is the inside of a dog nail, and pull straight, swiftly and firmly. A light bandage may be needed if the bleeding can't be stopped quickly.

WATERBORNE DISEASE:

Though they drink out of puddles all the time, if one contains the same "nasties" that make humans sick, like giardia, coccidia or cryptosporidium, it can cause diarrhea and/or vomiting in dogs. Keep your dog as hydrated as possible. Add electrolyte solutions, like Pedialyte, to your dog's water and add white rice to your dog's food if your dog starts to show symptoms. Blue-green algae, which often looks like foam, scum or clumps of red, green, or brown algae that smells musty or foul can cause a skin rash. Rinse your dog and equipment if it swims in this and if he or she shows signs of sickness, seek veterinary care. Algae can be toxic to dogs' kidneys, liver, intestines, and nervous system.

FOREIGN OBJECT IN THE EYE OR EAR:

If your dog is blinking excessively or rubbing its eyes or ears with its paws, it may have something lodged that it needs help removing. If the object is superficial, on the surface of the eye but not inside the cornea, or in the outer ear where you can see it, remove the intruder with forceps or tweezers. Be careful not to cause any additional damage. Flush the eye with saline solution. If you do not see anything in your dog's ear, don't dig around. It may have an infection and need antibiotics. Do not remove foreign objects buried deep in your pet's eye, get your dog to a vet.

BARBED WIRE OR OTHER SERIOUS CUT:

Attempt to control bleeding with pressure, clean the wound with antiseptic and antibiotic ointment, and wrap the wound with a bandage or by gluing or stapling it shut. If your dog is in danger of excessive blood loss, tie a tourniquet an inch above the wound with a ripped off section of a t-shirt, an ace bandage or whatever else you have on hand. Insert a small stick, pen or other straight, narrow object in the fabric loop and twist tight. Wrap the stick to the leg with tape or bandage. Loosen the tourniquet every 15 minutes for one to two minutes to allow blood circulation to the limb. Get the dog to somewhere that it can be sutured as quickly as possible.

PENETRATING INJURY:

Do remove an object you are certain is close to the surface by pulling it out the way it went it. But don't ever pull out a stick that's protruding from deep inside your dog's chest, abdomen or anywhere else. Removal can cause more damage than entry. If a stick is buried in your dog, hold the stick firmly, saw it off so that it doesn't cause more damage, keep your dog as quiet and calm as possible and get to a vet.

FALLING TRAUMA (BREAKS, SPRAINS):

Bind sprains with a figure-eight pattern with an ace bandage, but not so tight that your dog's paw gets cold or swollen. Stabilize obvious fractures with a splint or stick and get your dog to a vet while keeping it as quiet and calm as possible. Broken limbs swell. Sprains don't, and they're generally not tender to the touch.

HEAT EXHAUSTION/OVEREXERTION:

Treat as you would an over-exerted human, with rest, fluids, shade, and energy foods like molasses, which has long been used for hunting dogs. A soda can be also given to bring the blood sugar up and prevent shock.

ALLERGIC REACTIONS (RASHES, SWELLING, HOT SPOTS):

Administer Benadryl orally, around 2mg per pound every eight hours for allergic swelling. For localized reactions like rashes, wash affected area and apply hydrocortisone or steroid cream. The July 15, 2012, issue of the Journal of American Veterinary Medical Association provided new guidelines for dog CPR. If your dog is no longer breathing, and you cannot detect a pulse, perform mouth-to-snout ventilation, maintaining a ratio of 30 compressions to two breaths every two minutes. Be advised, CPR on dogs doesn't work as well as CPR on people. In a hospital scenario, about 20 percent of human patients respond to CPR, and about six percent of dogs respond.

CHAPTER 43
IMPACT INJURIES * BY MONICA WHEELUS
Originally appeared in the April 2014 issue of Tuskers Magazine

I grew up around hog dogs and have seen every kind of injury imaginable, some that even the best of vets couldn't have repaired. I know dog hunters generally take good care of their dogs and hate to lose one, but it happens. I am lucky to work for a vet who admits hog hunters can patch up almost anything with a well stocked cut kit. Through his years of practice, he has usually had someone working for him that understood hunting dogs, and their owners, are different than most of the clients that come in the front door. I am now the vet tech that crawls into dog boxes to give shots, asks few questions when we get a call saying that a hog dog is on the way in for an emergency and will carry that dog wrapped in a bloody jacket to a room. However, something often overlooked are injuries to dogs that suture and staples can't fix. With the development of cut-gear, and the constant improvements being made, dogs are hunting more frequently and longer than they ever used to. This is allowing other health issues to become more obvious. While those issues can be anything from arthritis to tick borne diseases, the one being seen more and more in the clinic where I work are spinal injuries.

From July 2013 to December 2013 our clinic saw several unrelated dogs, of various breeds, with similar symptoms;

Lack of energy
Lack of appetite
Difficulty standing or walking (buckling over)
Labored breathing
Showing signs of pain with an unknown source

After running basic blood work, and finding nothing significant, we took x-rays and found that all had signs of impact injuries with slipped/compressed/ruptured discs or a general narrowing of vertebral spacing. We treated all but one with a combination of muscle relaxers, anti-inflammatory pain relievers and IV steroids. Most of them reacted well to the treatment and were back hunting after a period of rest. We did make it clear to those owners that these dogs were on borrowed hunting time and eventually would not be able to go because of the damage already done. The two that didn't respond were in the worst condition when the treatment began and had irreparable nerve damage that led to the owners deciding on euthanasia.

After seeing so many in a short period of time, we wanted to find out what the connection was between all the injured dogs. With my vet's approval, I contacted all the owners and asked some questions about general health of the dogs before they started showing symptoms. There were two shared factors that stood out; what and how they were fed and the type of equipment used for protection.

I asked a retired veterinary radiologist, that specialized in working dogs, to look at the x-rays. After showing him the various styles of cut collars, and how they are supposed to fit a dog, it was his opinion that most of the neck injuries could be attributed to collars that didn't offer adequate support. If the collar was too soft, didn't fit snug enough, or was too long/too short, the neck would lose stability and vertebrae could be displaced. Looking at the x-rays of back injuries got more complicated. We looked at different types and brands of cut vests and discussed how a dog could suffer impact injuries to the body. Having a good idea of how hard a hog can hit a dog, we also considered a catch dog getting banged into trees. rocks and other solid objects. We were able to conclude, the better a vest fits the individual dog and the higher the quality of the vest, the better it distributed the force of an impact. That doesn't mean that good protective gear will prevent all spinal injuries, just that it can greatly lessen the severity.

However, the other thing noted was that all the dogs x-rayed were extremely tight muscled and thin. Most were being fed a predominantly raw diet and two were being fed a high protein dog food.

Six were only being fed every other day, a common practice in this area. Both vets agreed that the body condition of the dogs contributed to the severity of impact injuries, simply because there was not enough cushion to withstand the kind of force the dogs endured while catching larger hogs. In addition to the spinal injuries found on x-rays, there was also healed and fresh stress fractures where inadequate vitamins and minerals could have been a factor. Without advocating or endorsing any particular feeding regimen, it was just a general opinion of both vets that a well balanced diet, including fats, would be beneficial in preventing some types of injuries. As we all know, some dogs are naturally going to be thinner. However, like any type of athlete, a well muscled and well fed dog will have more stamina, better ability to heal and be able to endure more days of hunting.

The bottom line is, we all run risks of serious injury to our dogs when we hunt. Those type of injuries aren't always preventable, but we do what we can by using cut-vests and cut-collars. Any protective equipment is better than nothing, but it is always better to invest in something that will last. Pay attention to your dogs, if one is still not acting right after a couple days of rest, there might be something wrong that can't be seen on the outside. Keep in mind the symptoms I listed are just a short list of things we saw and can also point towards other ailments. Above all, you know your dogs and know what isn't normal behavior.

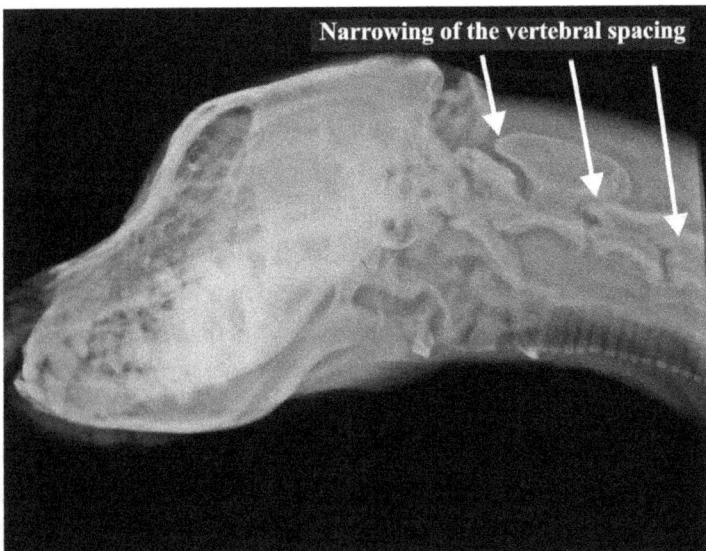

Narrowing of the vertebral spacing

CHAPTER 44

OLD TIME REMEDIES * BY ED BARNES AND MONICA WHEELUS

Originally appeared in the October 2015 issue of Tuskers Magazine

ED BARNES *

I cut my teeth hunting with dogs surrounded by old men. I guess I have an old soul and have always found that I prefer the company of old men over men my own age. I hunted with men in their 70's and 80's and I often found myself asking for advice from my great uncles that were in their 90's. Very often the advice of old men was at odds with what modern veterinarians told me. Being a reasonable man I would weigh the options but more times than not I sided with the old timers and for the most part the remedies they gave me worked. Often my vet would laugh, and tell me, "Try it, can't hurt, but it ain't gonna work!"

I started to see a pattern in the old cures and the new vet cures. I could see the science behind the old ways, it was more than backwoods dog witchcraft. The old cures stemmed from necessity, poor boys with poor ways, but the cures were not without merit.

What we are going to do here is I am going to give some of the old time cures for dog ailments and Monica is going to give the modern day remedies. I am only going to use the old remedies that I have personally used and seen used.

1. **Red mange.** I have gone around and around with red mange! There are a few old time remedies. The first, and the one most people know about is dipping the dog in used motor oil. Oil from a diesel truck works best. (Diesel works because of the sulphur, but with today's low sulpher fuel, it really isn't a viable remedy anymore.) You dip the whole dog in oil, it gets all over you, the

261

kennel, the dog house, it gets places on you that you didn't know you had. The dog looks pitiful, and about the time he starts looking better you dip him again! While some people would frown on this, it does work.

Another remedy involves polk sallet. You pick big ole polk plants, roots and all. After smashing them up best you can, you boil it all off into a soup and smash it some more to make a paste. The paste is applied over the entire dog, get it everywhere! Repeat every few days for a couple weeks. This works, but it is a lot of work. Now neither one of these are a "cure" as they just help keep the mange under control and the mange WILL pop back up next time the dog gets cut bad, or a dog next to him is in heat. Anything stressful seems to pop the mange back out. (Bitches with red mange should never be bred as it is hereditary, dogs should not be bred either.)

2. Ear mites, sore pads, bad cuts. This one always tickled me, not that it didn't work but these old men used turpentine to cure EVERYTHING! Like my grandma thought castor oil could cure a headache. When I was a kid you didn't make a fuss about anything or that castor oil was coming out of the cupboard. We've all run the pads darn near off a dog and then get that dog back out there in the woods and he just limps around and won't really get in the game because it hurts for him to walk. An old man I hunted with would carry turpentine in the truck and pour a little out in a dish or a cup we cut in half, you just hold that dog with all you got and dip his foot in it and hold it there 10 seconds. Maybe it is just that the dog wants to get away from you, but that dog will hunt like his foot is fine as frog hair for half a day before he goes back to limping.

Turpentine is also used for killing ear mites. Just like with most the over the counter medicines you put it in the ear, fold the ear over and rub to spread it around and then wipe it out.

On a bad cut turpentine is used topically as an antiseptic, it also constricts blood vessels and reduces blood loss. Again, you gotta hold that dog! I have used it a time or two on myself and it makes alcohol in a wound feel good. After a few minutes though the turpentine has a bit of a numbing effect and eases the pain, maybe it just seems that way 'cause it hurts so dang much at first. Either way, it does work.

3. Overheating. I had heard of this remedy a few times before I saw it used, I always thought it sounded rough, and it is, but I am here to tell you it is a life saver! Losing a dog to overheating is always hard to swallow, they die because they just have so much heart they won't quit, and that is pretty admirable. I have seen guys cool them off slowly with air temp water, but it was never very effective. I have seen guys cool them off fast with cold water and it was a 50/50 crap shot at best. Then one day I saw an old man take his pocket knife out over a dog that was dying. I honestly thought he was going to put it out of its misery. Instead he cut about a 1/4" off the tip of each ear. The dog bleed like a stuck hog! Then we pulled that dog's mouth open and gave him some coke and it wasn't 15 minutes later the dog was up and walking and out of danger. The trick here is in blood loss, it cools the body, the Coke (or any sugary liquid) staves off shock that blood loss can cause. Rubbing alcohol on a rag and rubbed over the whole body will also drop body heat fast through evaporation.

4. Worming. In the old days people wormed with what they had. There are a bunch of old worming strategies, I will only mention the ones here that I have used and seen used. Ash was a very common wormer. You get a good fire going of hardwoods and let it burn all the way down. The fine white ash is mixed with water to make a thick paste. You roll a ball about the size of a golf ball or a little smaller and get it down the dogs throat. This method was used on all stock, for cows and hogs you leave the water out and put the fine ash on something they will willingly eat. when hungry.

Tobacco was also a common wormer, and I still know a man that uses a good plug or twist of leaf tobacco to worm his mules. Pretty self explanatory, you just get it down em. With the price of good leaf tobacco today, this makes no sense from a money standpoint though.

Black walnut was also used as a wormer. You get the green hulls, before the walnut is ripe and soak them in alcohol for a few days. The liquid is used to do the worming. Black walnut is a good wormer, but it takes practice on the dose, as it is toxic if you use too much, so generally you start with a small amount and observe the dog and the dog's waste and adjust dosage.

5. Joint issues. Often, old dogs will get where they just don't move like they used to, or limp until they get warmed up or limp around after a good long hunt. Feeding the dog fish will often ease this if it is due to arthritis or just basic joint pain. I catfish a lot, so I take the catfish skin and fry it for the dogs in lots of oil. Fish oil pills also work, but we are talking about old time remedies here. I have also seen friends take the skin and everything that is left after cleaning fish and boil it all until the bones are soft and feed the whole lot to dogs getting up in age. My dogs lick their lips when they see fish on the diet, they love it, but when I add a new dog they give me a strange look when I plop a big serving in their dish - they eat it, but reluctantly at first.

6. Infection. Infection is something we as hog hunters have to deal with from time to time. We usually bust out the syringes and start poking and injecting, but the fix might be right in the garden. garlic aides the dog's immune system and will help in fighting off an infection.

MONICA WHEELUS

I agree, there is a lot of merit in the old methods. However, it often isn't the most ideal, easiest or even the right treatment for what ails a dog. I grew up listening and learning from old timers just like Ed did and I know there are a lot things that can be learned from them. I have seen or used many of the things he mentioned and now have the luxury of working in a vet clinic where I could learn the more modern and ideal treatments. With that being said, I work in a rural area for an old school vet that is a bit more open minded than most. As a clinic we try to give a client all the options that are within the realm of good medicine. So, I am going to try to give the example of ideal treatment and the alternative treatment that will often work.

1. Red mange. Most of us have gone round and round with Demodectic Mange at some point in our lives. The mite that causes it is on most dogs, but only dogs with weak immune systems have break outs. That weakened immune system can be from stress, injury, anesthetics, use of steroids for inflammation or BAD GENES. A weak immune system can be passed down and that is why dogs that had demodex as pups are often not bred...well, not unless you are a hunter. Inevitably, it is your best dog that has a predisposition to red mange and you are going to want a pup out of it.

I am familiar with the burnt motor oil treatment and it used to work great...messy, smelly and left a dog miserable in the summer heat, but it worked. You'll notice I said it used to work. Well, along came synthetic oils and they are low sulphur. Sulphur is one of main ingredients in the dips you can get from the vet and was part of why motor oil worked so well. The other reason is the smothering effect that the oil itself had on the mites, of course this also can cause the dog to overheat by trapping the dog's body heat and not allowing for proper cool down. I have heard of people still using this treatment and adding sulphur powder to it. My question is why? That seems like almost as much work as Ed's polk juice, which I don't doubt works. However, there are easier, more effective and longer lasting treatments out there. Ivomec injectable cattle wormer can be given orally daily and the dog can be dipped every 2 weeks in a lime-sulphur dip until all the hair grows back. Then there is Dectomax injectable cattle wormer that can be given as a weekly shot until all the hair grows back on the bald spots and no smelly dip is needed. Bear in mind, when the mites die off the skin can look worse for awhile. If a skin infection has developed it can be treated with either oral or topical antibiotics. It is important to determine that it is indeed red mange (demodex) and not an allergic reaction. Treatment with cattle wormer won't hurt the dog but, to be safe, a generic version of benadryl is recommended daily for the first couple weeks.

2. Ear mites, sore pads, bad cuts. Where do I start? Turpentine has been used to cure everything imaginable and yes, it works on most of them. However, it isn't always the best treatment.

The easiest ear mite treatment you can use is Ivomec and mineral oil. Squirt it down in the ear, squish it around and stand back while he shakes his head. Ear mites aren't always the reason a dog is shaking his head, infection from yeast and bacteria are the #1 culprit. Ticks are 2nd and then ear mites. The Ivomec will get ticks and mites, but the ear infection needs a different kind of treatment. I have included down at the bottom of this article a recipe for a concoction that a hunting spaniel breeder gave my boss and it works on most everything imaginable in the way of ear infections. The best part is a batch will last a long time and won't go bad.

Turpentine works good for sore pads because of the analgesic properties that numb the foot. There are things on the market like Tuf-Foot and Pad Tough that are marketed to toughen and treat sore feet. While these products are inexpensive, they can become costly if you have more than a couple dogs prone to sore pads. There is something hunters around here use that they call sole paint. It is equal parts pine tar, iodine, acetone and generic Listerine. We occasionally mix some up using formaldehyde instead of listerine. Any kind of phenol product can be substituted if formaldehyde isn't available and Listerine isn't strong enough.

Turpentine can be used around edges of a wound, but will actually slow down the healing process if used on the raw flesh. If you are wanting to suture or staple, it is best to flush with an iodine solution to clean the debris out of the wound and then fill with petroleum jelly if the bleeding is minimal. If the bleeding is heavy, try using some powdered tetracycline like is used in poultry waterers and leave the wound open. It is a good blood stopper and antibiotic to prevent infection. If all else fails, it is better to use the old purple/blue lotion topical antiseptic and let the dog keep it clean himself.

3. Overheating. Tipping the ears on an overheated dog works because it drops the blood pressure and takes stress off the heart. Dropping the blood pressure rapidly can also cause a dog to go into shock. Overheating is serious and in some areas a dog doesn't have to be working hard to fall victim. An overheated dog that goes into severe shock is almost impossible to save, so tip ears with caution.

The best advice is to be prepared. Keep water for humans and dogs on the ATV, UTV or truck and keep some old towels or strips of sheets handy. When a dog shows signs of overheating, wet the material and pack it around feet, belly, under tail and around ears/head/neck. Extreme cold can cause shock symptoms but it isn't as dangerous as the drop in blood pressure. You can always remove the cold wet towel if dog starts to shiver or seize. I learned a long time ago with any animal in a stressed situation that blood sugar will drop as the body tries to cope. We carry Karo syrup and a 30 cc syringe to give under the tongue in the back of the mouth. I have seen Gatorade/Powerade used and know a few people that buy the powder and make up a strong jug for day hunts when they worry about a drop in electrolytes.

Not every overheated dog can be saved because some dogs have too much heart to show signs until it is too late. Ideally, you get the dog to a vet so an IV can be started and temperature can be monitored. If your dog makes it home, but is still in bad shape, you can give subcutaneous fluids with a 16-18 gauge needle, 60 cc syringe and saline solution. Lactated ringers with an IV set is ideal, but many vet supply places won't sell that to some rough looking guy off the street. However, most will sell large bottles of saline and dextrose. You can make a lot of progress in saving a dog if you have those in your house or truck. (One old dogger I know as soon as he gets home draws up 20 cc of dextrose and 40 cc of saline and squirts it under the skin between the shoulder blades on EVERY dog that has been hunting in heat over 90 degrees.)

Once you get the downed dog home, put him somewhere that is a pretty constant temperature and not drafty. Do yourself a favor and invest in a cheap digital thermometer for the first aid bag. Check his temp every hour until it comes down to about 102 or below. Normal is 101.5, but anything under 102 is good. It is important to check on him, but if he appears stable let him rest. To bring a dog's temp down, the 3 most important places to keep room temperature damp rags is around feet, on belly and over ears. Always remember it is more important for an otherwise healthy dog to drink than it is to eat. A dog needs fluids to cool down just like a car needs water in the radiator to cool the motor.

4. Worming. This is one of the most over thought and over diagnosed reasons for a dog to be losing weight, off feed or any number of other symptoms. It is recommended to not worm a dog more than every 3 months unless they have repeated infestations of tapeworms due to fleas. (Flea treatment and prevention is subject for another day)

Ideally, vets will recommend worming with something that contains Pyrantel Pamoate and Praziquantel to treat and control roundworms, hookworms and tapeworms. There are some great, highly effective pills on the market. They are rarely needed because a 50/50 mix of liquid Strongid T and Panacur given for 3 days in a row will kill those same 3 types of worms. You will need something different if you suspect you have whipworms though. Many folks use paste horse wormer monthly and it works for the most part.

The reason that tobacco and ash work as a wormer is that they create an unfriendly environment in the GI tract. Using them causes irritation and the dog's natural defenses kick in and evict anything abnormal on the lining of the digestive tract. This also increases the risk for hemorrhagic gastroenteritis. That is where you are seeing blood in vomit and stool due to bleeding ulcer in stomach or intestines. Another reason to not try ash is some of the saps and resin residue can be toxic and cause more harm than good. The same can be said about modern tobacco, the residues are worse than anything the plant naturally has.

5. Joint issues. Ed is right about the value of fish in a dog's diet. There are countless joint supplements marketed that contain fish oil, meal and ground up bones. You can do just as well by going with the generic fish oil capsules and glucosamine/msm/bone meal products in the human section.

There are great products that can be bought through vet offices that work to increase the viscosity and fluid in old joints, but they aren't cheap. Anti-inflammatory products for dogs work well and MOST human versions are very toxic. I am not just reciting the song and dance that some folks think we give to get people to buy the pain pills from us. I have seen the liver and kidney damage that were caused by ibuprofen and acetaminophen. Buffered aspirin can be used and is a whole lot safer for a dog's stomach than regular aspirin.

6. Infection. Infection is not something to be taken lightly because there are a many causes for infection as there is treatments. The ideal is always seeking the assistance of a vet if you think your dog has a nasty persistent infection, however some injections of pen-G at home is often the first course of treatment. There are folks that use tetracycline powder once a month in the water to clear up anything a dog might be carrying that is penicillin resistant. Some broad spectrum injectable livestock antibiotics can be dosed down to be safe for dogs and are very cost effective if you have a large number of dogs.

Garlic is great for what ails a human, but the potential medicinal benefits are not really effective for our dogs. In fact, garlic can be extremely toxic to dogs and the consumption of even a small amount can lead to severe poisoning and if not treated in time, death.

Garlic, along with onions, shallots and leeks are in the Allium family. Unfortunately, dogs cannot digest these particular plants as we can. The ingestion of anything in this family by dogs causes a condition called hemolytic anemia. This condition is characterized by the bursting of red blood cells circulating the body. It may take up to four days after your dog eats garlic for symptoms to appear. Symptoms of garlic toxicity include breathlessness, lethargy, diarrhea, vomiting, pale gums, an elevated heart rate, an increased respiratory rate, weakness, exercise intolerance, and collapse.

One of the first symptoms is a dog losing interest in food. If the dog is already fighting an infection, the anemia will further weaken the immune response and your dog's body will have to fight harder to just keep up with the production of red blood cells needed for survival. A high iron diet can benefit any dog that may become anemic or large dose of an iron supplement can be given along with the garlic if you feel the possible benefits outweigh the risks.

CHAPTER 45
SHOCKING COLLARS

To start on a humorous note - I was hunting with an old man one day. He had his bib overalls full of everything but the kitchen sink, Tri-tronics hand held included, it was a 6 dog unit and you had to use the toggle switch to alternate between the three shocking buttons to reach all six dogs. I don't remember the infraction, or even which dog, but that controller came out and it was jostled around in his hand from Parkinson's disease. He was working that toggle and mashing buttons as he frantically tried to remember the color of the dog collar for the dog in question. Dogs still in the box were howling, and dogs in no wrong were flopping on the ground. I couldn't help but laugh! Hopefully those old dogs knew their owner well enough to not hold it against him - I think they did.

Joking aside - with most dogmen walking around with the Alpha, and the ability to shock their dogs at almost any minute, it seems fitting to cover some of the basics of how to use a shocking collar and how NOT to use one. God knows I have seen shocking collars used in the worst possible ways.

I will start off saying that I still use the old 320 Garmin, so I don't have the ability to shock while I am hunting unless I pull out the Tri-Tronics. I have an old 6 dog unit, and it is pretty high up on the shelf and has a fair amount of dust on it. My shocking system doesn't have dust on it because I have great dogs, it has dust on it because I work hard to not set dogs up for failure, but I am getting ahead of myself.

A shocking collar is a tool, and like any tool it is only as good as the hand it is in. I have misused collars, I admit. If you simply use the shocker as a way to inflict pain out of frustration you aren't going to have much success and you might as well forget dogs and move on to wrenching hot rods or something that doesn't involve animals or anything with a brain.

First you have to know what you are dishing out, so strap that collar on and give yourself some juice. Once you know the power of your shocking collar you can better tell what level each dog needs. "With great power comes great responsibility." If you don't think a shocking collar is "great power" strap a collar on and give the handheld to your wife.

Some dogs can be corrected with a bump from a very low level, some dogs you gotta mash and hold the button on "11" just to get their attention. I am after the lowest level of pain I can use to get the desired effect. If you crank on that 'soft-hided' dog at 11 there is a good chance that the lesson you were trying to teach will be missed. It is easy to lose sight that we are TRAINING not PUNISHING. Punishment is a part of training, but it is not the end we are after, a trained dog is. When I am shock training a dog my goal is not to inflict pain, it is less dramatic, I am just trying to get their attention. Always start on the easy side and move up as needed.

Most shocking collars have a vibrate or a tone button on them now. A good habit to get into is to hit the tone right before the shock, every time. There are a few advantages to this. Now I have heard folks baulk at the tone like it was some kind of tree-hugger feature, that is NOT the case. When we tone then shock we are "getting the dogs attention" like I said earlier. After a dog has been toned then shocked 3 times or 3400 (depending on how much the dog has upstairs) the dog puts one and one together and when it hears the tone it knows the shock is coming. Often the tone alone will bring up enough memories to stop the behavior that is warranting the use of the shocker. We are after a correction of behavior, not punishment, so if the tone works then our point was made. Punishment is best doled out with a switch and a clear understanding of it coming from you. I am not against dishing out pain to get my point across, I want to be clear- it has it's place, but it also can muddy up the water. When we get the dogs attention we have a chance to train, usually after punishing there is little chance of training.

Lets say we have a dog that likes to bark in the dog box. This is usually just about the excitement of the coming hunt, and in my mind shouldn't be punished severely, but I don't want a dog doing it.

(Before we had shocking collars we'd put a length of rope on the dogs collar and feed it through the side of the box up to the cab of the truck. When we got an unwanted bark, we'd yank that rope and rap a head against the side of the box.)

So we are easing down the road and the box barker goes to barking for no darn reason that we know of. We could mash the button, light him up, and hope he connects the dots. At the very best he is going to think that when he barks in the box it hurts. This might work and often does, but we really haven't fixed the problem we just covered it up, and a smart dog is going to learn that when he doesn't have the sharp pointy collar on (or the rope on his collar) he can box bark. I have seen old dogs that learned a shock collar and had to be fitted with a dummy collar made out of a block of wood and two probes, otherwise they were going to act out. I have also seen old dogs that somehow, by weight or something, figured out the dummy collar was a fake. These dogs reverted to bad behavior because they had not really been trained, only punished.

Now lets take a different approach at that box barking... we slam on the brakes and jump out of the truck after toning him and give him the command we use at home for kennel barking - everyone has one. This is going to increase the chances that the dog connects the dots and the behavior is stopped, collar on or not. Chances are when your dogs are barking at home you can stop them with your voice. That is training, not punishing. Now we could do the same command with a shock instead of the tone, and it would probably calm your nerves and you might even smile at the squawl... but, is the command really getting through to the dog while he's twitching his head and whining? I would bet that if I asked you 5 x 13 you could figure it out pretty fast. Do you think you could figure it out as fast if I hit you over the bridge of your nose with a t-post right before I asked? (Note: That command you use at the house to get dogs to quit barking is a powerful command and can be used for more than barking. It is the "tone" you use at home before you break out the bb gun, or put on boots. Your dogs know it is a disapproval of what they are doing right then.)

Another great advantage to the tone shows up in cases where the dog really isn't doing anything wrong but we need to stop their behavior. If your dog has been trained with tone then shock, the tone means something. So we are hunting and the neighbor to the north is a real piece of work and has been known to shoot dogs. We hunt on the south end but the dogs are rolling north headed for his place. A tone will get that dogs attention long enough to stop his hunting and hear your call to come in, maybe. The dog has not done a darn thing wrong, in fact he is doing everything right. A shock to get his attention could throw questions into a younger dogs head, he knows nothing of property lines. He could very well be on a hog track and get shocked just like the time he was digging that armadillo. Seems pretty logical, I know, but I have heard of folks shocking dogs off a bay because they didn't want to go in to the hog for whatever reason! In drastic cases where you might have to shock - older dogs are going to be able to handle this better, with less adverse effects than a young dog. If I had a 13 month old pup that was doing good on hogs but was of course new to running and the dog was running a hog into a dangerous situation I personally would roll the dice and stay out of the shocking or even toning business. The water is just too muddy and the possible backwards steps in training could potentially be nearly as bad as the dog getting shot.

Every single time we turn a dog out, be it a 9 month old pup or a 7 year old dog we are TRAINING (whether we know it or not) and we have to keep in mind the messages, or mixed messages we are giving our dogs. Think of dogs like you do a 3 year old kid, keep it simple and straight forward. Simple and consistent! We have to be consistent. If we are going to punish a dog for digging armadillos then we need to do it EVERY single time. If a dog gets away with it sometimes and sometimes not, then we are not giving the dog a clear understanding of what we find unacceptable.

So, about keeping it simple... lets say my "Sha-teet-a" pup is flat burning a deer up; 2 miles, wide open and averaging 11 MPH. I'm going to be a bit perturbed, and yet have a smile on my face. We drive around and I am close enough to light her up... but I don't. Instead I will stick it out, drive mile after mile, take the ribbing from my buddies and get the dog gathered up. I will not call the dog at all while it is chasing or hunting. If the young dog quits then I will call. I will load her after a few hours never saying her name. Once in the dog box I will let her know I am not pleased using only my voice and not over-doing it. The guys in the truck will laugh and poke fun and chime in, "I'd beat the dog PISS out of that HUSSY!" A lesser man will drag her in and thump all over her just to keep a hold of his masculinity, out of frustration, or to just not be seen as weak. (Remember we are talking about a pup, if it's an old dog thump away! They know better.)

If you are training in the woods you better be 100% sure your dog is running a deer, or whatever, before you mash that button! I used to shock in the woods, before a man got me thinking. I have been guilty of stepping on this fundamental. One day we had a good race going and drove the truck ahead of the dogs to where we thought they would cross. They had already crossed the road (this was before fancy tracking GPS stuff.) We could hear them bawling on the run and I jumped out and found fresh deer tracks with dog tracks over them. Well, I had been having deer "issues" with this dog an I got out my remote an starting laying into this dog. No more than I had let off the button and a bay was starting to develop and we took off to find they had a good boar. My dog wasn't ruined, he wasn't smart enough. Now I have to see, with my own eyes and be one hundred percent sure what is going on before I shock with a collar. That dog I just spoke of probably was running a deer when he dropped it for a fresh hog and then got shocked. But we have to correct in the present, not the past. Yet again, the running dogs could have just flushed deer out of the thicket as they ran a hog. I have seen it many times. Just because a deer is running ahead of your dogs does not mean your dog is chasing that deer! Watch that track pattern, and read that bark.

A couple days later I grab my trusty deer hide out of the

freezer and thaw it a bit. I make a drag with it and then hide it in the brush. I get Sha-teet-a out of her kennel and put her on a 20' rope with a shocking collar on. I let her run and bounce off the end of the rope a while until she calms, then I take her to the head of my drag. The pup gets a whiff of the deer and perks up and starts working it fast. Tone then shock on low without saying anything. If the shock was enough to interrupt her trailing I then take off straight to the hog pen. Now I will talk to her and let her bay from outside the fence, all the while talking to her and encouraging her. (One of the few times I will talk to a dog when they are working) I will pet her up and down and give positive sounding words. (Which brings up another tid-bit - never pat a dog, no matter how loving, dogs see this as a reprimand) Now back to the deer trail and we will repeat this 3 to 4 times if needed. If on the 4th trip to the deer drag the dog still wants to run it we will go back to the hog pen before ending the session. Rome wasn't built in a day, and most dogs are not broke off trash in a day. The dogs that are broke in one setting are usually ruined. Patience is the name of this game.

"Punishment" is not "Correction." Correction implies that you are saying, "Don't do this, but you can do this." (Correcting a dog off a deer drag at home and then praising them at the hog pen) Punishing dogs won't get you very far when dealing with pups. Old dogs we can punish, because they know better.

In the woods we cannot control the situation enough. When breaking off-game in the woods about our best hope to end on a positive is a simple "Come," and chances are very high that your negative mood will be plain to see for the dog, leading to confusion. They might contribute your negative attitude to their actions, but probably not. In the woods we are rolling dice. When we break off-game at home we have the ability to SHOW the pup the game we want and give them positive encouragement. Training is both positive and negative, not just a whole lot of "NOOO's!" The method I described of training with a deer hide can of course be used with any off-game.

Now lets change it up... when we drove around close to the dog burning up a deer and I did light into her with the shocking collar, she quit the deer and came in. Great! Problem solved! Right?

Maybe, maybe not and we might have got a good start on limiting the best trait in a hog dog. I imagine the dogs brain while she is having a blast running the deer - "DEER! RUN. HUNT! FUN! DEER." Then came that fire on the neck and ruined the fun. There are four words in her head, DEER. RUN. FUN. HUNT. The dog doesn't know which word, or action caused the pain in her neck, but she doesn't want that feeling again. We want the off game clearly connected to the unpleasant feeling the dog got. We want the dog to think that the deer somehow caused the pain. As in the example above, we can even link the smell of the deer to the pain. Now a dog isn't going to make this connection after one time, thankfully, but we are still setting them up for at most an educated guess even if we do everything correctly and don't muddy the water.

We have all seen a dog that has been shocked on a hunt come to the truck and the dog won't do anything the rest of the day - it is confused so it just shuts down. I have seen a boat load of these dogs, and they are very very hard to rehabilitate. I have seen dogs that would not do anything if they even had a shocking collar on. This is from an owner that didn't know how to use an E-collar.

It's a bit off topic, and a very large topic at that, but I mentioned it earlier so I will explain... I said if we burn that pup off the deer we might be limiting something? That "something" is bottom. The topic is a can of worms, with some saying bottom is bred in, some saying it is trained. As with most things, it is a combination of both. I think when you shock a dog off, even on off-game, you are training to quit. Dog hunting is not easy, grit your teeth and let that pup RUN until it catches or quits on it's own. Instead of curling your mouth downward, revel in the bottom and determination and dream of how that is going to help you in catching those old running hogs.

Most have heard of the old dog in a barrel method of breaking a dog. Many young folks think it is merely folklore. The method was to take a deer running dog and put them in a barrel with a deer hide and roll them down a hill. One day after an unusually aggravating hog hunt me and an old man returned to his house. He told me on the ride home he was going to deer break his dog when we got home. As a young man I sat up, ready to learn this mans ways. We led the dog into the barn and tied her up. The man went to the house and returned with a deer hide. I imagined he was going to toss it on her and go to thumping, instead he opened the door on a 55 gallon barrel contraption he had in the corner. "Bring her here," He barked! "Now help me get her in here." It was becoming clear. There was a motor hooked up to a pulley on the barrel. We got the dog inside and he found an outlet and plugged it in. The barrel began to spin, at first slow but gaining momentum. With every rotation I could hear the dog thud up against the side. His words were calm and relaxed, "Want a cup of coffee?" We went in the house and about the time he had the cups poured I asked if we ought to go get the dog out of the barrel. "Well hell no!" He hacked, "Gotta let her spend about an hour in there." "An hour?" I am sure the urgency and concern was heard in my voice, "She'll die!" "Might," he said, "Either way she will never run a deer again! You gotta make sure you do it good, 'cause after we take her out of that barrel she will NEVER be put back in again! Like putting a cat in a bathtub." It made sense. I drank my coffee fast. When we finally turned the motor off, (it wasn't a full hour) and waited for the spinning to slow and stop, he again barked at me, "Be ready." And he opened the door of the barrel. I expected the dog to bound out, and it did try but clumsily. The barrel was full of piss, and shit and vomit, and surprisingly an alive dog. Sadly, I don't remember if it cured the dog of running deer, but if I had to bet I'd say so. Those old men had hard ways!

While the above description might be harsh, it is just a less sanded version of breaking at home where the message is more clear. There is wisdom in the old ways, at the root if you dig enough.

As you have gathered I am not fond of shocking in the woods, but I am mainly talking about pups. With older dogs shocking in the woods is less risky. I will shock a dog in the woods when they have reached the stage where they know they are HOGDOGS, when they are just choosing to mess up and know better. On pups I say the longer you can keep away from shocking the better, at home or in the woods. I treasure those trashy pups, it shows me 'want to' and I won't waste time on a pup that isn't trashy. When a pup is running trash he is risking picking up habits, but they are not all bad habits. A trashing pup is learning lessons that will help it in the hog woods - they are learning the fun of the chase, they are learning the woods, they are learning to track and pick up on tricks used to ditch them, they are learning to get gone and come back. Trashing is a valuable tool, in moderation and at appropriate times, don't just look at the bad side of it.

Probably the best shocking collar advice I can give is to not set pups up to fail. Turn pups into areas you know there are hogs, feed them hog tracks so they don't get off on the wrong foot. Don't run pups with dogs that trash! I have trained quite a few pups that never once had an E-Collar on, and they turned out to be straight hog dogs... mostly.

My buddy Pat had a fine Plott x cur. The dog was a looker and conditioned very well. A man asked Pat one day after taking it out of the dog box what he was feeding it. Without hesitation or thought Pat replied, "Tracks!" We cast the dogs and the man still had a puzzled look on his face. He is still probably thinking about that one.

If you keep it in mind that a dog can't read your thoughts, and try to use an e-collar in the clearest way possible you should be alright. If you disagree with me put a collar on, give your wife the remote and tell her to shock you all day - anytime you do something she doesn't want you to do, or anytime you don't do what she thinks you ought to do - without any speaking. By the end of the day you will probably be a confused mess, hiding under the truck shaking.

It might seem I am some kind of softy on dogs, I am not! I carry a big stick and I will swing it. Most of these hog dog breeds are very, how can I put it? Self-assured! By their nature they are bold and dominating. If you do not have a disciplinary hold of your dogs most all of your training will be pointless. Remember that shy, humble, soft spoken substitute teacher from school? Don't be her! Be the coach that you KNEW would grab you by the shirt and yank a knot in your neck. Be a figure your dogs respect. My wife has troubled over the point for many years - one day I have to discipline a dog, and do a very thorough job at it, and the next day the dog is following me around and wagging that tail and is just my best buddy. She doesn't understand why they still like me. Dogs like the person that disciplines them. Clearly defined pack order is comforting to the mind of a pack animal.

I have said earlier that I came up running dogs with old men. That exposure has made an impact on me, and made me notice something that holds pretty true. Each generation seems to get a little softer on dogs. I have seen old men put a whooping on dogs and mules that would make the hangman drop his head! It might have been a small infraction, but those old men had only one level and it was full tilt. Their dogs also stood at attention when spoken to. A glance could make them stop in their tracks.

To train we have to have a disciplined dog, willing to bend to our will and knowing the consequences if he chooses not to, but training is not only about discipline. When we discipline we are the dad, and when we train we are the mom. Dad knocks the daylights out of you, and you run to moms comforting arms. She pets your head, and talks low but doesn't undermine the man, she just explains it in a soft tone. Your sniveling slows and if you aren't a blockhead it becomes clear. As dog hunters we have to be mom and dad. Dogs, like kids need that two pronged approach to training.

CHAPTER 46
TO BARR?

What we choose to do with a hog after we catch it is a question that often leads to arguments, hurt feelings and sometimes an air of superiority on both sides. The conditions that surround us determine what we do with caught hogs, the wishes of land owners, laws and of course our personal beliefs.

Personally I release hogs when the situation is correct. If we bay and catch a hog in a corn field we aren't going to release him. If we catch a hog on a ranch where the hogs are eating feed and rooting hay meadows we aren't going to cut and release either, out of respect for our neighbors and friends but if we are out in the hills and hollers where a hog does little to no damage we are going to release sows we don't want to eat, and barr boars.

Some faces surely curled up at reading of my admission of releasing caught hogs. As I showed earlier, we did not bring these hogs to America, and they are not our responsibility! Government agencies pay our tax dollars to state trappers to catch hogs, they also use our tax dollars to rent helicopters from private business to shoot feral hogs, they pay institutes to write lengthy reports on feral hog impacts, they buy hog traps from private companies to use to catch shoats - yet they simply 'expect' the blue collar hog dogger to just buck up and donate our services? By the account of most government agencies hog dog hunters don't catch many hogs anyway, so our small numbers of catch and release shouldn't effect the population. Of course, they want it both ways

- coming and going - just as their propaganda says feral hogs are infested with disease AND populations are on the rise.

For the nay-sayers I have an experiment lined up. Saddle that paint pony and ride out to your pasture or the pasture of a neighbor. Give a head count and then rope a cow. Now release the cow and give another head count. Has your herd increased?

When we barr a hog we are creating value. Big stinky boar hogs can be made fit for the table if cleaned and cooked correctly, but it is more work than most are willing to put in. When we barr a hog we are reducing his home range, taking reproduction off of his mind and leaving him only to work on getting food and in some cases to defend groups of sows and pigs. This makes a fat, tender big hunk of meat to take to the house. Working hogs in the woods is our southern tradition, and when you start engaging in it your view of hunting hogs takes on another level and feels more rounded and full, kind of like that barr hog.

One winter night myself and Kolby Ingram cast two dogs from near a road shooting them up a creek. After some time they caught a boar hog. After we had the dogs tied back and the hog hobbled we decided what to do with him. The boar was a good one, in the range of 240lbs. It was figured we would barr him. A couple days before we had made the same decision, and Kolby had been tasked with cutting and releasing him as I led dogs back to the truck. The release had been one of those heart pumping ones where the hog isn't just happy to trot off, but rather wants revenge against the man with the knife. With that experience fresh in his mind Kolby blurted out, "You're cutting this one!" I agreed after some joking. Kolby went 20 yards or so away and posted up next to a tree with a good branch to hop up on if things got western. I cut the boar then rolled him on his back. I had his two back legs against my thighs and began un-hobbling him. I had all the hobbles off and held his back legs high in the air to make him immobile. I eased my hand off of one of his legs and once again gave my path of exit another look over. With his free back leg the hog kicked and it landed right in my crotch, hard. The pain forced the air out of me and I dropped the other leg and grabbed at my pants, a mistake that was immediately noted! In a flash the hog was up and facing me. He bluffed a charge and I danced around.

He charged half-heartedly again, and again I danced in pain. I could hear Kolby laughing. Our stand off was just 20 seconds or so but it seemed like an hour. We were both sizing each other up. Finally he walked off and I got back to breathing regular.

One day I was hunting with Kolby, Tanner and Slim. It was a great day with a lot of hogs caught. On the last catch we decided we would cut a small boar. Slim had not been hog hunting that long at this point and I don't think he had ever cut and released a boar. Slim held the boar down, it wasn't very big, and I cut him while teaching Slim the correct way to barr a hog. I told Slim to look around for a tree, after he had one in sight I told him, "Now when I say, you let the hog go." I was still kneeling beside the hog and as soon as I said that, Slim bounded up in a run! The hog made it to his feet before I did and that barr hog ran me all over trying to get revenge as I kicked and cut figure eights. We all laughed and the story still brings a chuckle.

Cutting a boar is pretty straight forward but there are a few small things you need to do to get it 'right.' The first thing is the incision needs to be as small as possible. I have seen guys cut a boar and it looked like a slasher movie. We want the hog to survive. The second thing is how to cut the cords. Some pull them out but I don't subscribe to that. Most people just take their knife and cut them clean. I've had my head slapped for doing that! The 'right' way is to scrape the cord in two. You place your blade on the cord but instead of a cutting motion you rub the cord perpendicular to the blade while pushing down slightly. This creates a long surface area on the cord to clot the blood and the cord stretches and wrinkles - it naturally closes in on itself. Done this way it will heal much faster, lessening the risk of infection, and reducing bleeding.

We rarely get to control when we cut a boar in the woods. At the house, whether cutting hogs, horses, or dogs though, use the moon as a guide. The moon affects bleeding. When possible cut animals on a waning moon (shrinking) and there will be less swelling and bleeding.

CHAPTER 47
BUSTED BAYS

Busted bays are unfortunately a common occurrence in todays hog hunting. Our hogs are smarter, they are learning the game. Our game is a more stealthy one, grandpas hogs are gone.

Sometimes we bust the bay going in with the wind at our back. Sometimes we bust a bay with lights blazing and the loud trudging of ten people. Sometimes the reckless 90lb bulldogs break the bay as they crash in. Sometimes a 'baydog' breaks the bay with his over-enthusiastic catchy nature.

A hog breaks the bay when he knows the game, or when the dogs place too much pressure. Many of our hogs know the situation they find themselves in and are just hard to bay. I still stand my ground when I say most bays are broken by 'baydogs' that don't know their place, or we simply turn in too many dogs.

A few years back I said on social media that the number of dogs on a hog effected a busted bay more than any other factor. My friend Pat Lewing, who shared my view, set out to demonstrate that very notion in his 40 acre pen. First he sent two dogs and they bayed a hog. He then sent two more dogs to them, all loose, and the bay busted. The four dogs ran and ran the hog, as they ran he managed to cut off a dog on a road and catch it. Shortly the three dogs again bayed, and after turning a different dog into the bay it busted again. Pats experiment lasted half a day and at it's conclusion it was determined that two dogs could bay a hog in a shorter race than three or four of five...or eight!

Often I get a phone call or a message that deals with this common question. The fella tells me that hogs in his country just run and run and run and he wants some advice on getting them to stop. My first question is always how many dogs are on the ground? Often that question is answered with a scenario of starting with three then adding dogs and adding dogs until they end up with ten dogs on the ground running. While adding dogs seems logical at first glance, my answer is always to reduce the number of dogs. Pressure is the main ingredient in hogs running, they are dealing with a simple survival instinct. When we have a problem with a running hog our first solution should be to try to limit the number of dogs to two or even one. There are two approaches to hog hunting with dogs - force or elegance. We can force that hog to stop by dogs chewing, or we can lessen the pressure and make him feel safe in the face of one dog - elegance! While force might suit our manly nature, elegance is often the best answer to our questions.

We either run loose dogs or rough dogs, and a mixing of the two will lead to busted bays and cut down dogs. Pick a style and hold true and steadfast to it, mixing does not work!

Many years ago I hunted with two other guys. Myself and one other man had very loose dogs - the kind of dogs that would bay an 80lb shoat for two hours if it came down to it, and the other man ran rough dogs that would try to catch anything under 250lbs. We enjoyed each others company and had a great many fun hunts despite not catching many hogs. For the better part of a year we hunted together but caught very few hogs. I was ending up with loose dogs that were cut down, and bays that fell into races were the norm. All the while I would go hunting on my own and catch hogs regularly. Eventually there was a falling out with the guy that hunted rough dogs. Low and behold, me and the other man that ran loose dogs started catching hogs together - and the guy that ran rough dogs started catching hogs on his own. Mixing dogs does not work! You can remain friends with guys that hunt in a different style than you, but you shouldn't hunt together, or at least run each pack by themselves.

CHAPTER 48
KENNELS

The chain verses kennel debate is a long one. There are glaring pros and cons to each setup and it really comes down to what a man ranks as his priorities. I will hit on some of those pros and cons, but my main objective here is to give some insight into kennel design. First, I have to say I prefer kennels. There are many reasons, the least not being that I am a worrier. I can accept that fault in myself. Kennels help keep my anxiety down.

When the kennel verses a chain-spot debate rears its head the first comment out of every chain man is square footage. This is a legitimate argument - a 12 foot chain gives a dog 452 square feet, while a 6' x 15' kennel gives a dog 90 square feet. Square footage is by itself not a determining factor though. Kick the dog loose and he has the whole world at his disposal - limitless square footage and limitless dangers. While I downplay the square footage angle, I have to say that I feel 6' x 10' is a minimum as a single kennel spot for grown dogs. Pups are often whelped in much smaller kennels, say 4'x4', and I find nothing wrong with that up until about 2 months of age, after that a pup needs plenty of space to stretch out and get up to full speed. They have to figure out how those legs work. I used to hunt with a man that often kept a grown dog in a pup whelping pen. He started doing so when he ran out of room and the dog was somewhere around two. Immediately I noticed the dogs conditioning drop below standard, but the man wouldn't listen to me, and time and again we watched the dog drop out of races. Whether on a chain or in a kennel, much of the dog's self-inspired conditioning comes from solid pacing and jumping. Chain dogs will go to the end of the chain and jump against it, as well as running those earth eating circles at the end of that chain. Dragging that chain definitely helps in conditioning! Put a lazy dog on a chain and he is lazy, put a busy dog in a kennel and he will stay busy, most of this is determined by the dog. Neither setup alone will make a dog in top condition, that takes your work and dedication. Run the dogs enough and where they sleep has little effect.

Safety and control is where the kennel shines. When my dogs were on chains it seemed every week I had some mishap. I'd come home to find a dog rolled his water bowl. I'd come home to see a dog standing in the rain because his chain was wadded up and he couldn't reach his barrel. Then I'd find a dog slipped a collar and bred a gyp I didn't want bred. I have dogs get out of kennels, nothing is 100%. I forget to latch the door, pups slide a panel, or the such. What I like about a kennel is when the dog gets out he still doesn't have access to the other dogs, and he is in that big wide open world where he can do his best at fending for himself. He can find shade, some water, and a varmint to harass. Chain mishaps often end in death. With a chain it was always a balance of keeping the water and house on the outskirts of the chain so that things didn't get wrapped up, and then a stick fell and wrapped the chain where the dog couldn't reach the water or barrel. I think in that way the kennel outshines the chain. That said, many top-notch dog men use chains, if for no other reason than pure economics. There is nothing wrong with chaining dogs!

Sanitation is another category to consider, but kennels take a lot of upkeep if you want them sanitary. That waste doesn't disappear, you have to deal with it. While many see this as a downside I look for the positive in sweeping and hosing out that dog squat. It might seem unsightly, but I have a constant conversation with my dogs poop. Often a dogs stool is my first insight into a health issue and I can catch a problem before I see it outwardly in the condition of the dog. On a chain the poop is mauled by the chain, in a kennel it is sitting there screaming at you. If you don't have the means or determination to clean kennels every couple days they can be far more unsanitary than raw dirt and a chain spot.

Conservation of energy is a southern tradition - do it as easy as you can. A good friend has taken a job overseas and often I find myself at his house to medicate dogs. These 7 dogs are on chain spots and while not a terrible chore, it takes a bit of doing to hit each dog, as they are on 12' chains with a few feet buffer zone between. In my kennel setup I can walk a 50' straight line and hit each dog. I find comfort and ease in having all of my dogs in such close proximity. In the summer months I can set a single water sprinkler in front of my kennels and hit each kennel with it to cool the structure and my old dogs that are smart enough to stand where the sprinkler hits them. To do that with a chain gang of 8 dogs would take at least 3 or 4 sprinklers; again, doable, just more work.

I built my kennels 15 years ago. I am glad I did, but if I were to build again I would do it slightly differently. My kennels are 48' x 16' on concrete, closed in on three sides with the open side facing my front door so that the barking reverberates and shoots straight at the house. The orientation I would keep the same, I can swing that front door to the house open or just stand in the window and the old dogs hit the barrels silent as a mouse! Obviously, with concrete my kennels are stationary, that I might change given the need to rebuild.

That brings up the two main choices in kennels; permanent or movable. As with everything there are advantages to both. Concrete floors have a few advantages to dirt or wood.

1. Sanitation. You can completely disinfect concrete. It can be sanitary or it can be a cesspool, but that is up to you.
2. Longevity. It will last forever. Wood rots, steel rusts, concrete last forever.
3. Parasites. Dogs on concrete are much easier to keep worm and external parasite free. Keeping parasites off of dogs is relatively easy with attention to the dogs body, dog house and the immediate area surrounding.
4. Pads. This one is a big one for me, because it directly effects a dogs performance. (parasites obviously effect a dogs performance too, just in a less touch it and feel it way) In the many years I have had my dogs on concrete I have only ran the pads off a dog a few

times. Both those times it was in high heat, high humidity and I wasn't running dogs like I should have been.

The downside to concrete is -

1. It is permanent. You better put it right where you want it!
2. Joints. Concrete can be tough on a dogs joints, just because of the hardness. Joint pain will come up in older dogs.
3. Disconnect. This may seem a bit weird but I feel it to be true... a disconnect from the earth. I like to sleep on dirt, it's hard to explain but it seems to put me in connection with the natural world and I feel more a part of the world and not above. Sleep a night on the dirt and I promise you will wake with a feeling like you are part of the world. I have to think this link occurs in dogs too.

Kennels on skids, or movable do have some advantages. My permanent kennels are great in winter for shedding that cold north wind and weather, but in the summer months they get more of the hot afternoon heat than I would like. It is just a simple compromise at my place. I compensate with sprinklers and misters but it is a battle in July and August. If I had movable kennels I could easily move them from winter to summer and the dogs would get optimal shade in the summer and wind break in the winter. The other advantage of movable kennels is the smell. My kennels are built on a pad with a slight incline so that as I hose them out the waste goes out the back. Without a septic system on my kennels the waste gets thick so that I have to take a tractor and grade out the backside every couple months or so to keep the build up and smell down. The waste graded over my pasture feeds well, but it is a bit of work. With a movable kennel one could just move the kennel every so often to feed the ground, a task easier than spreading the manure. The downside to movable kennels is the wood floor. A wood floor is going to rot, no matter what treatment. The second negative is the sanitation. Wood is going to hold bacteria and you are never going to get the level of sanitation as on concrete, though wood floor will be far more sanitary than dirt. I have recently seen some kennels with a grated plastic floor and they are even removable - these could be very sanitary.

A couple years back one of my neighbors got a new trailer house, and like most around here, they just put a match to the old one. I drove past the frame of the old trailer house a few times and then one day it hit me - that thing would make a great floor frame for a movable kennel! Like most, they planned to put a cutting torch to it and haul it for scrap, but it continued to sit there. They told me to take the dang thing. Free, just get it out of here. I declined, but my point is that one can be found very cheap or free. In a good day a man could have it decked with wood. On a wood floored kennel you are of course going to want to use a treated wood. Which though, I don't know, because I have never done it. I can say that my pressure treated lumber in my kennel has stood up to 15 years worth of water and urine and looks to be going nowhere soon. You are going to build it pretty much like a deck, with staggered joints and screws not nails - nails will back out and cut pads, it's a given. While we are talking about movable kennels, I have noticed that a good many movable kennels are short, too short for a man to stand up in. Going upwards is relatively cheap, make them where you aren't crawling in there, because you ARE going in there, OFTEN! Here in tornado alley it is a given, but I will say it anyway. Movable kennels, especially if walled, need some way of securing to mother earth! In a three sided kennel I would imagine some straight-line winds could even pick them up.

Once you have settled on permanent or movable kennels the next consideration is whether to enclose them or not. Kennels can be completely enclosed, just a roof, or a roof and any number of walls. For me the roof is a must, with no advantages to not having one. When you frame the roof, go ahead and extend it about two or three feet past where your kennel doors will be. My overhang is just about 18" and if I were doing it all over, that would be three to four feet. When you are feeding in the rain it is nice to have that little cover, plus it can be added shade and to keep the front of the kennels a little more dry. The walls, unlike the roof, have pros and cons. Those walls sure help in the winter, and hurt a bit in the summer. Where I live that winter weather that falls from the sky doesn't just fall, usually it comes in with wind and it is sideways. That is why I chose walls. In the summer months the walls do cut the breeze, and the kennels are probably a few degrees hotter than they would be without them. The other con to walls is again about the limited breeze, it holds smell more than it would if open. So climate is probably the biggest factor in whether to wall your kennels or not.

My walls are made of "R" panel, just like on a pole barn. They go to the roof but stop short of the concrete pad by about 3". There is a "frame" on my post at that level to stiffen up the sheet metal so that a dog cannot squeeze through or get access to that sharp edge of the sheet metal. The 3" gap allows you to hose out, and also allows for a small amount of circulation. It also allows some dogs to paw at the ground outside and drag in dirt for you clean up, another reason extending the pad past the kennel by a few feet might be worth the added cost.

Orientation of the kennels is a very big consideration if you are building permanent. You want kennels as close to the house as your woman will put up with, but you also want them far enough that you don't smell it every time a dog farts. Placing them where you can easily pull a truck close to load and unload dogs is also important. You don't want to build them in the very edge of your property where you can't at a glance know what is going on when the racket starts 40 times a day. You also want to place them in an area where you have room to add to them in the future, to hold more dogs, or maybe fence an outside yard for the dogs. When I built mine I made six holes and used the end, 12' x 16' as a storage area for feed, a wheeler, and junk I should have thrown away. It didn't take me long to gut that end and add two more kennels.

After convenience, the more important part of orientation is about that blazing star in the sky that tries to kill us every summer, and that north wind that wants to shatter our bones. Obviously we don't want our open side (if walled) facing north, that part is easy. The other three directions are where the real consideration comes in. My open side faces west. Now most of our bad storms come in from the west, so it might not sound logical, but. With my open side facing west, my largest closed side faces east, the sun gets it in the morning, but with my trees by 10am the shade hits it and doesn't come back until about 4pm in the summertime. Unless you are lucky, sun is going to hit your kennel, and it NEEDS to, for the sake of dogs; if you can choose, pick the morning sun over the late afternoon version. Yet another consideration are your utilities. Water at the kennel is a MUST, and electric is very nice! Lights you can click on too see those dogs in the winter is a plus. If you are like me, in the winter, it is dark when you leave for work and dark when you get back.

Before I had permanent kennels I had a few chain link pens. They were not cheap, and I was proud as hell when I got a couple. Within a few weeks that had worn off in a big way. Chain link might cut it for beagles, or bird dogs but my hog dogs literally chewed dog-sized holes right threw them to get out and harass the hogs in the pen, go on a date, or run to town for a few beers. In my kennel setup now I used hog panel. They aren't chewing through it! They come 16' long and 32" or 34" tall. From the bottom up the spacing is something close to 3 - 2", 3 - 3", 1 - 4", 2 - 5", and 1 - 6". Two panels will get you about 5' tall, not tall enough for most dogs with some gumption, 3 will take you all the way to roof. Go to the roof! With the small holes of the panel at the bottom, on each panel when stacked, most 40 to 50lb dogs will not be getting out. When you price panels your jaw will drop when comparing hog panel to horse panel (2x4). It will hurt, but you will thank me later, make at least two kennel spots out of the horse panel. These spots will be for your pups, and those dogs we all come across that can somehow get out of anything you put them in.

Earlier I said if I had to build my kennels over I would do a few things different, here are my changes.

1. My kennels are simple post and frame construction, just like a pole barn. I wish I had built concrete block stem walls about 24" tall as dividers between the individual kennels and then went with the frame and panels on top of the stem wall. There are a couple reasons for this; when I wash kennels I get one clean and then move to the next and of course while spraying I get the first kennel a little dirty and I have to go back and give it a quick hosing. While this is just a minor inconvenience, a solid barrier between kennels would better quarantine dogs and limit cross contamination when bringing in a new dog, or when only one dog comes down with something. Secondly, the short wall limits fighting and fussing between kennels. 24" is not going to STOP fighting, but it would limit it. You could easily go higher, but I like the dogs in the pens to have at least some access to other dogs. I

don't think it is a good thing to have dogs in solitary confinement. I would build one kennel with 4' stem walls for that special dog that likes to get grouchy, or new bulldogs. This concrete block stem wall would also eliminate the need for a 2x4 paneled pup pen.

2. I already said I would have extended my roof out a few feet as a weather break, but I would do the same under foot. Three or four feet of concrete in front of the kennel would be nice. As is usual, I can still do this, but don't give me too much grief, it's only been on my long list for ten years or so! It's always easier to do it right the first time.

3. I'd install a septic tank. Now where I live no one cares WHAT you do, no inspections or the such. Two barrels plumbed together and 50' of lateral line would serve me for years. If I lived somewhere it had to be done 'legit' I would probably pass on the septic though just because of hassle and cost. A man I knew had a homemade septic on his kennels. On the backside, long end of the kennels he put a 6" pipe cut in half longways, right up against the concrete and had it on about a 6" drop over 40' and flowing into an underground setup. He sprayed the kennels out from the front and after went to the back and shot the waste down the troff into the septic tank. It was a really good setup, and cheap. He got a divorce and had to move and leave the kennel. When he told the story of his divorce, the kennel always came up, and ranked very high on his regrets in life. The old man and his wife split over dogs, so I am sure it irked her up until her death that the divorce conversation even centered around dogs in his mind. (She killed all his dogs and that is what spurred the D.I.V.O.R.C.E. pony out of the barn, BUT that is a story for another day.)

4. Across the 16' side of my concrete pad I only put about a 1" drop. I wish I had gone a minimum of 3" and I think my clean out time would be much less.

Inside the kennel there are also layout issues, its not as simple as throwing a barrel in there and a water bucket. The first

293

consideration is not an easy one, and it is one I have not yet worked out in my kennels in a way that I like. Dogs are not inherently nasty animals. A dog wants to do his dirty business far from where he eats and sleeps. In an enclosed kennel my access is limited to the front, obviously, so for MY convenience I want to feed and water in the front so that I do not HAVE to enter each kennel. In 99% of the kennels you see the barrel is in the back and the man feeds in the front. It just seems logical, until you stop and think about it. If the feed and barrel are together in the front then most dogs are going to mess in the back and make cleaning much easier, as well as easing the dogs mind.

I like a raised dog house inside the kennel, with a 'porch' so that the dog can easily get in the barrel and also have a perch. The raised barrel stays clean. Barrels on the ground become havens for turds to hide under, and just get plain nasty. They can of course be cleaned, but again we go back to that great southern tradition of avoiding unnecessary work. The raised barrel also stays warmer in the winter as the earth and concrete do not become a heat-sink. Lastly, that 'porch' is a jumping point and helps keep dogs in better shape, plus they all seem content to sit on the porch and watch the world going on. A couple years ago I had some pups in a kennel and I had taken the barrel down so they had a place to sleep they could get to. I was in there cleaning one day and moved the barrel to spray and there was a three foot copperhead coiled up under the barrel! So lastly, barrels on the ground give creepy things a place to sleep.

Cleaning kennels in the winter is really not a good time. I have a hydrant right at my pens and hard as I tried, when the real cold weather came I always forgot to un-connect it and I'd go out to water and clean and it would be frozen. I'd haul water and put off spraying out kennels, or when motivated I would drag that frozen hose into my shop and thaw it out. I got to thinking there had to be a better way. So I plumbed a contraption. From a splitter at the hydrant I ran 3/4 inch PVC up and then ran the length of the kennel with a down-shoot of PVC at each individual kennel. I put a PVC cap on each down-spout with a 1/4" hole drilled in it and aligned the water buckets up with each. At the lowest point of the mainline I put a valve that I can use to drain the whole system after I am done so that it doesn't freeze. So at water time I just turn a valve and all the dogs are getting watered, at the same time, and I don't drag a hose, I can do other things.

I have also installed misters, the kind you see in fancy horse barns where a very fine mist kind of hangs in the air. They are cheap to buy and there is nothing to it. I just ran them along the back 1/3 of the kennels along the roof joists, careful that the mist didn't get inside the dog houses. In the heat of the summer the old dogs will just stand under them. You don't want a swamp, so if you do this just use them in the heat of the day, say 2pm until 6pm, when it's hot enough that everything isn't dripping wet. A dogs pads can't take constantly standing in water. (The dryness of concrete is in part what makes dogs on concrete have tougher pads)

Most every farm store has hard plastic "Hook Over Feed Buckets." They are usually about 2 gallons, kind of square, and have large hooks on the back that are meant to hang on panels. These are GREAT water buckets for a kennel. It is close to impossible for a dog to get them off the panel, so no knocked over bucket leaving a dog panting all day while you are panting at work.

Any good setup for dogs takes a few bucks and a lot of head scratching. The payoff comes when you see your dogs safe, comfortable, and things are easier for you. For me, kennels are about my peace of mind.

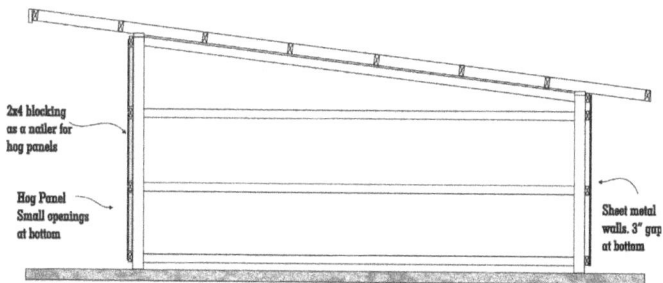

2x4 blocking as a nailer for hog panels

Hog Panel Small openings at bottom

Sheet metal walls. 3" gap at bottom

Side Elevation

CHAPTER 49
HUNTING MANNERS
Originally appeared in the August 2014 issue of Tuskers Magazine

A lot of the older guys, or even younger guys that were raised around hunting dogs will get this and may even think this is all common sense and a bit of wasted space, but we are going to talk about hunting manners. For many years before Tuskers Magazine I hunted either by myself or with one or two other very close friends, I would never hunt with anyone else. Partly because I am kind of like that, social interaction with most people is painful for me, but also because the few times that I would step out of my box and hunt with other people the manners on them left a bad taste in my mouth. Another thing about hunting with different people are the dogs, and I wont just throw my dogs that I have worked hard to make hunt the way I want in with dogs that I know nothing about. Now since we started Tuskers Magazine I find myself hunting with lots of different people in new and interesting places, sometimes they are with us, sometimes we are with them. That last part is important when talking about hunting manners. There are things you can do when you are on your place that you can't do when you are invited and hunting with others on their place.

First we are gonna talk about dogs. If stranger "Billy" invites you to go hunting you don't show up with a box full of dogs! If you want to bring dogs then you need to ask Billy before you go. Now me, I don't even want to bring dogs. Sure, you've seen Billy post pictures of hogs, an he has a pretty good reputation of having some darn fine hounds on the computer, probably way better dogs than you have you think, but let me tell you from numerous first hand experiences - don't believe any of that until you see it with your own eyes. Before I throw my dogs on the ground to hunt with someones dogs I want to be dang sure these dogs aren't going to drag my broke dogs into a deer race or show them all the fun they been missing killing dillos, treeing coons or runnin' to town to drink beer all night while I'm off in the hills yodeling for them all night. Lets take Billys side - he invited you to hunt with him and he don't want your hounds running his dogs to town to drink beer either! Now, when most people go hunting, they want to run their dogs, an I get that. So you showed a good bringing up and asked Billy if he minded you bringing 2 dogs and he agreed. The classy thing to do when y'all get out to the corn fields is to let Billy run his dogs on that first cast, tie one and then ask if you can run yours. If Billy's dogs impressed you and hunt in a way you like then turn your dogs in with his, if not maybe suggest his take a breather and run yours by themselves. Most dogmen will box their dogs without being asked out of caution. After Billy has seen your dogs hunt, if he throws his dogs in with yours then take that as a compliment.

I guess I got a bit ahead of myself, so lets back up and talk about NOT BEING LATE! If y'all agreed to meet at the truck stop at 9, then I would be there, truck gased, beer on ice and mens room already visited by 8:45, ready to roll. Now we are talking about hunting with new people, I don't ever like being late, but with old friends stuff happens and sometimes it's funny to be fashionably late. We are talking about first impressions, after that you can cuss, spit an make fun of fat wives.

Sometimes if the place your hunting is a good ways off, you might catch a ride. If you do, PAY FOR HALF THE GAS! Gas is high and guided hog dog hunts are even higher. I have taken guys hunting and they didn't do this, and take a guess how many times I called them after that to see if they wanted to go?

So you're a veteran hog hunter that just moved and you met Billy at the feed store and your hunting with him Friday night just to meet some local guys and get to know people an so on. We get it, you've been hog hunting with dogs for 2 decades, but SHUT UP! No one likes a blow hard, so show Billy how much you know about hog hunting with your actions and let your darn mouth rest for a minute. That brings up another thing, DON'T BAD MOUTH A MAN'S DOGS unless you got one right there that's a better dog. Now me, I've rarely bad mouthed a mans dogs, the few cases I have, it's been because the man was a bigger jackass than his dogs. We all have a ton of time in our dogs, and even the guys with less than great dogs are proud of them, so let the boastful talk of your dogs rattle in your head, not his. Talk is cheap.

So you didn't bring dogs, you were on time, and you haven't ranted and raved about so-n-so an his 'bring you a beer' dogs. Billy's dogs got in a foot race, crossed 2 counties, 9 rivers, it's 5AM, you gotta be at work at 7, and the dogs are bayed in an underwater cave and Billy's truck has a flat and is stuck in a mudhole... YOU HUNT 'TIL THE HUNT IS OVER! You don't hunt part of a hunt, you don't get to tag along as long as things are peachy and then split when you get tired or hunting hogs gets a little too hairy ofr your taste. This one is a very big hang up I have, and a sure way to never see me again. It seems pretty obvious to me, but I have seen it more than a time or two an it gets my blood boiling.

It don't matter if you have been hog hunting for 20 years or never been, if you are hunting with another man, YOU DO WORK, YOU DON'T WATCH WORK! There is a lot of work in hog hunting with dogs; there are hurt dogs that need carried, there are hogs to drag a quarter to the road, there are bulldogs that need led. The man that watches me work won't do so but once.

FOLLOW DIRECTIONS! Even if you don't do it that way when you are hunting. When you are hunting with another man on his ground you do things the way he wants them done, chances are he has a good reason for doing them that way.

We all hunt for different reason, for some it's for pork, for some it's about dogs, for some it's varmint control, for others it's a social event. Sometimes I enjoy talking, not as much as most, but I do enjoy it sometimes, but there is a time and a place. So Billy cast his mutts towards the river and he's standing by the Ranger staring at his Garmin and you and 15 other guys are talking about the virtues of the running walker as a hogdog or Jim's fat wife. About 1000 yards in the bottom one of Billy's pound bred cur x bird x poodle dogs opens just once. SHUT YOUR MOUTH! The "social" aspect of hog hunting just ended in the heartbeat that dog opened, we are hog hunting now and there are couches all over Texas, Oklahoma, Arkansas, Louisiana, and probably a few other states where talking is allowed. We don't hog hunt in your living room, don't talk over our hog hunt. This one always gets me, and usually leaves the question in my head, "How fast can I get my dogs hollered in and loaded up so I can go home?" Sure, we have Garmins, we know where the dogs are, an have an idea of what is going on, but NOTHING replaces good ole fashioned ears for letting us know WHAT is going on. When a man knows his dogs he can read that one little bark like the Bible. It tells him whether we need to load up and get close, stay back and let it get worked out, haul butt and get a bulldog ready, or *cough*- get the Tri-Tronics out of the glove box. When you are talking while a man is trying to hear his dogs you are increasing the odds that he won't need that mule tape tonight.

So here is the short version on manners when hunting...

1. ASK BEFORE YOU BRING DOGS.
2. DON'T BE LATE
3. BUY GAS IF YOU CATCH A RIDE
4. STOP BRAGGING
5. STAY 'TIL HUNT IS OVER
6. DO WORK
7. FOLLOW DIRECTIONS
8. SHUT THE *(^$ UP WHEN YOU HEAR A DOG BARK!

CHAPTER 50
DOG HUNTERS CODE OF ETHICS

Our code of ethics as houndsmen is our bond, and it is a code that we should all adhere to and urge other houndsmen to follow. Our code of ethics is based on care for dog and game; it aims to help secure our future.

1. I will provide proper care for my dogs including food, water, medical care and shelter and will firmly insist other hunting dog owners do the same.

2. I will provide proper identification and contact information on all of my dogs at all times.

3. I will work to retrieve my dogs by the end of the hunt, recognizing it is my moral and ethical responsibility to retrieve every dog as quickly as possible. If I cannot locate a dog by the end of the hunt, I will do my best to retrieve it as quickly as possible.

4. I will only release my dogs on property on which I have permission to hunt and will not tolerate others releasing dogs on property where they do not have permission to hunt.

5. I will find a proper home or shelter for any dog that I determine I cannot or will not keep. I will not abandon any dog and will not tolerate any one who does.

6. I will consider myself a guest of the landowner, whether private, state or federal, always seeking permission up front, and will conduct myself so I will be welcome in the future.

7. I will do my best to tread lightly while afield, to carefully use only established roads and trails, to leave any gates as I find them (open or closed), and foremost to leave no litter.

8. I will promote fair chase of game animals and ethical treatment of hunting dogs.

9. I will strictly follow the rules of safe gun handling and obey all game laws and regulations.

10. I will actively encourage young and new hunters to participate in and enjoy the thrill and camaraderie of hunting with dogs.

11. I will always be mindful that I am the public face of all dog hunters when afield or in the community. I will strive to hold myself and others to the highest standards of behavior when hunting with my dogs so we all reflect well on the ancient and honorable tradition of hunting with dogs.

12. I will be mindful of the negative impact to our sports that improper post on social media can have on our future.

EPILOGUE

As hog hunters of the late 20th and early 21st century we hold a unique position in history. Men all over the world have hunted hogs with dogs for a couple thousand years at least. There are cave drawings of man chasing hogs, and old world Europe holds many statues of man and dog battling with Sus Scrofa - yet in America we are at the front of a changing landscape, species, and social agenda when it comes to hog hunting with dogs. We are in a different moment in time, a more complex and extended game in history than our grandpas were. We are at the forefront of a new sport. We are breaking new ground and pushing dogs in a new direction. The hog hunter is pushing new dogs further than any other dog hunters in America at this time - simply out of necessity. We will go down in history if we hold true. Ours is a new venture; in beast and dog. We are breaking ground. As the hogs evolve, and the hunt changes with laws pressed onto us by government agencies, we too must evolve and press our dogs to stay ahead of the swinging curve of history.

Our future as houndsmen, the future of our sport, and future of our endeavors to create new dogs is in jeopardy. We are left-overs from another time and another mindset; a time and mind when man lived in and with nature and not against it. Our future will find us in constant battle to maintain our lifestyle, and insure a future for the next generation of hog hunters. Our candle faces many winds!

It is every houndsman's burden to take this fight, if not for himself, then for his children, and grandchildren and legacy. If we show the fight, grit and bottom in ourselves that we command of our hounds we can win the fight, and how can we ask more of our dogs than we ask of ourselves?

EPITAPH TO A DOG
~ Lord Byron.

Near this Spot
are deposited the Remains of one
who possessed Beauty without Vanity,
Strength without Insolence,
Courage without Ferocity,
and all the virtues of Man without his Vices.

This praise, which would be unmeaning Flattery
if inscribed over human Ashes,
is but a just tribute to the Memory of
Boatswain, a Dog
who was born in Newfoundland May 1803
and died at Newstead Nov. 18th, 1808

TERMS AND DEFINITIONS

Air - (generally used when talking about catchdogs) Ie. That dog has good air. Meaning that he has good lungs / muzzle and does not tire easily or snort and puff when exerted.

Babbling - When a dog constantly barks and there is no track. Pups often babble when older dogs are farther ahead of them.

Backtracking - When a dog runs a track in the wrong direction, getting further from the game.

Backdooring - When a hunter steals land from another hunter by going behind his back and talking to the landowner.

Barr - Slang term shortened from the word Barrow. A castrated male hog.

Barren Sow - A mature sow who has not had any litters of pigs and has no maternal inclination. They often take on a very boar-like body shape and often have small tushes.

Bawl Mouth - A long and drawn out style of barking.

Baying - Barking at a hog, or any animal which has stopped running on the ground. Baying is also used as a short term for the sport of bay penning.

Bitch - A female dog that has had a litter of pups. Generally older terminology and not widely in use today.

Blanketback (or Saddleback) - A color pattern in dogs where there is a large black marking on the back that goes from the neck to the tail in a way that looks like a blanket has been laid across their back.

Blooded hog - A hog that has a large amount of domesticated blood in his breeding, or a fully domestic hog used to 'tame' the blood of wild hogs and give the offspring a more table friendly body type.

Boar - An uncastrated male hog.

Bottom - A dogs ability to stick with a hog as long as it takes to get it to bay up. This is not to be confused with range, but often is.

Broke Dog - A dog that has been broke off of undesired game, or Trash, and will only run the desired game.

Brood Bitch - A female dog used primarily for breed purposes, often but not always retired from hunting.

Brucellosis - A disease of the reproductive system. Dogs can get it from coming into contact with saliva or mucus from an infected hog. It can cause sterility and death.

Busted Bay - When the dogs have a hog bayed and he chooses to run again. This term usually used to refer to a dog being the reason the hog went back on the run.

Cast - A style of hunting where the dogs are sent in a direction and hunt out away from the handler. Ie. We cast the dogs towards the river.

Cat Footed - A dog that has a small round foot, with toes that are tight together. Usually a cat footed dog will stand high on their toes. A good trait in a dog that makes them more agile.

Coon Footed - A dog that sits back on the heel of the foot with toes splayed apart. The opposite of Cat Footed, a negative trait in a dog.

Catchdog - Any dog whose job is to physically catch and hold the hog. Generally a Bulldog but other large breeds and even Curs are sometimes used to catch.

Check-in - When a dog returns to the handler after a distance or time of hunting if no game is found and they goes back out to continue hunting.

Cold Nosed - A dog that can and will take an old track.

Chop Mouth - A short and choppy style of barking, common among curs.

Crossbreed - A dog that is a mix of one or more breeds of dogs.

Cut Hog - A boar hog that has been barred. (castrated)

Dam - Mother of a litter of pups.

Dog - Male dog, a term used more in the past.

Ear Dog - A catchdog that usually catches a hog on the ear.

Finished Dog - A dog that is fully trained, requiring no more training.

Gameness - the willingness to persevere regardless of what state or condition the mind or body is in. Generally a bulldog term.

Gilt - A female hog that is young and has not yet had a litter of pigs.

Grade Dog - A dog that does not have papers, they can be full blood or crossbred. The term does not indicate they lack ability.

Gyp - A female dog, specifically one that has not yet had puppies.

Help Dog - (Also called a Pack Dog or a Me-Too Dog) - A dog that does not have the ability to take his own track and trail a hog.

A help dog merely follows along with strike dogs and helps once they strike or bay a hog. Some Help Dogs do not follow along with the strike dogs but wait to hear a bark and then go to them.

Hot Nosed - A dog that works fresh, or hot tracks.

Hung papers - Falsified papers to show a dog is either registered when they are not, or showing the wrong lineage of the dog.

Lead-in Catchdog - A dog that is led into the bay, or close to the bay and turned loose to catch the hog. A lead-in catchdog does not participate in the 'hunt', chase or bay of the hogs, his sole job is to catch after the baydogs have got the hog bayed up.

Listed hog - A hog with a colored band across the midsection of the body. Generally points towards evidence that the hog has a good amount of domestic blood.

Locate bark - A bark that a dog gives once or twice when a track has been started, and sometimes intermittently as the race goes on. This does not mean running open.

Long Range - A dog that hunts approximately 1000 plus yards from a handler.

Loose Bay Dog - A dog that bays from further back on a hog and almost never has physical contact with the hog.

Loose Mouth - A dog that opens when there is no track. A loose mouth dog might bark when you let him out of the dog box, then again when he finishes cleaning out and sees the other dogs far ahead. He uses his bark for other reasons than hunting.

Marked Hog - A hog whose ears have been notched by man to show ownership.

Meat hog - A hog that is fit for eating. Usually barr hogs, or sows and boars under 150lbs.

Medium Range - A dog that hunts approximately 500 - 1000 yards from the handler.

Open / Open Mouthed - A dog that barks on track, in sign or when giving chase.

Pig - Other than the obvious umbrella term for swine, "Pig" is used to describe unweaned or very small babies. Ie. The sow had a whole bunch of pigs on her.

Piggy sow - A sow either with a litter of fresh born pigs or a sow that is very close to having a litter.

Pup Trainer - An older dog, usually past it's prime, that is used to train pups. The pups can keep up easily and the dog is trusted to not get them on any trash.

Rally - When a group of hogs gang up on dogs to fight instead of running off after individual hogs have been bayed or caught.

Rig Dog - A dog that can strike a hog from on top of a dog box, on the hood of a truck or ATV, or from a boat.

Roading - Putting dogs on the ground in front of a truck or ATV and slowly driving. The dogs stay ahead and close until they strike.

Rolling Out - When a baydog immediately leaves the bay to continue hunting after the hog has been caught.

Rough Dog - A dog that is not a catchdog, but will 'lay a tooth' on a hog at a bay. Often Rough Dogs will help the catchdog catch the hog.

Running Catchdog - **(RCD for short)** - A running catchdog can strike and run his own hogs or he can run with bay dogs. The running catchdog physically catches the hog as soon as he his able with no baying. The RCD is loose on the ground as opposed to the lead-in style catchdog.

Saddleback (or Blanketback) - A color pattern in dogs where there is a large black marking on the back that goes from the neck to the tail in a way that looks like a blanket has been laid across their back.

Semi-Open - A dog that barks on track but not with the full on regularity of an open dog.

Shoat - A young hog, male or female that has been weaned. Regularly used for any pig under 50lbs or so.

Short Range - A dog that hunts close to the handler, approximately 1-300 yards.

Silent - A dog that takes a track or runs a hog with no barking until the hog has been stopped and bayed.

Sire - Father of a litter of pups.

Snout Dog - A catchdog that usually catches a hog on the snout.

Sounder - A large group of hogs that travel and live together. Sometimes called a 'Wad."

Sow - An adult female pig, generally referring to a female that has already had a litter of pigs.

Stop Dog (or Shut Down Dog) - A dog that bites on a hogs rear in a race to get him stopped from running. A Stop Dog will let go of the hog once it has quit running and go to baying.

Strike Dog - A dog that either from rig or ground, makes first contact with a hog track and begins pursuit. Generally the term is reserved for dogs that are very close to finished or finished. A pup might strike a hog, but he's not really a Strike Dog until he can be depended upon to regularly and accurately do his job.

Tight Bay Dog - A dog that bays very close to a hog.

Trash - Any animal that a dog might give chase or catch that is not wanted by the handler.

Tushes - An older term for Tusk, or Cutter. The long lower tooth of a hog that extends outside of the mouth.

Walking bay - When a hog is not running and the dogs are in close baying but the hog continues to walk at a slow pace. Generally shows a hogs disregard or lack of fear of the the dogs.

Wetter - The curved tusk on a hog that extends out from the upper jaw. The wetter is used to sharpen the Tushes by grinding. In the abscense of the Wetter the tushes will grow very long.

Winding - When a dog is tracking and leaves the actual step-by-step track, by taking a straight line to the next track scent that the dog has found by the movement of wind. It is a shortcut.

www.ingramcontent.com/pod-product-compliance
Lightning Source LLC
Chambersburg PA
CBHW020825270326
41928CB00006B/445